*The Social Face of Buddhism*

# The Social Face of Buddhism
## An Approach to Political and Social Activism

Ken Jones

Wisdom Publications · London

First published in 1989

WISDOM PUBLICATIONS
23 Dering Street, London W1, England; and
361 Newbury Street, Boston, MA 02115, USA

*British Library Cataloguing in Publication Data*
Jones, Ken H.
 The social face of Buddhism: action and
 analysis
 1.   Buddhism
 I.   Title
 294.3  BQ4012
*Library of Congress Catalog Card Number*
 88–40562

ISBN 0 86171 062 2

Set in Palatino in 10½ on 13 point by Setrite Typesetters
of Hong Kong, and printed and bound by Eurasia Press of
Singapore.

# Contents

Dedicated to
all Followers of the Way


*Go forth on your journey, for the benefit
of the many, for the joy of the many,
out of compassion for the world, for the
welfare, for the benefit and joy of
mankind.*


The Buddha (*Vinaya* 1, 21)

# *Foreword by His Holiness the Dalai Lama*

In this work the author examines ways in which Buddhism and social activism can contribute to each other. This is a timely and potentially fruitful field of enquiry, for they have much in common. While the main emphasis of the Buddha's teaching is on inner development, that is no reason for Buddhists not to participate in the society in which they live. We are all dependent on others and so responsible to others. The fundamental aim of Buddhist practice, to avoid harming others and if possible to help them, will not be fully achieved simply by thinking about it.

The phenomenon of social activism is an attempt by like-minded people to alleviate social problems through drawing attention to them and trying to change the attitudes of those in a position to affect them. Whatever the problem may be and whatever form the activism may take, it is important that the individual activist has a sound motivation. In this, Buddhist training, with its methods for developing a calm, clear mind and a kind heart, can certainly be of help. However, this is not a quality exclusive to Buddhists, for it is a positive feature of social activism that particular issues bring together people of many different beliefs in a common cause.

All human beings want happiness and have a right to pursue it. Thus, it is important to create a just, equal and peaceful society. I hope that this book will help readers to appreciate this and the complementary contributions Buddhism and social activism can make to realizing it.

THE DALAI LAMA
*Thekchen Choeling*
*McLeod Ganj*
*Himachal Pradesh, India*
*4 August 1986*

# Foreword by Venerable Ajahn Tiradhammo Thera

We are living at a very important time; when the cacophony of discordant views intimates a wave of change about to surge into human consciousness.

In our 'post-industrial' society the plethora of emotive issues entering into discussion can quite simply be defined as those between 'quantity' and 'quality', that is, the 'quantity of material possessions' or the 'quality of life'. And if humanity is to survive it is becoming increasingly clear that 'quality' must take precedence.

If we look at the world's problems from the perspective of our ordinary, rational minds, solutions seem despairingly impossible. Seen, however, in terms of human spiritual evolution this situation is challenging us, indeed chasing us, into a totally new way of relating. We are now impelled into an urgent need to question the very basis of human existence as experienced in our own minds.

In attempting to formulate the basic questions confronting us we are turning over many foundation stones of our assumptive world view. For some people it is a painful and heartbreaking task to address our naked humanness. For others it is a stimulating adventure of discovery. Only by opening up to the very roots of our despair are we able to understand and reach beyond. This is the way of liberation.

Towards a clearer understanding of basic questions (and possible solutions) there has evolved a body of literature concerned with what I call the 'paradigm revelation' − an awakening of human consciousness revealing a new world

11

view. One link in this momentous process is the effect of Buddhism upon Western culture. Archetypally this is the engagement of East and West — who knows what kind of marriage, if any, will ensue!

Buddhist perspectives are quite different from those of the West on many fundamental themes.* This is valuable, firstly, as a reflection for views and attitudes conditioned by Western culture and, secondly, as a challenge to discover an all-encompassing, holistic perspective.

One area of very fruitful exploration between Buddhist and Western attitudes is that of social action, that is, how Buddhism can contribute to and influence the transformation of contemporary Western society. Keeping in mind the Buddhist 'goal' of spiritual Enlightenment, this endeavour is at once positive and problematic.

As an introduction and preliminary discussion of social action this book is a virtual compendium comprising a comprehensive exposition of the principles of Buddhist practice, social theory and history, and the meeting of Buddhist principles with contemporary thought and action. Here we have the whole spectrum of background information, many encouragements and warnings, and practical possibilities. Although principally addressed to Buddhists and social activists, this work can be of valuable service to all who are concerned with caring attitudes.

This preface is not written by an expert or authority but simply by another concerned human being offering their own personal reflections. I very much appreciate Ken's finely balanced perspective matured by many years of meditation and personal involvement with social issues. This work not only resonates with the author's particularly graphic language but is enlivened by his special flair for addressing practical, root issues without letting 'slippery eels' get away.

---

*See, for example, the introductory essay in *Buddhist and Western Psychology*, ed. Nathan Katz, Pranja Press, 1983.

The book covers a lot of ground, but what I found especially valuable is that in explaining the intersection of Buddhism and social action the author is able to profitably point out many confusions and distorted ideas about Buddhist practice, for instance the dangers of pietism, the motives of morality and the 'Quietist Fallacy'. The elaboration of special Buddhist contributions to social action such as the 'Higher Third' and monasticism, enables him to perceptively weave in the relationship of Buddhist perspectives with contemporary thought, for example, 'Indra's Net' and permaculture, meditation and Transpersonal Psychology. As well as discussions of past and present Buddhist-inspired social movements, Ken also bravely tackles more controversial topics such as Buddhism's relationship with the humanistic therapies and the need for a distinctive 'Western Buddhism'. (Should the reader feel somewhat weighted by the 'Analysis' of the first half of the book, I suggest a temporary move into the 'Action' of the second.)

In the discussion of Kamma I should like to emphasize that what is really needed for a true understanding of 'moral causality' is meditative reflection upon one's own actions. I would also suggest that although Buddhism has been mostly associated with *nonviolence*, the Buddha's teaching is more precisely directed towards complete *harmlessness*.

This work is of particular importance for Buddhists as a timely reminder that spiritual practice occurs in a cultural context and is coloured, both psychologically and socially, by that context. Thus practice can include helping to create an environment supportive of spiritual values for oneself and others. In the way of liberation one needs to come to terms with one's conditioning before freeing oneself from it. In a sense, then, the writing of this book is a milestone in the history of Buddhism in the West. It marks a certain stage of maturity where Buddhism is seriously concerned with the relationship and response to its adopted culture.

I speak of a stage of maturity but I would also maintain that it is metaphorically only that of adolescence, compared to its venerable old age in the East. Thus we find Buddhism in the West oscillating between dependence upon Eastern parents and the assertion of its own culturally relevant character. This has resulted in a diversity of expressions from sectarian to universal, fundamental to esoteric, orthodox to heterodox — such is the ambivalence of adolescence!

For Buddhism, coming to terms with social issues is similar to an adolescent coming to terms with the world, and in the process developing a distinctive character. Buddhism in the West is in a unique position. This is a time when its character will be developed, a time when we will see if Buddhism still has a living heart. And if this character is to be of benefit to human beings it must be rooted in the Buddha-Mind — all-encompassing, exclusive of nothing. Buddha-Wisdom is universal wisdom. People in the West today appreciate Buddhism because they recognize *universal* human truths within the Buddhist form. These are the truths which speak to all Humanity to awaken spiritual wisdom, the wisdom which sees the unity of all things.

At this time in history we find a diverse array of Buddhist traditions gathered together in one 'culture'. In this rather unseasoned state, hatched, as it were, from comfortably Buddhist cultures, one still finds awkward and artless responses to the indigenous culture and other Buddhist traditions. This is the inelegance of adolescence which gives rise to such responses as 'tinsel tolerance' and 'myopic compassion', especially as Buddhism drifts away from its universalist outlook and into the guise of a special sect (more, of course, the psychology of insecurity than Buddhism!).

The Buddha's Awakening is a universal remedy for the human condition, yet there is still much quibbling over a 'Western Buddhism' as opposed to an 'Eastern Buddhism', or Mahayana Buddhism rather than Hinayana Buddhism. Just as our social consciousness must evolve to encompass the 'Global Village', so must 'Buddhist' consciousness evolve to include everything; not in the way of conversion or looking for 'Buddhist' similarities, but in the way of the Awakened Buddha-Mind. This is the *real* meaning of Buddhism — the Teaching of Awakening!

Much energy has already been wasted looking for 'Buddhist' responses or in trying to push a particular 'brand' of Buddhism rather than bringing Buddha-Wisdom into the world. As we cultivate spiritual practice and learn the joy of sharing our experience with others — friends and enemies — a relevant, situational response will necessarily unfold from the compassion of living wisdom, rather than from the 'compassion' of compulsion.

In responding to contemporary social issues one is forced to return to basic Buddhist principles to distinguish the 'spirit' of the Buddha's teaching from the mere parroting of the 'letter'. And this takes more than just learning *about* Buddhism. This requires that one put the teachings to the test of experience. That is, one must guide one's practice by the 'letter' in order to experience the 'spirit'. Thus I heartily agree with Ken Jones in emphasizing the need to refer back to 'root Buddhist teachings'. Unfortunately much harm has been done to Buddhism by apologists and 'reductive modernists' who, in their support of Buddhism, have been rather heavy on the 'ism' and light on the 'Buddha' (that is, 'Awakening'). They have frequently ended up merely adding another ideology to an ideology-afflicted world.

Basic Buddhist teachings also provide the unifying link between the various Buddhist traditions. Their emphasis thus inclines one away from sectarianism, while reference to principles such as tolerance, harmlessness, compassion etc., inclines one to a universal approach so necessary for the transformation of human consciousness, personally and socially. This is the challenge of trying to practise the Buddha's Teaching at the present time — to be a *living* example of Awakened Buddha-Wisdom, rather than some cultural anachronism. Certainly if Buddhism cannot be lived Here and Now, best it were left in the museums!

When Buddhism was first introduced to the West its perspective seemed rather strange and unique, that is to say, God-less and soul-less! At the present time, however, with the recognition of similarly inclined perspectives appearing from various quarters such as physics, biology and psychology, many Buddhist principles are becoming more fully identified out of the menagerie of cultural accretions. We can thus translate Buddhist principles into modern language as organismic, holistic, ecological, pluralistic, egalitarian, self-reliant, etc.

It is necessary for Buddhism to learn to appreciate, and co-operate with, the expressions of its basic principles in a much wider context without necessarily compromising its unique approach. Otherwise there is the danger of implosion into its own narrow, traditional confines and drying up for want of nourishment and relevance, or even of its becoming a divisive culture. If Buddhism is not able to encompass all things, it is not really Buddhism but merely some faded interpretation. The Buddha was a teacher of human beings, rather than a teacher of Buddhists! In this way Buddhists can join helping hands with noble-minded people of all backgrounds together trying to build a world based upon human spiritual values.

Here we can recognize the Buddhist contribution to the principle of equality − unity in diversity and diversity in unity. We can respect each individual's unique response to the realization of the One Truth. A Buddhist, to me, is not someone who merely recites appropriate formulas or wears the right uniform, but one who lives their life as best they can in the true spirit of Truth. This is the whole purpose of the Buddha's Teaching, and the ultimate purpose of ALL spiritual teachings! A Buddhist social activist then is someone who is living Wisdom and Compassion in a social context; learning to share selfless spiritual treasures with all beings.

At the present time, as we are groping for new responses and ways of relating to the fundamental nature of human existence, one link in this interrelated network of discovery

will be the evolution of Buddhism from a culture-bound
creed to a living expression of Awakened Human Consciousness. This book is an invaluable contribution towards
this process.

May all beings be well; may all beings realize peace.

BHIKKHU TIRADHAMMO
*Harnham Vihara*
*Northumberland*
*England*

# Acknowledgements

For fundamental orientation in the Buddhadharma I am grateful to Venerable Myokyo-ni (Irmgard Schloegl). My indebtedness to fellow Dharma activists will be evident throughout the text. In particular, many valuable suggestions for improving the typescript were made by *Ajahn* Tiradhammo, Noragh Jones, Garry Thomson and James J. Hughes. Thanks are also due to my editor at Wisdom Publications, Robina Courtin, for her encouragement, support and patience.

I am grateful to His Holiness the Dalai Lama and to Venerable *Ajahn* Tiradhammo Thera for contributing the two Forewords.

# Introduction

This book is about the contribution of Buddhism to under-standing and transforming society. It is written for both Buddhists and non-Buddhists. It is particularly a response to the many Buddhists who feel their hearts split between the requirements of a personal, privatized Buddhism and their deep concern for the suffering in the world and the need for direct and positive response to it. It attempts, therefore, to show that a distinction between personal Bud-dhist practice and social activism can be false; there is only one practice to be done. The book is also written for people who are trying to understand society, are concerned to change it and who know nothing about Buddhism, but would like to explore beyond the horizons of our familiar landscape of secular rationalism. And particularly it is writ-ten for those who suffer frustration and despair at the prospects for our planet and our seeming inability to do much about them.

Although the book focuses sharply on various aspects of Buddhism and its practice, in many places it opens wider spiritual and humanistic perspectives, in keeping with the pluralistic and open spirit of Buddhism. Thus I have made free use of other beliefs and theories wherever such *dharmas* (truths, teachings) would best illumine the Buddhist context (the *Buddhadharma*). Existentialists, Quakers, Marxists, Phe-nomenologists, Anarchists, 'Greens' and many others will therefore come across what is both familiar yet seen in a different light.

In recent years there has been quite a lot of interesting writing which, implicitly or explicitly, suggests affinities between Buddhism and contemporary developments in physics and biology, and also in psychology and psychophysical therapies, even though the connection may be more problematic than is sometimes implied.[1] Similarly, Buddhism suggests directions in the development of alternative lifestyles and strategies for social change, whether it be the Buddhist tradition of nonviolence or Schumacher's discovery of 'Buddhist economics'. And as a transcendental humanism it bridges the gap between the dominant secular humanism of our time and the theistic spirituality and social activism of the other great world religions. It can throw some light upon what Dr Ursula King has described as 'in a way, the greatest religious problem today...how to be both a mystic and a militant, as Adam Curle has expressed it; in other words, how to combine the search for an expansion of inner awareness with effective social action, and how to find one's true identity in the synthesis of both.'[2]

However, it seems that there has so far been little attempt to sketch out a Buddhist theory of society in the light of contemporary social theory (that is, if we discount the various attempts to demonstrate how 'modern' Buddhism really is, [see Chapter 26]). Such a project could be very fruitful.[3] This book offers some preliminary and exploratory ideas to meet a growing interest, in hope of stimulating discussion and as a development of two earlier pamphlets.[4] If these ideas are challenged, refined, varied and extended by others better qualified spiritually and intellectually, then the book will have served one of its purposes. And there is a particular need, I suggest, to develop and apply some of the perspectives introduced here to such contemporary fields as ecology, economics, education and feminism, taking in the scatter of preliminary contributions that have already been made.

This book shares a number of concerns with Ken Wilber's 'transpersonal view of human evolution', *Up from Eden*,[5] which I have found very stimulating. More tangential to my purpose is Wilber's *A Sociable God*,[6] which systematically examines sociology and the sociology of religion from the standpoint of transpersonal psychology, and which is addressed primarily to the academic community. Although it is hoped that the latter will find this book of interest I have written it mainly with social activists and spiritual practitioners in mind, attempting to assess the social significance of the Buddhist diagnosis of the human condition (and especially the contribution of the Mahayana dialectic) and to outline a radical Buddhist activism.

I have been generally critical of attempts to 'update' and 'reinterpret' the Buddhadharma, and am concerned, instead, to examine social phenomena and problems of social transformation in the light of root Buddhist teachings. Buddhist social activism − 'Engaged Buddhism' − is not seen as some new kind of Buddhism, but simply as the logical extension of the traditional teachings of morality and compassion to twentieth-century conditions.

The exposition unfolds through the analysis of the first half of the book and the activism and perspectives on social transformation of the second half. The book starts with the Buddha's diagnosis of the human condition (Part One). This diagnosis is then extended socially; the process of social change is examined, and there is some discussion of the implications of Mahayana Buddhism for our understanding of social phenomena (Parts Two and Three). The second half opens with Part Four on Buddhist training and lifestyle, being the prescription relating back to the diagnosis in Part One. Part Five is both a vindication of Buddhist social activism and a description of the different forms it takes. Attention shifts in Part Six to contemporary Buddhist societies, with a discussion of some Asian Buddhist thinking and social developments. Part Six also refers to the testimony of the Theravada Buddhist *suttas* (scriptures), to the attempt by the Emperor Asoka to create a model Buddhist society, and advice given by the great philosopher Nagarjuna to the same end. Parts Seven and Eight range over questions of violence, peacemaking and conflict resolution, the values and characteristics of a Buddhist Good Society, the prospects for a transformation to some such society, and, relevant to that end, Buddhist affinities with contemporary (and mainly Western) movements, spiritual and secular. There is also some discussion of the relevance of oriental spiritual traditions to the transformation of contemporary Western consciousness, for the fundamental social change argued earlier in Part Eight must, we maintain, depend upon such a personal transformation. The Epilogue is about the gates of despair, and beyond.

# I  Understanding

*The main point to remember is that all the Buddhist teachings are the outcome of a warm heart cherished towards all sentient beings and not of a cold intellect which tries to unveil the secrets of existence by logic. That is to say, Buddhism is personal experience and not impersonal philosophy.*

D.T. Suzuki[7]

*Part One*
Living a Life

# 1 'The Hound of Heaven'⁸

'Suffering, and the Way out of Suffering, I teach.' We begin where Siddhartha Gautama, the Buddha or Awakened One, began in the fifth century BC, with the problem of being a human being, of having to live out a life. 'Suffering' is the usual translation of the Pali word *dukkha*. It is unavoidably misleading, as will become clear as the compendious and suggestive meaning of *dukkha* unfolds.

There is the suffering that arises from gross physical and mental affliction (*dukkha-dukkha*), the 'objective' pain of disease, famine, bereavement and so on. There is the suffering that arises from change, from the vicissitudes of life, from the impermanence of phenomena (*viparinama-dukkha*), whether it be the prospect of death, the sadness of a departure, or the disappointing reality of a long-imagined arrival. As the Zen saying goes, we are all fleas on life's hot griddle. The fleas that jump must fall, and the fleas that fall must jump. And most fundamental, and drawing in the other forms of *dukkha*, is the suffering arising from the struggle to synthesize the flow of transient physical and mental energies into an enduring sense of self (*samkhara-dukkha*).

The Buddha's Second Noble Truth was that suffering arises not from these afflictions themselves but from our characteristic response to them, which is to try to escape from them, and to get less of what we don't want and more of what we do. Whereas we tend to feel that it is the affliction or deprivation itself which causes us to suffer. You may like to confirm the Second Noble Truth by undertaking a simple experiment. Identify in your life some small but strong and well-established indulgence, such as the regular enjoyment of a particular food or drink or some treasured habit. Now deprive yourself of it and continue to do so until you can feel the raw emotion of frustration, irritation and longing almost as a physical sensation. If this experiment is done with a bare, unmixed attention, it will become clear that it is the *feeling* of frustration, the *feeling* of being deprived that causes the suffering and not the *fact* that we have to go without. Contrariwise, it is our frustrated attempts to *evade* what is unpleasant which cause us suffering, though it appears to be due to the unpleasantness itself.

The Third Noble Truth is that suffering disappears when its cause is eliminated. If somehow we cease our (ultimately futile) attempts to try to escape *from* what we don't want *to* what we crave for, then either our sufferings will cease entirely or, in the case of gross physical and mental suffering, we are at least likely to suffer in a different and more positive way. Very different individual responses to much the same painful illness are a case in point. This, as we shall see, by no means implies that by ameliorating these gross forms of affliction we should accept the fact of them with an 'oriental' indifference and do nothing further to remedy them.

As we may discover, perhaps in meditation, perhaps in a personal crisis, all our specific fears go down to one tap root of Fear, growing out of an underlying sense of vulnerability, of transience, and of all that is Other but which resists our efforts to control, possess or reject. And Fear itself conceals an underlying sense of meaninglessness, of existential emptiness. The nature and origin of the self-delusion characteristic of the ordinary human condition are very precisely defined by Rilke:

> Strange, alas, are the streets of the City of Suffering
> where, in the sham silence of sound drowned by

sound, there swaggers the cast poured forth from
the mould of emptiness.[9]

This terrifying sense of emptiness stems from the human
paradox of having an animal body and yet being vividly
conscious of the fact; and from being able, at least some of
the time, to dissociate mind from body and reason from
emotions.

Most people are impelled from the depths of their being
to evade the experience of reality and their evasion takes the
form of whole constellations of behaviours and imaginings
in forms provided by their particular historic culture. Those
who struggle but are unable to share the problematic support
which these delusive constructs give are labelled 'neurotic'.

It was Kierkegaard who dramatically highlighted the existential paradox, which has been central to much subsequent
psychology (the schools of Jung, Fromm, Rollo May, Maslow,
Norman O. Brown are examples). But it has been left to the
poets to express it most graphically — as in Rilke's 'Ninth
Duino Elegy': 'Oh, why *have* to be human, and, shunning
Destiny, long for destiny?' This was particularly so of many
Renaissance poets, who were acutely aware that man's
new-found sense of mastery brought with it a yet deeper
sense of alienation and helplessness. And today, at the end
of an era, many of our poets testify to the unbearable depths
of that paradox. Thus, Shakespeare on the 'Expense of Spirit'
and the Suffering of Alternation:

> The expense of spirit in a waste of shame
>     Is lust in action; and till action, lust
> Is perjured, murderous, bloody, full of blame,
>     Savage, extreme, rude, cruel, not to trust;
> Enjoyed no sooner but despiséd straight;
>     Past reason hunted; and no sooner had,
> Past reason hated, as a swallowed bait,
>     On purpose laid to make the taker mad:
> Mad in pursuit and in possession so;
>     Had, having, and in quest to have, extreme;

A bliss in proof, and proved, a very woe;
  Before, a joy proposed; behind, a dream.
    All this the world well knows; yet none knows
      well
    To shun the heaven that leads men to this hell.

And here, three hundred years later, is Philip Larkin on 'The
life with a hole in it' and the Suffering of Impermanence:

Life is an immobile, locked,
Three-handed struggle between
Your wants, the world's for you, and (worse)
The unbeatable slow machine
That brings what you'll get. Blocked,
They strain round a hollow stasis
Of havings-to, fear, faces.
Days sift down it constantly. Years.[10]

Both *in* nature and yet transcending it, man has to live his
own life; it is not lived for him, as with the animals. He is
doomed never to find real peace until he has faced and truly
responded to the human paradox – that is, until he has
wholeheartedly accepted his humanity.

# 2   *The Lifelong Lawsuit with Reality*

Every kind of human ingenuity is exerted, all unconsciously, to mask and deny what we are. The normal, characteristic human condition is that of delusion, of inauthenticity. Delusion is sustained by the drive to acquire, to possess, to cling to all that will apparently strengthen our sense of self, and to reject all that threatens to undermine it. Whether it be a wave of depression, a bronchial condition, being without work, or unhappiness in a close personal relationship, we instinctively struggle to maintain something of an inviolate and separate self, whether outraged or saintly. 'I' tend to respond as if somehow separate from my condition, making the threat into an alien 'thing' − my bronchitis, my unemployment, my disagreeable marriage. This has the effect of making the condition even more alien and threatening. We are instinctively opposed to what could bring relief and enable us to cope better, through a total acceptance of the depressed me, the wheezing me, the idle and frustrated me, the self-pitying and guilty me. We feel we would become too vulnerable, would 'lose control'.

The struggle to sustain delusion is carried on with ill will, aggressiveness, bitterness and anger, and in the virtuously repressed and transmuted forms of these emotions which will make them socially acceptable and relieve us of guilt. 'When we structure our world we stake out an area which we regard as our territory and the rest we define in vague and general terms − "not my concern", "not worth bothering about", "not our sort of people". We want our territory to be clearly structured, controlled and predictable. When it threatens to be not so...we become aggressive. That is why men go to war and women give their families hell.'[11]

The incessant coping with threat and the feeding of desire to keep the sense of well-being and control is our biographical (and historical) project, our lifelong lawsuit with reality. True, diversions, drugs, entertainments, day-dreams, the playgrounds of what was and what might be, are not unimportant, but there is no doubt that for most people most of the time 'coming to terms with life' amounts to building up and fortifying a strong belongingness identity and 'making your mark in life'. The lifelong formation of belongingness identity is described as follows by Adam Curle: 'We become what we belong to and what belongs to us: our civilization, our nation, region, family, church, political party, wife and children, school, university, neighbourhood, community, house, land, books, profession, clubs and societies, social standing, investments, tastes in music and literature, views on the meaning of life and the immortality of the soul, preferences for brands of cigarettes or gin, friends, reputation, dress, eccentricities, honours, hobbies, way with the opposite sex, pictures and a thousand other things. From these we fabricate a sense of self, an identity. It is by this that we define ourselves to ourselves. It is this form of awareness we must be emptied of in order to achieve the objective awareness of the observer'[12] − a plain awareness identity.

Note that we find our (inauthentic) self-identity both through association but also through 'standing out' and 'making our mark', whether as president of the golf club or wearer of plum-coloured trousers. The most favoured and more or less socially licensed ways of 'standing out' have not changed much since St Augustine of Hippo in the fourth century AD identified them as the acquisition of more power, prestige, wealth and sex than the next person. Similarly, in AD 1984 the twentieth-century luminary, Helen Gurley Brown, editor of *Cosmopolitan* magazine, claimed that 'what every woman yearns to learn' is how to have for herself 'love, success, sex, money'.

With all these belongings and acquisitions what is significant here is not necessarily the mere fact of them but what impels us to need them and our use of them as 'things-out-there' for the aggrandizement of self. Behaving ultimately out of a fear-driven self-need we tend to use all that is other not in terms of itself but in terms of our lifelong project of self-confirmation and reality-denial. As we shall see, that is why much of human history for most people much of the time has been so hellish. Like other great religions, Buddhism teaches that each of us has a True Nature, a Buddha (Awakened) Nature revealed when we become aware that mortal fear is not a necessity of the human condition. More, or less, masked in each of us, this True Nature is always there, always our potential, and always capable of manifesting itself. But it is best not dwelt on, since there is nothing that the hungry self (Small Mind, as we say in Zen) would wish to dress up in more than in that Big Mind. The devil has long been reckoned a cunning fellow, especially in matters of idolatry. And so, in each of our lives, what we do out of self-need *may* indeed be alloyed with a relatively selfless fellow spirit which partakes of our True Nature, in service and in friendship. Buddhism is not a religion of Good warring against Evil, which all too easily becomes the top dog of ego beating hell out of the bottom dog of id for not being good enough. If, through meditation, we become more aware of that self-need that had previously and all-obliviously powered and carried us, and conscious of its destructiveness, then the way forward to integration as a full human being is through the befriending and gentling of it — 'the despised and rejected Shadow' as Jung called it.

As a kind of meditative exercise, you may now like to doodle the details of your own lawsuit with reality on a large sheet of paper. Stick to the facts, allow the associated feelings to surface, do not obstruct with meanings. Watch how it turns into another game for the self to confirm (or disconfirm) the self. For what would happen if there were *no* reflection in the mirror!

In the high-income, high-technology consumer societies when material acquisitiveness palls there is the historical and multicultural supermarket of something different, an array of new ideologies, mysteries, causes, with variants of all the conventional trappings listed by Adam Curle above. With arrivals so much facilitated, eventually finding nothing *really* new or satisfying becomes a bigger and bigger let down. The era of convenience, speed, choice, time saving, and instant access increasingly removes all impediments to the self confronting the nothingness of the self, like Ibsen's Peer Gynt peeling the onion of self to discover what was in the middle. Deluded, wilful and unprepared, this is the beginning of madness, not the dawn of enlightenment. Don Cupitt amplifies:

> In effect, the development of critical thinking and of the scientific outlook has now demythologized or demystified all the things that people have traditionally lived by. Religions, ideologies, moralities and even such basic institutions as marriage and the nation-state have all been reduced by sceptical analysis to complex cultural transforms and masks of the raw biological will to power. The sceptical biological naturalism of Machiavelli, Hobbes, Nietzsche and Freud has prevailed, and the realization of the extent to which human beings as we know them are ultimately motivated by egoistic will-to-power has coincided with our actual acquisition of destructive power on an almost unimaginable scale.[13]

Finally, our sheer, vibrating busyness, being 'on the go', is available to confirm that we are alive and well and here. It can be observed in meditation how, as the mind stills, and the speed of this cinematographic projection slows down, empty gaps begin to appear between the frames and there is

no longer a reassuringly continuous picture. The operator
gives an alarmed start, and the picture speeds up again.

At bottom, all of the foregoing analysis is experiential
rather than intellectual. If it speaks to the reader's condition
this will be because it 'makes sense', and not because 'it
sounds reasonable'. Most people are doubtless, much of the
time, getting sufficient self-reinforcement out of their lives
and are sufficiently unaware of the process, as to find little
truth here. And indeed Buddhism itself may provide such
reinforcement, and thus may take you into a meditational
practice where you become aware of that motivation.
Christopher Isherwood observed that:

> Not all the socially underprivileged are dissatisfied,
> as every reformer knows, to his despair. And this is
> even truer of spiritual poverty than of economic
> lack. Life contains a number of vivid sense-
> pleasures, and the gaps of despondency and bore-
> dom between them can be filled more or less
> adequately by hard work, sleep, the movies, drink,
> and daydreaming. Old age brings lethargy, and
> morphia will help you at the end. Life is not so bad,
> if you have plenty of luck, a good physique and not
> too much imagination. The disciplines proposed
> by the spiritual teachers are drastic, and the lazy
> will shrink from them. They are tedious, also, and
> this will discourage the impatient. Their immediate
> results are not showy, and this will deter the
> ambitious. Their practice is apt to make you appear
> ridiculous to your neighbours. Vanity, sloth and
> desire will all intervene to prevent a man from
> setting his foot upon the path of religious effort.[14]

However, the purposes for which this book was written do
not include conversion. It is simply that people will take from
expositions such as this whatever they find of value. The
value of the book does not altogether depend on your taking
the Buddhist diagnosis personally; that is a matter for you.

The argument of Part One is resumed in the following passages from the Thai meditation master, *Ajahn* Buddhadasa. Of human delusion, which is a key idea in this book, he writes:

> The covering that makes the Buddha-Dharma, or Truth of Buddhism, invisible to us is threefold.... The outermost is the attachment to sense objects....Instinctively our sense organs seek incessant satisfactions. People think they are masters of things, but, on the contrary, they are really the slaves of their senses....The intermediary covering is attachment to and belief in ideologies, creeds or cults of one kind or another. Belief is something that a worldling cannot do without....To take refuge in something other than ourselves is an incomparably strong instinct....The Buddha teaches us to be *attasarana*, or to take refuge only in oneself....The last or innermost covering, [which] is to think in terms of self or 'I' is the most subtle.... To be free from suffering is to destroy the very misconception of an 'I' or self who wants to be free from suffering....['I' or self] is very difficult to gain insight into, because it is suffering itself. It is like the fish swimming in water of which it has no awareness.[15]

And so it is that when

> A fool once searched for a fire
> With a lighted lantern,
> Had he known what fire was
> He could have cooked his rice much sooner.[16]

This brings us to the prescription for the remedying of the human condition as diagnosed above, though the instructions for the remedy — the Buddha's Fourth Noble Truth — must wait till Part Four. This liberation can, from the delusive starting point of the Way of practice and training, only be an 'inconceivable liberation'. It is the total acceptance of, and opening up to, the transience and fragility of our human condition. It is the emptying of wants and desires of the clinging, agitated and opinionated 'I', so that the world is experienced undistorted and unfreighted by self-need. All that is Other is then seen in its *own* light. The self is restored to the self, to the body and to 'the ten thousand things'. Then 'things become beautiful, but not desirable; ugly, but not repulsive; false, but not rejected; a task may be boring and trivial, but we do it without anxiety or alienation.'[17]

In the awakening to the realization that there is no fear, there is a great sense of release and gratitude, although, at the instant, this transcendence seems a leap into oblivion. When we cease to struggle, the water buoys us up, and then we are ready really to learn to swim, instead of thrashing about to keep afloat in the belief that we are getting somewhere.

This 'coming home' to reality and our restoration to our True Nature is the dawning of what Buddhists mean by Wisdom. And the transpersonal, social face or aspect of this revelation is Compassion, which arises as deep fellow-feeling for the driven folly and suffering of humanity and all living things.

Delusion and suffering can only be personally and individually experienced. And they are perennial to the human condition; they are *existential* phenomena. However, individuals live out their lives as social persons; their endeavours to satisfy their existential needs, whether these be physical or spiritual, are social endeavours. Phenomena such as delusion and suffering therefore take on a secondary, social aspect, which amplifies or supercharges the existential experience described in this chapter. The traditional Buddhist picture of personal delusion karmically sustained over many lifetimes must now be supplemented and seen also as a social process sustained through successive historical cultures. Society in the Buddha's time lacked the kind of dynamism and complexity that might have stimulated such awareness. This only came into existence in the West in comparatively recent times, with the emergence of the social sciences. Our next step in this book will therefore be to extend the fundamental, existential *dharma* introduced in Part One so that it engages with the social process as we understand it today, and to show how it powers the evolution of human cultures and societies. This is the subject of Parts Two and Three.

*Part Two*
The Dynamics of Delusion

# 3   *The Driven Historical Drama*

In its unfolding, human history has been shaped and powered by millions of individual hungers to *exist* as persons who need not only food, shelter and protection from enemies but who also hunger for the *feeling* of existence, of selfhood. Ignorant of the nature and origin of this hunger that rises from the depths of their being, men and women have struggled to assuage it in inauthentic and fear-driven ways, within their minds, in their personal responses, and historically in an awesome collective social drama. This powerful Will has been expressed in different schools of psychology variously as the Will to Pleasure (Freud), the Will to Power (Adler), Fromm's Will to Have (instead of the Freedom to Be), and the Will to Meaning of the existentialists.

This deluded struggle for psychic survival throws up social creations, whether they be institutions or ideologies, which appear to take on a life of their own, become things-in-themselves, whether it be the 'blind' workings of the economic system or a war's 'inevitability'. With gathering momentum and increasing complexity, human history appears to move episodically through successive societies and cultures towards a tragic climax, with grand flourishes of vainglorious folly along the way, whether of imperial might or of technological achievement. Will the climax militarily or ecologically cripple us and lay waste almost beyond recovery? Or will our predicament somehow spring us into a collective awareness of reality analogous to the mystic's

Awakening out of the Dark Night of the Soul?

This chapter looks more closely at the historical process. Chapter 4 analyses the global crisis in some detail, since this is the context of Buddhist and other spiritual activism. And Chapter 5 first examines the Buddhist idea of *kamma* (*karma*) in its traditional meaning and then discusses how this might be extended to inform our understanding of the nature of human history.

For most of recorded human history productive capacity has been so low that famine, poverty and disease have been endemic. With limited sources of power, the use and control of the natural environment was marginal and precarious, though in many ways skilful and resourceful. For most, starvation was never further away than the next failed harvest. However, recorded history has traditionally been about the doings of rulers and especially about the wars which they waged. Beyond the alleged necessities for taking up arms, wars have always had something of a blood ritual about them. To be willing fearlessly to face death and to triumph over death by successfully slaughtering others is perhaps the most powerful existential self-affirmation, or so the culture of warrior societies would suggest. The mass of the population struggled to scratch a living from the soil, their tiny surpluses above subsistence level being appropriated by their rulers. From time to time they rose in vengeful revolt, slaves and peasants threatening order with chaos. Within and without, 'all is burning' proclaimed the Buddha's Fire Sermon, and another ancient scripture warned that 'due to sensuous craving, conditioned through sensuous craving, impelled by sensuous craving, entirely moved by sensuous craving, people break into houses, rob and plunder, pillage whole houses, commit highway robbery, seduce the wives of others. Then the rulers have such people caught and inflict on them various forms of punishment. And thereby they incur death or deadly pain.'[18]

Subsequently the nation-state replaced the church in providing the most powerful and bonding belongingness identity for rich and poor alike in the West. Previously somewhat disreputable, the 'private vice' of unvarnished mercantile greed was proclaimed a 'public virtue'. In the last four hundred years the peoples and resources of the whole planet have been laid open to an exploitation that epitomizes the ancient Buddhist 'Fires' of greed, aggression and delusion more dramatically and unequivocally than in any previous culture.

The fact of exploiting and exploited social classes so pungently laboured by Marx seems such a gross commonplace to any traveller with eyes to see, or to anyone with a little knowledge of the history of the common people of his own district and the evidence he can see on the ground, that it is remarkable that it should be considered controversial. Yet this phenomenon of social class exploitation is inexplicable solely on economic grounds, and only becomes credible if the analysis is carried beyond Marxian economics. For, having made provision for their physical needs, the powerful are *still* driven by an insatiable existential hunger fed by wars and triumphs, pomps and shows, great works and monuments to confirm 'in perpetuity' the high and mighty power of the personal and collective selfhood of ruler, ruling class, and State (and much high art, literature and music has been culled as by-product). For most of human history this 'psychic greed' (or existential need) has been the prime mover working beneath and beyond Marx's 'historical materialism'. Indeed, at times, as 'prestige' and 'honour' it has overridden both political and economic concerns. Governments will go out of their way to exhaust their wealth and even hazard their existence on some point of national honour. A relatively recent example is the British—Argentinian conflict over some economically worthless islands of bog and heather situated on the edge of the world and with a population no greater than that of an English village. In the capitalist era feudal ostentation has given way to a more calculating and single-minded acquisitiveness, clothed in the sombre morality of Protestant industrial Christianity, with its philanthropic righteousness, immense self-control, and quiet desperation beneath the hypocrisy. And today in the world's rich countries there are millions of people who are wealthier than the princes of old yet nine-tenths of their consumption is a self-confirming satisfying of an endless round of newly created desires.

Yet amidst all this the record testifies that in all ages there have been the less deceived, the eloquent witnesses to the folly and the tragedy, the celebrants of the black existential comedy, the open hearted and the open handed, those who have *known* but undefeated have done their best, whether wise sceptics or saints who have lived before God as if He did not exist. These have testified to the potential to *see through* historically amplified existential conditioning. The drama is not inevitable. But the poor and the oppressed also suffer existential hunger, so much so that in trying to satisfy it they have subordinated the satisfaction of physical needs and even given their lives. To this end they have (from a Marxian view like that of Marcuse) colluded with their oppressors (whether Sargon King of Kings or Adolf Hitler and the Third Reich) in order to share the exalted belongingness of our war, our race, our religion, our ideology, our country. To suppose these are mere Marxian opiates and ruling class conspiracies is entirely to misunderstand and underestimate them. It is a commonplace that authority cannot long be maintained by force or the threat of it; authority originates in those who obey and conform, not in those who govern by it. The 'false consciousness' that is powered by existential fear and existential greed is much more profound and all-embracing than is the socio-political phenomenon identified by Marx. And in this lies the ultimate futility of the Marxist remedy.

From the examples given so far in this chapter it will be easier to appreciate the phenomenon of *antithetical bonding* as the principal social and historical means of personal and collective self-affirmation. We have seen in the previous chapter how the individual seeks both the self-confirming assurance of group membership and the self-affirmation of standing out separate from all that is other. This is socially enhanced through antithetical bonding, that is, by bonding together in a group where the common belongingness identity is more deeply established and exalted by the subordination of another group or competition with it. This antithesis may be an economic, political, cultural, racial, religious or − most persistent − sexual phenomenon. History is the history of us and them, though with ulterior rather than overt expression. The relationship between social identity and historical events has been analysed by Tajfel and others, [19] and a number of earlier classic experiments[20] testify to the ready resort by individuals to antithetical bonding on the slightest pretext or encouragement. Once in train, both the bonding and the conflict tend to intensify; all other goals and values are subordinated to that of ascendency of one's own group; leadership is consolidated and deviant ideas within each group are suppressed; differences between the groups are exaggerated and what they may have in common is ignored or denied. Antithetical bonding is the means by which the destructive potential of existential delusion is realized, culminating in Cold War between two groups large enough to span a shrunken globe and offering a prospect of mutual destruction in preference to the most modest kinds of existential self-denial.

Readers who attempted the exercise in the previous chapter might now like to extend it to sketching in their own cognitive map of *their* in- and out-groups, opening to the associated feelings and the underlying sense of *needfulness*.

Whether within the group or by one group over another, the very activity of ordering and controlling, of bending others to our will, and even rejoicing in their vulnerability, fear and pain, has about it a gratuitous lust, a thick-blooded need, which goes beyond what may be functionally necessary or even socially and morally sanctioned. This is very evident in certain insecure and rigid types of personality but it is an impulse that appears to exist in most of us, revealed as one of the bitter first-fruits of meditative awareness. It is a matter of common experience in police forces, prisons and armies, where it is given some functional and moral licence, but also occurs quite commonly in the whole range of everyday superior—subordinate relationships, as in professional and client, landlord and tenant, teacher and pupil, parent and child, official and citizen. Always there is both the tendency to merge into the role, and so avoid exposing our vulnerable humanity, and also the urge to exploit it beyond the functional requirement. This may range from the tangible satisfaction of the civil servant who formally regrets his unhelpfulness because he is 'tied by the rules' through various kinds of (aptly called) bloody-mindedness to the cool efficiency of the government torturer now found in most of the world's states.

Although it is the same existential hunger that drives humanity through successive eras of its history, the cultural evidence indicates that it is experienced through an *evolving* consciousness. Ken Wilber has outlined such an evolution in his remarkable book *Up from Eden*. From the neolithic agrarian revolution and the beginnings of civilization he distinguishes (in the West) low, middle and high egoic periods of evolution, 2500 to 500 BC, 500 BC to AD 1500, and AD 1500 to date, respectively. Among the 'new and expanded potentials' of the egoic era he includes 'the possibility of rational comprehension; a final transcendence of nature and the body; formal operational thinking; a capacity for intro-spection; a new form of, and potential respect for, morality; the beginnings of the sanctity of personhood.' But these potentials Wilber balances against the 'new terrors *necessarily* brought' by the egoic structure, which is 'more vulnerable; more aware of its mortality; more guilty in its emergence; more open to anxiety. *And* the new terrors *inherent* in the ego, when coupled with the new *powers* of the ego, resulted in the *possibility* (not necessity) of even more brutal terrors exercised *by* the ego: new substitute sacrifices, mass homi-

cide, oppressive exploitation, massive slavery, class alienation, violent inequality, hedonistic over-indulgence and
wildly exaggerated substitute gratifications.'[21]

Wilber assumes that there is a necessity in this evolution
whereby the egoic powers must be developed to the full
before they can be transcended in a breakthrough to authentic experience. In this he contrasts with currently fashionable 'wrong turning' views, which hark back to various
possible Golden Ages before 'the Fall' of Technological Man.
Wilber's view has interesting implications which are taken
up at the end of this book. His tidy evolutionary assumptions
are very much open to question, however, as is suggested
by a footnote on page 187 which explains the two basic
reasons why 'the story was somewhat different in the East'.
'The East developed and implemented on a large scale techniques for transformation into the superconsciousness
realms, which acted as a counter-balance and release from
the exclusive tyranny of the ego; on the other hand, masses
of Eastern peoples never truly developed beyond membership societies, with heavy emphasis on pre-egoic ties and
communal values.' Societies that enabled techniques for
spiritual transformation to be implemented on 'a large scale'
surely cannot have been marked by a 'low' level of consciousness development?

# 4   The Culmination

The global civilization brought forcefully into being in the twentieth century can be characterized as follows.

1. There is a central belief in material progress, founded on society's apparently limitless capacity for technological development.

2. This runaway productive capacity is cutting deeply into the natural resources of the planet. It is also poisoning the environment with its waste products, and threatening ecological equilibrium.

3. The seemingly endless satisfaction (and stimulation) of consumer expectations has become the main preoccupation of the richer countries and the goal of the poorer countries.

4. The ever-increasing wealth, however, is increasingly concentrated in the richer countries and, more particularly, in the hands of the world's governing élites (including the rulers of the poorer countries). The indebtedness of the poorer countries, the impoverishment of the mass of their peoples and the destruction of indigenous cultures are accelerating processes. It is estimated that when the world's population stabilizes at about the end of the century, the Third World will have ninety per cent of the world's people but only twenty per cent of its wealth.

5. The four-hundred-year evolution of nation-states and their balance of power has culminated in the Cold War between two superpowers and their satellites, driving, and driven by, an escalating military technology of genocidal capacity. This mutually suicidal relationship has at least part

of its origins in the fears and ambitions arising from competing influence in the Third World countries, which are becoming increasingly unstable both economically and politically.

6. Less well known is the creeping militarization of global society, in terms of the increasing economic importance of arms manufacture and trade, the power of industrial, and scientific and military vested interests in this sphere, and the increase in size and power of the military and police bureaucracies concerned, even in the democracies, with civil surveillance and control. It is estimated that in any twenty-four-hour period the world spends £1½ billion on arms whilst 10,000 of its people die of hunger.

7. In several countries, various forms of socialism (ranging from Soviet communism to Swedish social democracy) have appeared as purposive and systematic attempts at counter-vailing 'social engineering', designed both to relieve the suffering caused by unbridled capitalism and to make bene-volent use of the productive capacity it has developed. This is the classic secular industrial response to the problem of human suffering, and it has engaged much noble idealism and sacrifice, as well as much hatred and vengefulness. It is at once the most hopeful and the most disappointing social phenomenon of our century, and deserves the respectful and critical attention of Buddhists. This line of enquiry is resumed in Chapter 10.

8. American capitalism and Soviet communism display equal and opposite virtues and vices, but, overall, each distorts and impoverishes humanity. And in much the same ways they amass world war arsenals, ravage the earth's resources, and trample on human rights. E. F. Schumacher has characterized the *industrial materialism* that they share in common as follows: 'If greed were not the master of modern man — ably assisted by envy — how could it be that the frenzy of economism does not abate as higher standards of living are attained? How could we explain the almost uni-versal refusal on the part of the rulers of the rich societies —

whether organized along private enterprise or collectivist enterprise lines – to work towards the *humanization of work*? It is only necessary to assert that something would "reduce the standard of living" and every debate is instantly closed.'[22]

In its metropolitan countries of origin (though less likely in its neo-colonial client states) capitalism is associated with representative democracy and human rights. Together with much else of value, these democratic cultures provide a climate in which new departures of all kinds can at least *begin* to grow and where many invaluable phenomena can flourish. The fate of Buddhism in Tibet and Vietnam as compared with Thailand and India springs to mind. The production and distribution of this book now in your hands is an immediate example. Contrariwise, the restrictions and repressions in communist countries contrast with their education, health and housing services available on a basis of need rather than greed, and with their full employment and absence of grinding poverty. A grim Czechoslovak joker concluded that 'in the final analysis, in democracy man exploits man, in communism it's the other way round.'

However, for better or worse, the dominant driving force in the world today is surely transnational capitalism, with the United States providing the main thrust. Where it is well established, communism tends to run to uneasy and defensive conservative bureaucracy, preoccupied with internal problems. Although given to bouts of aggressive paranoia and military adventurism (Soviet Union in Afghanistan, Cuba in Angola, China in Vietnam), the weight of expert opinion[23] does not support the view that there is some kind of innate Soviet thrust to global domination. The Palme Report makes the point that 'Eastern bloc transnationals talk about royalties instead of profits and report to government commissions instead of shareholders, but they are organized on the same global scale and participate in the same global resource wars motivated by the same obsessions with open-ended growth.'[24] There is, nevertheless, no comparison with the much greater resources, dynamism and global coverage of transnational capitalism. Today, so-called 'international communism' rather than being a global pace-setter tends, instead, to erupt as one possible Third World response to the intolerable pressures of the transnationals and their often oppressive local client regimes. Subjected to military and economic pressures such *national liberation* movements (for example, Cuba, Nicaragua, Laos, Angola) tend to be pushed into the Soviet or Chinese communist sphere of influence in order to survive. For example, in Nicaragua 'The most popular slogan is still "Patria libre o morir" — freedom or death. . . . Mention the word *socialismo* and the average Nicaraguan peasant will probably look blank or say he wants no part of it!'[25]

Capitalism is a system of wealth creation, but it is also an historic form of response to existential fear and frustration which makes public virtues of the ancient Buddhist 'Fires' of acquisitiveness and aggression, in the form of the maximum freedom of individuals and groups to pursue wealth and status, to fight it out in competitive conflict, and to exercise great power over their fellow men and women, as both wage workers and consumers. At least in the rich countries, the institutional violence of modern, corporate capitalism is restrained, masked and refined as compared with its nineteenth-century antecedents, and it is in the poor countries of the world that its presence is most grossly evident. The characteristics of this social system have been eloquently summarized by two Western Buddhists each writing out of a lifetime's first-hand experience. David Brandon, a British social worker, writes of social structures and institutions that 'reward and encourage greed, selfishness and exploitation rather than love, sharing and compassion. . . . People who are relatively successful at accumulating goods and social position wish to ensure that they remain successful. . . . Both in intended and unintended ways they erect barriers of education, finance and law to protect their property and their interests. . . . These structures and their protective institutions continue to exacerbate and amplify the basic human inequalities in housing, health care, education and income....Certain people's lifestyles, characterized by greed and overconsumption, become dependent on the deprivation of the many.'[26] Similarly, for Gary Snyder, a much travelled American Zen Buddhist and poet, 'The "free world" has become economically dependent on a fantastic system of stimulation of greed which cannot be fulfilled, sexual desire which cannot be satiated, and hate which has no outlet except against oneself, the persons one is supposed to love, or the revolutionary aspirations of pitiful, poverty-stricken marginal societies like Cuba or Vietnam.'[27]

As we try to unravel that global crisis which is the field and context of Buddhist social ethics and action, using guides like *The Global 2000 Report*,[28] the two Brandt Commission reports[29] and the Palme Report,[30] the conclusion of the last becomes more and more evident, namely that the large transnational corporations are the principal agents of today's global exploitation − undifferentiated growth, the arms race, political dominance, perpetuation of the inequitable distribution of wealth, exploitation of both people and nature, and destruction of the biosphere.

Let us now examine more closely the facts of this global crisis, considering first the situation in the poorer countries of the world and then the other intertwining strands of the nuclear arms race and the ecological degradation of the planet.

In the Third World traditional cultures in their rich diversity are being rapidly undermined and destroyed. Cash cropping for export is pushing the peasantry out onto the poorer marginal tracts, and increasing soil exhaustion, deforestation and malnutrition. For example, seventy-five per cent of all Central American forests have been destroyed since 1975 in order to produce beef for export to the USA. Yet beef consumption in Guatemala was halved over that period, and seventy per cent of Central American children are undernourished. The United Nations Food and Agriculture Organization reports that out of a world population of some 4500 million, 500 million are actually starving, most of them children under five years of age. There is an unemployed and marginally employed slum proletariat swollen annually by the increasing numbers who can no longer make a living off the land. In order to sustain a middle-class Western lifestyle (and, hopefully, to provide basic welfare and education services for their people) the local élites in the Third World countries must promote the low-cost exploitation by the multinationals of foodstuffs and raw materials, to which end their lands and rivers are being ravaged and contaminated on a scale which would be unacceptable in the rich countries. The destruction of the world's great rain forests is a well-known case in point. 'Aid' programmes provide the roads, harbours, dams and other infrastructure, and inflate bureaucracies which include many sincere planners and administrators for whom no practicable alternative development model exists. Indebtedness to the rich countries has reached crisis proportions, with renewed demands from the creditors of the International Monetary Fund to lower costs and push down living standards.

The Third World countries have also suffered extensive militarization in recent years, whether it be to combat, or to sustain, 'people's liberation' or 'communist subversion', or out of fear of destabilization by more powerful states, or to fuel the several national, racial, civil and tribal conflicts which add to the afflictions of Third World peoples (for example, Iraq/Iran, Ethiopia/Eritrea, Uganda, Lebanon). The following poignant episode was reported from the remote Uganda–Kenya frontier area. There the traditional tribal raiding parties were once armed with bows and arrows and depended on stealth and fleetness of foot. Now they have been able to acquire automatic rifles. A journalist has reported the result, from a Catholic mission hospital in the region: 'Down one side of the ward were the Karamajong; down the other side, six feet away, were their enemies, the Turkana: both smashed to pieces by dum-dum bullets.'[31]

The world arms trade now makes two-thirds of its sales in the Third World countries, which spend three times as much on arms as on health care.

Rich countries and poor are very much part of an indivisible economic system, as the shelves of any supermarket make clear. Should not the peoples of the rich democracies find more effective and fundamental ways of making common cause, in shared humanity, with 'the wretched of the earth', as Fanon called them? While one hand gives marginal, charitable support, the other pays taxes to warehouse the various surplus food mountains.

The nuclear arms race and ecological crisis are seen rightly as the great threats to humanity, but it is Third World exploitation and conflict that powers them. It is in the Third World that superpower fear, acquisitiveness and triumphalism are most specifically located. Of the ten military nuclear crises that have occurred in the last twenty years all were in the Third World, where there have been all the major wars or dangers of war since the end of the Second World War. In my view the momentum of the nuclear arms race is to be found in the endeavour of the United States to achieve an overwhelming military superiority in order to safeguard absolutely the global concerns on which its prosperity depends. The bizarre 'Star Wars' project (Strategic Defence Initiative) is the most recent and sensational example. Thus two American foreign policy experts have argued that 'For us, peace finally exists when the world is safe for American businessmen to carry on their business everywhere, on terms as favourable as can be made, and in settings managed preferably by native middle-class governments, but if need be by oligarchic and repressive ones.'[32] The arms race momentum is also sustained by the huge arms industry and the associated scientific and governmental bureaucracies: the Cold War is their business, their way of life. True, it takes two to make a race, and the Soviet Union can be a no less truculent and uncompromising partner in it. But, as we have argued earlier, this is a partner that struggles anxiously to keep up, rather than one that sets the pace. Poor economic and technological performance, numerous other internal problems, unreliable allies, and the potential threat of China all suggest that the Soviet threat is one of paranoiac adventurism and panicky pre-emptive strike rather than any inherent drive for global hegemony.

The Cold War thus has existential roots as the ultimate, global expression of antithetical bonding, and a strong economic and political trunk. Trying to lop back the thick foliage of mutual fear and mistrust is well worth doing, but should not be mistaken for an uprooting of the tree.

It is important to appreciate that the policy of Mutually Assured Destruction (MAD), which for many years provided at least some kind of consolation and mad rationality for the nuclear arms race, has now, in effect, been abandoned by both sides. Each is now perfecting nuclear weaponry like the American MX system that is intended to be fast and accurate enough for a pre-emptive knockout of the adversary. Worse still, the USA is evidently abandoning the previously tacitly accepted policy of maintaining some kind of 'balance' of nuclear terror. It has made a dramatic bid for unchallengeable superiority by proclaiming its intention to create an impregnable 'Star Wars' shield in space. This would enable it to make a first nuclear strike with impunity, since even if the knockout of the Soviet capacity for retaliation were not total, any retributory missiles would be intercepted. However technologically impracticable this hugely expensive project may be, there is no doubt that it has worsened the Cold War, frustrated disarmament negotiations, caused deep apprehension in the USSR and in Europe, and created a deeper sense of despair and incredulity in the world as a whole.

The rich countries of the world are now spending $17 billion a fortnight on arms, a sum that could provide adequate food, water and health services for every man, woman and child on earth. So great is the mutual overkill capacity that East and West could dismantle fifty per cent of its nuclear weaponry without any military disadvantage. Yet it has not been possible even to agree a (readily verifiable) freeze of the development of new weapons and a comprehensive test ban treaty (though the USSR *does* favour both). All but the smallest towns in the USA, USSR and allied countries now have hanging over them by a thread the Sword of Damocles of specific targetting. With six minutes warning time, a bilateral nuclear war would take about twenty minutes to complete. Within thirty days ninety per cent of Americans, Europeans and Russians would have died as a result of initial blast, fireballs, radiation sickness, starvation, psychosis and grief. Conservative and independent estimates by both Western and Soviet scientists point to the climatic catastrophe of a planet shrouded in nuclear dust. The resulting arctic climate would combine with other conditions to make the continued survival of humanity (and many other species) improbable.[33] To the possibility of war precipitated by computer failure or human error must be added the more long-term certainty of the proliferation of nuclear weapons to countries such as Libya, Iran, Israel and South Africa by the end of the century.

Most experts believe that nuclear war is more likely than not to occur before the end of the century, but this prospect of the laying waste of our civilization and the termination of the human race is more than the imagination can reach to, or than it could bear if it could. Despair is variously masked by helpless apathy, wilful ignorance, obsolete rationality, and other forms of denial. It is as if we are resigned to our fate as to a possibly terminal illness but through which we pretend to carry on as normal. Yet the sickness of humanity need not be fatal, if only we can find a way beyond both denial and despair.

The third of the intertwined strands of global crisis is ecological. Although an environmental crisis undoubtedly exists, its nature and future development are more problematic than they appeared to be some years ago, with much conflicting evidence and supposition. Most notably, the claim that planet Earth would become a spent, depleted shell if the present rate of exploitation of its raw material resources continued for a few more decades is now no longer tenable. These resources are indeed finite, but, when needs be, modern science and technology have a great capacity both for making little go further and for developing alternatives. Schumacher himself did not believe in the general depletion theory and put the weight of his argument for alternative technology upon the imperatives of a global energy crisis.[34] The falling price of oil (and of world consumption of it) over the last ten years, together with the recent discovery of huge supplies of cheap coal world wide, have now negated this argument also. Conservationists themselves have maintained that the absence of an energy crisis makes nuclear power stations unnecessary. What is certain is that on present trends sooner or later we shall lose valuable planetary resources with results that are at best unpredictable. The loss of our tropical rain forests early in the twenty-first century would be particularly grievous. Nevertheless, it now appears that the ecological crisis is less about the absolute exhaustion of resources and more about how resources are used, in both environmental and social terms.[36] World population and food supply is a case in point.

World population growth is expected to stabilize by the end of the century, and sufficient food is already being produced to feed everyone adequately were the economic system to be based on simple need. However, for reasons noted earlier in this chapter, in the Third World more food is now being produced, but there is less of it to eat. The problem is not the redistribution of food, or even overseas aid, but the redistribution of control over agricultural resources. And *that* is a brutally political problem. Here the economic situation has forced the unwise use of resources, which are suffering an absolute depletion. A combination of profit-hungry agribusiness on relatively good land with over-cultivation of marginal land by the displaced poor is in many areas impoverishing the soil. According to a recent United Nations Environmental Programme survey, one third of the surface of the earth is in danger of turning into desert, and 470 million people living there are now seriously under-nourished or actually starving.

Whether or not resources are being seriously depleted, their reckless large-scale exploitation to maximize profit out of artificially stimulated needs undoubtedly contributes to the pollution and degradation of the land, sea and air. Agribusiness is increasingly controlled by the petrochemical industry, with extensive use of toxic fertilizers and pesticides to boost the production of increasingly over-processed 'junk food'. The United States alone produces a thousand new chemical compounds a year, many with uncertain long-term effects on human beings. Toxic wastes and pollutants are an increasing hazard in land, sea and air. Acid rain is a well-publicized example. The dangers of nuclear technology in particular are becoming more and more alarmingly evident. Thus, Dr Helen Caldicott goes so far as to argue that 'nuclear technology threatens life on our planet with extinction. If present trends continue, the air we breathe, the food we eat and the water we drink will soon be contaminated with enough radioactive pollutants to pose a potential health hazard far greater than any plague humanity has ever experienced.'[36]

It will be seen that the better use of global resources is about three kinds of concern. The first is the need to reduce environmental hazards and degradation by employing safer and less destructive alternative resources and technologies, as in the case of organic farming and wind and solar technology, and by modifying such conventional technologies as may be worth retaining. The second concern is for greater social justice in the control and distribution of wealth, that is, concern about the *relative* shortage or availability of resources. It is no longer credible to assume that if more and more wealth were created enough of it would inevitably trickle down to make the poor comfortably off. The poverty and beggary of the world's richest city, New York, comes as a shock to visitors from European 'welfare states' where trickle-down has been enforced and equitably distributed by legislation following political pressure. In the Third World there are short-term, marginal developments that can help the poor to make the best of their existing situation, for example, sinking wells and introducing drought-resistant crops. Such basic self-sufficiency should indeed be pushed to the limit, but in some countries landlordism, usury, profitable large-scale cash-cropping, the pressures and inducements of the multinationals, and local governmental policies combine to narrow the limit beyond which power politics have to be challenged, and that is a move into a dangerous, complex and intractable area, whether for the Third World poor or for their supporters in the rich countries. A preference for working for development aid or endangered species is understandable but may to some extent be an evasion of the hot, socio-political, fear-and-greed-and-power problems that are the prime mover of our multiple crisis. Outside the violent, confrontational ideological games of conventional politics we need to find means of persuasion and pressure, upon the multinationals and governments, to help the poor in the Third World to shift the balance of power more in their favour. Writing Oxfam cheques and not bringing South African oranges home from the supermarket are both worthwhile, but is this good enough?

In the third place, campaigns against nuclear power, artificially processed foodstuffs, the destruction of areas of beauty and wildlife, and against new ways of increasing speed, convenience, quantity and novelty at the expense of beauty, simplicity, tranquillity and self-reliance, are all reactions that are at the same time positive aspirations towards a society of harmony and peace instead of exploitation and violence. For Buddhists, these values relate to our 'True Nature', our authentic, fully human potential.

Beyond gross and subtle physical violences wrought by

a driving, technologically armed, power-seeking greed there is a spiritual deprivation to be noted. In Chapter 2 we observed how the restless search for greater understanding, control and rationality has stripped bare traditional beliefs and institutions so that, paradoxically, people now find less and less in their world that is truly Other in a meaningful and supportive sense. Similarly, humankind is busily creating convenient, easily available means for the satisfaction of our wants. But this is at the cost of losing a kind of environment that was once sufficiently Other for us to *have* to work with it, go with its grain, and become more aware through doing so. Now we are able all too easily to impose a potent − but alienated − selfhood upon it through our omnipotent technology. Compare, for example, a fibre-glass boat with one crafted out of timber, or a concrete bridge with the necessary arching curves of a bridge built of bricks or stones. And the heart's ease is found not only in the making of these things, or even only in their use, but in the daily company of their shape, texture, weight. The often more convenient, and certainly cheaper, plastic simulations are only sad day-dreams after such realities. In my innocence yesterday I went out to buy deal planks for book shelves as I had done years ago, but was offered only degraded composition wood. Tongue-and-groove room lining and stripped pine furniture of the servant class are now in demand for middle-class homes because we are able to salvage less and less of such *reality* even from the commonplace past. Rilke warned that 'live things, things lived and conscient of us, are running out and can no longer be replaced. We are perhaps the last still to have known such things. On us alone rests the responsibility not only of preserving their memory (that would be too little and unreliable) but their human and laural value' ('laural' in the sense of household gods).[37] In our loss we are becoming aware of the significance of the traditional Buddhist reverence and gratitude for even the humblest things that are themselves and truly *other*. If we have the humility to honour them in the way we keep company with them and use them, they honour us in return and warm our hearts. This is a wisdom known to every craftsman and crafts-woman. It is the wisdom and compassion of a Buddhist ecology.

Before concluding this chapter I should like to clarify this villain-of-the-piece called transnational capitalism. I use this and similar terms with reluctance because they bring with them many ready assumptions and are the signal for readers to start taking sides. A phenomenon like transnational capitalism is seen as a thing-out-there or, worse still, as a collectivity of walk-on villains (or heroes) out there, available for some heart-warming hatred (or applause). We tend to swing readily into such objectivizations, with a sense of relief at knowing where we stand and recognizing that everything in our mental/emotional landscape is in its familiar place. Such solid objectivizations, in strong and contrasting colours, have a compelling quality, which appears to take us out of ourselves away from the quicksands of self-awareness.

Transnational capitalism is a network of economic and social relationships, few of which are face-to-face. These relationships are lived out, variously, with defiance, resentfully, ignorantly, gladly, greedily, purposively or even altruistically. They are thus variously lived out by the Latin-American plantation worker, his boss the plantation owner in his hacienda, the banana company executive in an air-conditioned office a thousand miles away, the shareholder whose income depends on such investments, and the supermarket assistant through whose hands pass a huge range of the cheap tropical produce of Third World wretchedness. In fact, the network of relationships is infinitely more impersonal and more institutionally labyrinthine than this. Clearly some kind of historic crime is being perpetrated, or at least some great wrong, but so many of us are implicated; even the banana eater is an accessory. But such institutionalized, role-entrenched crime goes on being institutionalized unless the institutions are changed (in which case the 'criminous' will try to turn to something else). However, even in the case of commonly recognized institutionalized crimes, such as war crimes, there is usually some allocation of responsibility, some recognition that free-will exists even if it is conditioned by 'just doing my job', 'not my responsibility but his', and so on. Buddhism, however, while being rigorous about personal responsibility, is the more compassionate in blame by virtue of its recognition of the rooted, deluded, and *driven* condition of unawakened humanity.

Those who, world wide, hate transnational capitalism (with good reason), and work to destroy it, are in fact more actors in the same play, working out of the same script, than they are aware. And so are we all. It is a script whose different parts are made up of violence, domination, dogma, hypocrisy, apathy and despair, but these mentalities are shared out more equally between the 'heroes' and the 'villains' then they were in the old stage plays. They are more, or less, substantially in evidence in Moscow, New York, Havana, Tehran, Jerusalem and Copenhagen. People have given their lives (and are doing so now) to create social orders in which people are less afflicted by these mentalities. However, it is questionable how far new social conditions have or could give any *fundamental* relief from these afflictions, or could dissolve the global crisis. It is also questionable whether such superficial 'liberation' is not selling humanity short of its true potential.

# 5   *Kamma: The Dynamism of Delusion*

The last two chapters have been concerned with the socio-historical expression of the characteristic individual struggle to escape from fear by acquiring, achieving, belonging and aggression. This chapter and the next examine the personal and social dynamics of that response. In Buddhism this is the phenomenon of *kamma,* and I use the Pali word here because the better known Sanskrit *karma* has acquired Hindu meanings of 'fate' and 'justice' which have nothing to do with Buddhism.

A central tenet of Buddhism is the dynamic interdependence of phenomena, which are in process of continuous mutual redefinition. As we shall see in the next Part, in Mahayana Buddhism this is a paradoxical dialectic, but for our present purpose it will be sufficient to understand that interdependence in terms of cause and effect. The Buddhist literature distinguishes five different orders of conditioning, of cause and effect. They are:

> *utu-niyama,* physical inorganic order;
> *bija-niyama,* physical organic (biological) order;
> *mano-* (or *citta-*) *niyama,* non-volitional mental order;
> *karma-niyama,* volitional mental order; and
> *dharma-niyama,* transcendental order.

The relationship between the different *niyamas* is complex, though at a gross level they are accessible to common observation and scientific investigation. All, however, are also expressions of a Universal Consciousness, *alayavijnana*. The 'law' of kamma and the 'law' of cause and effect are thus not synonymous in Buddhism. Kammaic 'law' is simply one kind of cause and effect relationship.

Kamma is volitional mental activity which may leave in the personality a trace or influence (kammaic 'fruit', *kamma-vipaka*), as in the case of feeling bloody-minded towards somebody. It is important to distinguish between kamma and its effect; the latter becomes the ground for further kamma. Such activities interact and such traces cumulate, shaping a personality marked by dispositions and tendencies, a character with habitual and predictable patterns of feeling, thought and behaviour. An old saying has it: 'Sow a thought and you reap a habit; sow a habit and you reap a personality; sow a personality and you reap a destiny.'

Since most of us are root-deluded and alienated from others and from our very selves, our kamma tends to be *akusala* – unwholesome, that is egoistic, aggressive and acquisitive. However, our mental acitivity is conditioned by our existential fear and the whole superstructure of response that stems from it, and therefore it would be better to describe it as *wilful* rather than willed. We may be so carried by our kamma as to be unaware of our bad habits, and when we are aware we may find we have little or no control over our 'wilfulness'; hence expressions like 'I did it without thinking', 'I just couldn't help myself', 'I didn't really mean to do it'. There is, however, always the potential to develop good kamma, expressed in ethical behaviour, even if only through fear of punishment. Buddhist morality, however, is concerned with personality formation, with character building from which ethical behaviour will arise naturally and spontaneously, rather than with the willing of good behaviour. Nevertheless, this last is necessary to avoid harming others, as part of conditioning good kamma, and, most important, as part of a system of spiritual training through which a deepening awareness ripens an unalienated and intrinsically good personality (the 'cleaning' of kamma). This theme is explored more fully in Chapter 14.

Traditional and canonical Buddhism extends the span of kamma through successive rebirths. The succession, however, is that of a vital energy, not of a reincarnated personality, and it has been likened to the phenomenon on the billiard table when one ball suddenly stops dead when striking a second that immediately speeds away. A contemporary Buddhist scholar writes that 'Buddhism, while granting that "the laws of heredity" (*bija-niyana*) condition, on the whole, the physical and physiological characteristics of the person, holds that the temperament and such personality characteristics including aptitudes and skills are, on the whole, conditioned by the psychological past of the individual.... According to the texts there is mutual interaction and integration of the two in the formation of the new personality. It is said: "Just as much as two bundles of reeds were to stand erect supporting each other, even so conditioned by the (hereditary) psycho-physical factors is the consciousness and conditioned by consciousness are the psycho-physical factors." (Samyutta-Nikaya.II.114)'[38] Although modern social scientists differ about the relative significance of nature and nurture, all would give considerable weight to nurture. The notion of the two sheaves quoted above is now no longer adequate, and instead we have a tripod of Nature (hereditary physiology plus reborn consciousness) plus Environmental Nurture equals the Personality. But this is only a preliminary and mechanistic way of looking at the problem, for the social environment is itself substantially recreated by successive generations. Each individual inherits at birth certain kammaic social conditions, a collectively created past at work in the present. These conditions include those which belong to the non-volitional mental order (*mano-niyama*) noted earlier (for example, belief systems, ideologies). They are non-volitional in that the individual potentially has some freedom to act independently of them; (under a fascist regime one is not bound to be a fascist). Neither is kamma deterministic. This theme is developed in the next chapter; here we are concerned with an altogether more primitive notion about the social signifi-

cance of kamma: the retributive belief in *karma* (as we must
here call it).

Viewed as retribution, kamma is reduced to destiny, a
fate, a *deus ex machina*, a process in which the seemingly
random fortunes and misfortunes of this life are believed to
be rewards and punishments for (unknown) virtue and evil-
doing in previous lives. The poor, the powerless, and the
diseased are therefore assumed to owe their misfortune to
moral transgressions in past lives, no matter how virtuously
they may strive to improve their condition in this life. This
mystification is applied also to whole peoples and nations,
the present misfortunes of countries like Vietnam and Kampuchea being attributed to unjust wars and other historical
national turpitudes. This retributive belief encourages fatalism and devalues self-help, which is seen as unavailing in
the face of an ineluctable fate which, moreover, has moral
authority. Similarly the political and social status quo is
morally legitimized, no matter how evil and oppressive it
may be.

This retributive view of kamma is quite alien to canonical
Buddhism, as Buddhist scholars and teachers have made
clear on many occasions. Thus Walpola Rahula notes its
theistic overtones (which are quite alien to Buddhism) and
warns that in the context of kamma 'the term "justice" is
ambiguous and dangerous, and in its name more harm than
good is done to humanity. The theory of karma is the theory
of cause and effect, of action and reaction; it is a natural law,
which has nothing to do with the idea of justice or reward
and punishment. Every volitional action produces its effects
or results. If a good action produces good effects and a bad
action bad effects, it is not justice, or reward, or punishment
meted out by anybody or any power sitting in judgement
on your action, but this is in virtue of its own nature, its
own law.'[39] These remarks refer to *karma-niyama*, the volitional mental order of causes and effects, but biography and
history are subject no less to the other orders of cause and
effect listed earlier in this chapter. In repeatedly condemning

the notion of fatalism, the Buddha declared that although he taught that every willed action may produce an experienced effect he did not teach that all experienced effects are products of willed action (*kamma*). Thus, for example, a fatal but unexplained aeroplane crash may occur because of metal fatigue (*uti-niyama*), or an oversight on the part of an overworked ground controller (*mano-niyama*), or even a covert suicide wish by the pilot (*karma-niyama*), recently argued as a possible cause of air disasters. The kammaic condition of each of the passengers is surely the least likely cause. And it is contrary to the whole spirit of Buddhism to go hankering after some 'meaning' for the 'coincidence' that it was those particular passengers of the thousands safely flown by the airline who booked onto that 'fateful' flight.

In the retributive tradition, 'good karma' tends to be equated with fortune and success in the world of the three traditional 'Fires' of greed, ill will and delusion. Since these are the values that measure success and are designed to achieve success in such a world, would it not be the *bad* karma accumulated in previous lives that explained material success in this one!? The retributive belief surely encourages a superficial fear-and-acquisitiveness ethic in which good actions (as prescribed by a specific culture) are undertaken in order to accumulate merit in one's karmic bank account. Sufficient investment may ensure, for example, a favourable rebirth in a more wealthy station in life. This meaning of kamma has been well documented in such studies as that made by Spiro of Burmese Buddhism: 'Many Burmese keep merit account books...these are exclusively concerned with *dana* [offerings to the monastic community]...almost any villager can say to the last penny how much (and for what) he has expended on giving.'[40] Derision, however, is too easy. This could be read as what Marco Pallis calls an accommodation in the doctrinal field 'in order to bring various truths within the purview of an average mind'.

It is perhaps the prevalence of the vulgar, retributive form of kamma that has helped incline many educated

Eastern Buddhists to reject the doctrine of rebirth. In a study made by Gosling in Thailand this was accompanied by a complete rejection of Buddhism only in an insignificant number of cases. 'Parallel with tendencies towards new patterns of social involvement go doctrinal changes which seem to underline a pronounced this-worldly emphasis. It is therefore not surprising to discover that other-worldly notions such as rebirth, Nibbana, and, to a lesser extent, kamma, are no longer taken very seriously.'[41]

In Thailand and elsewhere there are those who maintain that the doctrines of rebirth and kamma were incorporated into Buddhism simply because they were part of the taken-for-granted cultural currency of the Buddha's day, and they were not developed as intrinsic elements of Buddhist doctrine. It is recalled that on several occasions the Buddha encouraged a critical and pragmatic approach to his teaching, which was not to be taken as once-and-for-all revealed wisdom but rather to be tested and retested against experience. On the other hand, belief in rebirth appears to be gaining credibility in the West, where it has a distinguished pedigree going back to the Greeks and the Christian Gnostics, though broken by the long centuries of exoteric Christianity.[42] None of the arguments advanced in this book require either rejection or acceptance of the notion of rebirth. Kamma, however, seems to me to be both a logical element in fundamental Buddhist teaching and an interestingly suggestive idea in the discussion of Buddhist social theory.

# 6    *Delusion Institutionalized*

Chapter 3 discusses ways in which the personal (and ultimately frustrating and fruitless) drive to meaningfulness is socially translated and embedded, with antithetical bonding as arguably the most significant expression. This chapter extends the discussion further, in the light of kamma.

To paraphrase Marx, men make their own history, but they make it not of their own accord, or under self-chosen conditions, but under given and transmitted conditions; of these being human – the existential, human condition itself – is fundamental. The root existential condition of each person is, however, *socially* conditioned by the cumulative kamma (in turn socially conditioned) of previous and living generations, creating social relationships, structures, institutions, beliefs, values, and even nurturing appropriate feelings. Whether or not each newborn child inherits a personal kammaic condition through rebirth, she or he certainly inherits socio-historical kammaic conditions. These provide normative forms and channels, specific to time and place, through which the struggle to make meaning of life and reality of self can be carried on with social support and approval. But note also that these *social* forms are also appropriate to specific and successive historic expressions of *existential* suffering. For example, in Ken Wilber's 'high egoic' period in the evolution of human consciousness in the West (AD 1500 onwards), the self suffers extreme existential exposure in that it 'stands out' from strong membership cultures and other traditional forms of ego support. It is supported, however, by a culture that makes an economic, political, religious and aesthetic virtue of such individualism, in terms of capitalist private enterprise, freedom of the individual, everyone's direct access to God, and art as personal rather than communal communication. (There is, of course, only one human condition or state, and references to the 'existential' and the 'social' are only an essential convenience for understanding its nature.)

Each specific historical culture compounds within itself the myriad wills of its individual members, expressive of their existential needs, but at the same time socially channelled and modified to ensure the integrity and continuity of that culture. The culture is a normative optimization of opportunities for its members to express who and what they are, for the most part in the traditional deluded forms of acquisitiveness and aggression — and at the same time make a public virtue of it. Thus the undertow of rancour within each of us finds a useful social outlet in the penal system (of which, however, it is possible to become an equally rancorous reformer). In England, for example, there is a body of opinion well known for the vehemence and strong feeling with which it demands harsher punishments for criminals, including flogging and hanging. Similarly, aggressiveness, acquisitiveness and dominance are encouraged in the male but are channelled into the various approved forms of patriarchal dominance, entrepreneurial competitiveness, and patriotic soldiering.

Let us look more closely at exactly how the growing person assimilates the social inheritance willed by previous generations (and thus becomes a *somebody*). This is of particular interest to Buddhists, with their concern for *how* a well-fortified sense of self arises in deluded response to the root human predicament. Phenomenological sociology has demonstrated how this self and the 'objective' reality that confirms it as established and separate, is very much a dynamic social construct. This reality is created by the intercommunication of members of the same culture of inherited (and evolving) meanings of shared experiences, for example, life and death, fear, the authority of the ruler, the nature of work, the cause of rain, the justification for war. Only through extensive acceptance, everyday sharing and more formal sanctions (for example, the imposition by force of 'revealed' religious truths) is 'reality' solidly established. This dialectical process of reality construction is expressed by one social theorist as follows: 'The behaviour of men and women is "caused" not so much by forces within them (needs, drives, self-actualization, existential aspiration, etc.) or by external forces impinging upon them (social forces, deterministic internalization of norms...) but by what lies between − a reflective, socially derived interpretation of the internal and external stimuli that are present.'[43] Thus, paradoxically, a world is produced unknowingly which is then experienced as something other than a human product.

Through this *monist*, unified process a *dualistic* 'reality' is created, the reality of self *and* a solid, objective reality 'out there' that serves to confirm self's separateness. The sense of self is further assured by one's fellows, for whom one's self is a recognized and needful part of *their* reality, and it is interpersonally consolidated yet further through interlocking roles (see below). Shared meanings are consolidated and refined as common vocabularies, frames of reference, ethical values, bodies of 'objective' knowledge, ideologies, and so on. Certainly for the dominant social group, a comfortable and stimulating cultural home is furnished for ego.

To the extent that the egoic need for a solid and assured identity recedes, a person needs less the support of the above kind of reality. Reality is then experienced as trans-situational, inter-subjective *awareness*; there is my truth and there is your truth. This theme of a sense of reality unweighted by a strong self-need is resumed in Chapter 8. But note that what is implied here is not that only the subject exists and the object is illusory (which would simply be a suppression of one half of dualism), but that subject and object exist in a paradoxical dialectical unity (monism).

Of the 'shared meanings' that structure reality, roles are of particular importance. A role is a set of behaviours, attitudes, thoughts, and feelings relevant to a person's particular situation or occupation. They are maintained more or less consistently and are more or less acknowledged by others (the role set), who can be relied upon to respond in a predictable way. For example, in youth we pick up the cues and learn how to play the role of a diner and meet the role expectations of the head waiter and the wine waiter. Or in the social security benefit office we learn to play the role of claimant interlocking with that of claims clerk behind the glass partition. Lightly carried, role is a convenient, instant shorthand for everyday transactions in complex societies. Played lightly and humorously it can even be a bridge between strangers. More commonly, however, the existential, expressive use of role is to dig-in the persona of Fortress Self and arm it with some socially permitted, guilt-free, safely long-distance weaponry. Roles ensure a secure, orderly world in which even subordinates may be glad to 'know their place'. The white coat, the peaked hat, the official smile and a whole range of other nonverbal signals ensure that we shall at least be recognized as *some* kind of somebody. To the extent we are so recognized, we shall be 'dressed in a little brief authority' to be exercised over others. If it is to do them good, it will be even more satisfying, but in any case it will be socially legitimated. The uses and misuses of role are nicely illustrated in the case of spiritual teachers and their students. Here the most profound authentication of experience is what is being transmitted, but particularly in the early stages role can be employed as a skilful and expedient learning aid and awareness of role by both teacher and student can be extremely valuable.

Like the Jungian persona, role goes much deeper than the formal social contexts exemplified above. For example, the child who feels neglected may win recognized status for his habitual petulence and, as he grows up, may learn to manipulate it in more subtly rewarding ways. In adulthood he uses it at work to play 'No Win' games of the kind described by Eric Berne,[44] with variant forms at home to blackmail affection and retain control over his family. The ultimate delusion of the persona or role is when it takes over the whole identity, so that the person is dependent for his entire personhood on his roles: he is his persona. 'One could say, with a little exaggeration,' writes Jung, 'that the persona is that which in reality one is not, but which oneself as well as others think one is.'[45]

Role, then, is a compelling device by which individuals are inducted, gratefully or reluctantly, into their kammaic social inheritance. Historically an engine for both sustaining and instilling existential delusion, society therefore reinforces the root *human* evasion and illusion through which the spiritual search must penetrate. Different societies offer more — or less — favourable kammaic conditions for undertaking the Long Search, though always to some extent discounted by particular individual aptitudes. For example, the Nazi indoctrination of 1933—45 was clearly a deeply alienating and negative kammaic experience for the German people, relieved only by a handful of remarkable spiritual witnesses like Dietrich Bonhoeffer and Alfred Delp. Contrariwise, for much of its history Tibet was a spiritual incubator of unparalleled kammaic power. Although the human condition itself is the prime kammaic mover, the positive or negative *social* reinforcement to good or to bad kamma is of profound importance in establishing a rationale for Buddhist social activism. And if kamma is given its full canonical amplitude as the successive rounds of rebirth, each of these is a birth into a specific culture, which itself has kammaic power to support or block the personal quest for authentic awareness. True, only persons can experience kamma, and whatever its origins, it will just be kamma. But it is also evident that kamma cannot be regarded simply and solely as a personal, asocial phenomenon. To the extent that kamma is a social phenomenon, the spiritual project of freeing humanity from bad kamma, from the historic momentum of greed and violence, necessarily includes the creation of positive social conditions and hence the transformation of whole social structures.

Cumulative social conditioning can kammaically blind us even to an elementary ethical awareness. For example, in the terrible famines afflicting parts of Africa in recent years, although there have been significant voluntary and individual contributions to relief funds the aid offered by democratic states has been negligible when set against their enormous resources. And yet they have not only the necessary surplus foodstuffs but the technological resources that could have brought great benefit even if mounted only on the modest scale required to fight some minor war to uphold national prestige. All appeals to reason have fallen upon a kammaically conditioned deafness. On this scale nation-states wage wars and not relief operations.

Buddhism is a *radical conservatism*. It is conservative in its recognition of the deep kammaic inertia in the persistence of acquisitiveness, authoritarianism, exploitation, secrecy and many varieties of violence even after social revolutions. But Buddhism is also radical, in proclaiming the possibility of a revolution that goes to the very roots of the human condition.

*Part Three*
# The Dialectics of Delusion

# 7    The Janus Syndrome

Part Three explores further the theme of the delusive character of social reality as ordinarily experienced. It focuses particularly upon the social insights that come from understanding the paradoxical play of opposites, of *this* and *that*, and draws on the Mahayana Buddhist dialectic in Chapters 8 and 12. Chapter 9 locates Buddhism in the two historic 'mentalities', paradigms or 'world views', with particular reference to problems of social analysis and social change. The 'Social Fallacy' of Chapter 10 is the belief that social change can itself effect fundamental change in the human condition. This is followed in Chapter 11 by the discussion of the dominant contemporary secular assumptions in the light of Buddhist and related spiritual perspectives.

The Janus syndrome, named after the ancient two-faced god, draws attention to the relationship between the *instrumental activity* and the more shadowed face of *expressive behaviour* of individuals, groups, organizations and nation-states. Expressive behaviours attempt to build and defend a strong, well-being sense of self, through belongingness identity, through 'standing out', through power and possession, through drinking deep of satisfaction, and, in short, through the whole delusive and ultimately frustrating *expressive project* described so far in this book. This behaviour is expressive of the fact of human existence. Expressive behaviour is manifested through such *instrumental* activities as getting on in a career, competing successfully with a new product, and winning a war, and includes the systems, institutions and cultures developed to support these activities. As we have seen, instrumental activities are *socializations* of individual expressive behaviours in that they channel them so as to support the integrity, survival and well-being of society or organization or group or individual.

Some of the instrumentalities of our time, discussed in Chapter 4, are inherently alienating and destructive (for example, nuclear weapons systems, poisonous industry). Others, such as the social services of 'Welfare States' are benevolent and, at least in some sense, an authentic open-handed, open-hearted attempt to relieve affliction. Some instrumentalities may be used expressively or authentically, depending on who is using them. A fast road may enable me to drive from A to B with the convenience of a shorter journey time, and perhaps more safely, though probably not more pleasurably. And that is all. Or the fast road from A to B may be an instrumentality through which I can feel a sense of power, prestige, and mastery and cut a few precious minutes off my journey time, forcing confirmation from other road users by my aggressive style of driving. In the latter case I shall need an impressive-looking, high prestige, executive motor with the speed, performance and expensive high technology to provide the necessary instrumentality for my expressive needs.

Even when the instrumental fire *could* burn with a clear, benevolent flame there is usually a lot of expressive smoke obscuring it. It is difficult for the 'I' just to do what the situation needs. Also, or even instead, I have to do what *I* need, thereby obscuring and spoiling the situation. The left-hand face of Janus (portrayed in the accompanying diagram), is mostly the potentially superfluous dance of delusion. And the right-hand side is mostly its frightful, bloody-minded outcomes. The Buddhist 'ideal model' society is a benign, single-faced one, in which behaviour is authentic, at-one response to the needs and possibilities of situations.

Professionalism is an illuminating example of the Janus syndrome. Instrumentally, professionalism is about good

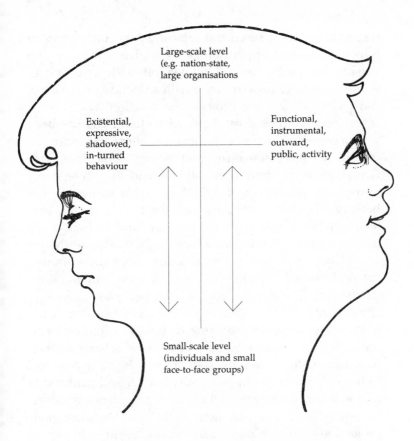

Large-scale level
(e.g. nation-state,
large organisations

Existential,
expressive,
shadowed,
in-turned
behaviour

Functional,
instrumental,
outward,
public, activity

Small-scale level
(individuals and small
face-to-face groups)

Diagram to illustrate The Janus Syndrome

and reliable standards of service to a client given expertly and impartially, and free of profiteering. Expressively, and particularly in the high prestige professions like medicine and the law, ego gets a huge multiple reinforcement which it will feed on more or less hungrily. There will, however, be some − 'the professionals who cast no shadow' − by whom these reinforcements are not taken up or are felt to be irrelevant; action is solely out of awareness of need and opportunity, unspoilt by identity hunger. The reinforcements include a highly respected role in society, strong professional belongingness identity, a sense of power in respect of clients, assured and substantial income, a sense of achievement, and opportunities for leadership inside and outside the profession, all topped off with a feeling of service to society in accordance with an ethical professional code. How in fact the professional function has to some extent been corrupted by these existential needs has been well documented as part of the growing client and consumer critique of professionalism over recent years. Long ago George Bernard Shaw drew attention to the professional 'conspiracy against the laity'. Professional monopoly has been exploited to protect incompetence, to maintain professional 'mysteries' from lay scrutiny, and to inhibit the development of alternatives which might threaten orthodox ascendancy. In Britain, the expensive damage done through the professional arrogance of town planners and architects (abetted by greedy property developers, prestige-hungry city councils, and the technological hubris of the construction industry) is now widely recognized even by the professionals themselves. For example, several housing schemes which have been failures from the start are now being dynamited, to be replaced by traditional small houses and gardens. In rich societies, consumers collude with providers and advertisers in discovering ever new 'needs' and the prestigious professions are in a particularly strong position to exploit the movement towards 'the apogee of the modernized service society, when the professionals can say to the citizen: We are the solution to your problem; we know what problem you have; you can't understand the problem or the solution; only we can decide whether the solution has dealt with your problem.'[46]

Another example of the Janus syndrome is the behaviour in committees, teams and other small work groups. Instrumentally, there are agendas, objectives, and objective problems to be resolved, and these are the overt subjects of group activity on which the members feel they are focusing their attention. But the other side of this instrumental functioning is in the hidden personal agendas of more or less urgent emotional business that each person brings to the meeting. Much time in the meeting may be taken up in satisfying, frustrating or otherwise processing the participants' emotional needs, but in only partial awareness and through the medium of 'the business'. Training methods for overcoming the Janus effect in group work are noted at the end of Chapter 31.

The last example is a reminder that in any group there will usually be found a spectrum of personalities at different levels of consciousness, ranging from the endless hunger and frustration and paranoia of the 'difficult personalities' to those whose expressiveness is a warm welcome and who can get on with the work — or the play — without having to scratch the irritating parts of their personality all the while or, *in extremis*, to wield it as a problem-solving weapon. As we shall see, there are many different stages along the Way of consciousness evolution, from a blindly driven delusiveness to awakening to complete authenticity of being. Just being easeful enough with oneself to be able to be easeful with others would for example, make a world of a difference. (Between levels of psycho-spiritual maturity and organizational and social seniority and authority there is, of course, no correlation and, in some circles, an inverse correlation.)

Janus's left face (in the diagram) tends to be shadowed even from self and inturned from others, including organizational outsiders and unauthorized persons. The successful careerist will be largely unaware of the deep springs of ego need that drive him, for they *are* him, and it would need an Ibsen to do justice to their ultimate tragic quality and to the dark hungers that are not fed. Bigger and bigger doses of promotion, recognition and so on are needed until he finally storms up beyond the limits of his real competence, thus once more vindicating the Peter Principle (that people tend to be promoted up to the level of their incompetence). All this will be encouraged by colleagues as laudable ambition, contributing to organizational success and benefiting society (as indeed it might do).

Beyond the individual, groups and organizations and networks and cultures, strongly fortified in the antithetical bonding described in Chapter 3, manifest a corporate expressive behaviour in their struggles to survive and prosper and dominate, related in each case (and often in very complex, paradoxical and ambiguous ways) to their overt instrumental functions. Thus, the Forestry Commission does not only manage forests; the motorway lobby does not only build motorways. At corporate as well as individual level expressive behaviour is usually not widely or well known even within the organization. It belongs rather to the realm of 'home truths' that investigative journalists seek to penetrate, because it is about doings other than overt corporate function and which may be against 'the public interest'. Such 'home truths' are usually personally experienced or passed on by word of mouth, behind closed doors. Such 'open secrets' tend to be anecdotal, specific and to tell what went wrong. This may be personally malicious, politically motivated and unreliable, but at least it is not the face of public and institutionalized lying. The public, instrumental face dispenses generalized, formal knowledge, prefers to stick to success stories, is inspired by wish-fulfilment and upholds and boosts personal and corporate prestige. It is essentially paternalistic in that it presumes, on the principle of Plato's 'Noble Lies', that knowing too much may be bad for people.

It will be noted that in the diagram the double face is divided into upper and lower parts, referring to large-scale and small-scale activity respectively. The distinction and the interrelationship are significant. Short-term, small-scale expressive behaviour (bottom left) builds up, usually more or less blindly, to the long-term, large-scale instrumental consequences in the top right quadrant of the diagram, along the arrowed directions. Historical events, for example, are the resultants of many different wills, but not necessarily willed by any one of them. Small events, whose expressive origins are generally below the level of awareness, and

whose instrumental implications may only be appreciated with hindsight, can accumulate into unimaginable follies. Buddhists will recognize here the kammaic parallels in the unfolding of a person's life, and will be inclined to discount history as the unfolding of grand and rational designs or of deep conspiracies. Human affairs, whether of individuals, organizations or states tend to be reactive, piecemeal and short term in character, what Charles Lindblom called disjointed incrementalism, or 'the science of muddling through'.[47] Much of this may be rationalized so that people do *feel* they are in control of events (or their own actions). There is a powerful myth of rational, calculative planning and control carried over into social affairs from technology. For 'high egoic' modern man it is an *essential* myth. Someone surely has to be in control, and it isn't God any longer...
There have, of course, been many examples of grand design social engineering, latterly supported by the ultimate rationality of the computer, but all have foundered more or less badly on the rocks of social reality.

The kammaic process of disjointed incrementalism is most frighteningly illustrated by the international build-up of defensive alliances and deterrent armaments designed to make going to war 'unthinkable' but which eventually make it 'inevitable'. Paul Bracken writes: 'In broadest terms, the danger facing the world is that the superpowers have institutionalized a major nuclear showdown. They have built the most complex nuclear apparatus ever conceived, without thinking through its purpose or how to control it. The resulting conflict system is strongly reminiscent of the institutionalized conflict mechanisms of the early twentieth century. World War I was a war waiting to happen at any time in the decade before 1914...the fact that it didn't happen was taken as a sign that all was well.'[48] A small group of British researchers — the Oxford Research Group — has identified some eight hundred nuclear decision-shapers in the five nuclear countries. Most of them are not politicians or diplomats but government scientists, defence ministry officials, military officers and industrialists. Each has his own restricted field of interest, such as improving the destructive power of a particular nuclear armament, developing a new system of military deployment, managing some arms-related industry vital to the national economy or just maintaining the pre-eminence of their arm of the services, keeping their missile research and development team together, 'carving a niche', crowning a successful career, and so on. This group's research suggests that nuclear defence policy is 'at best a post-hoc rationalization for the development of weapons systems whose *raison d'être* has become institutionalized'. One problem is the time scale. Nuclear systems take fifteen or twenty years to develop. 'By the time a minister...becomes aware of a system of development, so much has already been spent on it, both in terms of finance and the careers of individuals, that the momentum for this continuation in inevitable.'[49]

In many other fields as well as that of nuclear defence technological development has become a thing-in-itself regardless of the end to which it may lead − a self-sufficing source of personal achievement and intellectual fascination for groups of specialists. Writing out of much personal experience, E. F. Schumacher concluded that technology 'has become a force of its own; it has shaped man, a vast number of men, into little parrots that twitter and push and scrape to make things more and more complicated. And when they have found something that can actually be done, no matter how futile or dangerous it may be, such as Concorde or nuclear power, then they create a kind of mafia to make sure it gets done.'[50]

The Janus syndrome is a warning of the need, when we come to examine social problems, to turn our attention to the existential roots of society, that is, to the characteristically deluded and driven response of individuals to their human condition − the *expressive project*. In each case it is necessary to trace how this is expressed in group and organizational and other sub-cultures, how it accumulates in social impact and over time, and how it is expressed in overt social functions, instrumentalities and norms, in the conventional and reassuring 'normalcy' that both blinds us to the reality of the everyday world and makes it tolerable. It is hoped that the preliminary Janus that has been sketched here will encourage further investigation within the Buddhist perspective.

# 8    Finding the Higher Third

This chapter draws upon the philosophy of Mahayana Buddhism, which is most familiar in the West in the form of the
Zen and Tibetan Buddhist 'traditions'. The Mahayana or
Northern School of Buddhism originated in India arguably
somewhat later than the Southern School, which is represented today by Theravada Buddhism, with its Pali scriptures. For four centuries, from the Buddha's death in 480 BC
to the appearance of the first Pali and Mahayana scriptures,
Buddhism existed only as an oral tradition.[51] The Pali scriptures contain a considerable amount of explicit social teaching to which we refer in Part Six. For the present my concern
is to develop some analytical perspectives based on a fundamental, perennial Buddhism outside culturally contextual
teachings. This chapter introduces the dialectical relativism
of the Madhyamika and Yogacara Schools of the Mahayana.
The Avatamsaka and Hua Yen are represented through the
phenomenological interdependence of Indra's Net in
Chapter 12. At their different levels of abstraction Theravada
and Mahayana Buddhism offer, in my view, complementary
rather than opposed perspectives on Buddhist social theory
and activism.

From the fundamental Buddhist idea of existential ignorance or delusion, there evolved the critique of ideology
as absolute truth that has parallels in Kant's critique in
eighteenth-century Europe. Already present in the Pali
canon, the critique was perfected by the Madhyamika
School in Nagarjuna's Doctrine of the Void (*Sunyavada*)

(second century AD). Phenomena exist only through their mutually defining relativity. Black is black because white defines it, and so with good and evil, long and short, empty and full. It is difference that defines phenomena; 'False-imagination teaches that such things as light and shade, long and short, black and white are different and are to be discriminated but they are not independent of each other; they are only different aspects of the same thing, they are terms of relation, not of reality. Conditions of existence are not of a mutually exclusive character; in essence they are not two, but one' (*Lankavatara Sutra*). In Chuang-Tzu's words:

> He who wants to have right without wrong,
> Order without disorder,
> Does not understand the principles
> Of heaven and earth.
> He does not know how
> Things hang together.
> Can a man cling only to heaven
> And know nothing of earth?
> They are correlative: to know one
> Is to know the other.
> To refuse one
> Is to refuse both.[52]

Phenomena are therefore 'empty' of independent, intrinsic being (*svabhava*). The word 'emptiness' in this context is used not as the literal opposite of 'fullness' but with the specific meaning of 'empty of self need'. By attributing separateness and solidity to phenomena and emphasizing their differences we seek to confirm self through strongly affirming all that is other. The strong contrasts and opposites reflect the pull and push of attraction and aversion in the hungry and fearful ego. The nature of reality as commonly experienced is thus a (distorted) reflection of existential need, and this applies no less to what we do with concepts, such as Buddhism, God, democracy. These also become more solid, more separate, more contrasted, the greater our fear is that reality is somehow denying us our existence.

This relative definition of reality is paradoxical and impossible to grasp intellectually. In words it is no more than a suggestive expression of the meditative insight of the philosopher mystics who originated it. Hence it can only be experienced through our own meditative awareness in which 'I' recedes and dependence is reduced on making the myriad distinctions between *this* and *that* and solidly structuring our experience. Freed of the struggle to make of reality what it is not, awareness opens gladly to the contingent, insubstantial and ephemeral nature of reality:

> As stars, a fault of vision, as a lamp,
> A mock show, dew drops, or a bubble,
> A dream, a lightning flash, or cloud,
> So should one view what is conditioned.
>
> *The Diamond Sutra*

However, launched upon a sea of relativities without even an horizon for comfort, the 'I' anxiously attempts to create out of one relative pole an absolute as a landmark, be it Nirvana, or God, or Humanity. But the project is never wholly successful, for *that* relative has been made into an absolute precisely because its opposite is so threatening: and it doesn't disappear. Only those who hunger after security can know the profound misery of insecurity. Our fears are also our desires. When we cease to pursue the one, the other loses its power. Then the absolute truly stands forth as the one reality, the unity of this and that.

Though strenuously denied by its monk-scholars, there was in the Madhyamika a tendency to nihilism — 'the dialectical dissolution of everything', as Conze puts it.[53] This was countered in the Yogacara (Vijnanavada) School, and particularly in the Ch'an (Zen) Buddhism of China, whose Third Patriarch warned that:

> If you get rid of phenomena, then everything is
> lost;

If you follow after the Void, you turn your back on
the very substance of things.[54]

Building on the Madhyamika theory of knowledge, the
Yogacara bore witness to three kinds of experience. The
meditatively evolved experience of reality of a human being
who has opened to the higher levels of consciousness embraces both relative forms (*paratantra*) and also the 'emptiness' or absolute quality (*parinispanna*) inherent in them.
'The ten thousand things' are dissolved in meditative trance,
emerging from which emptiness, the void, is likewise dissolved, as the ten thousand things return into consciousness, but this time in their inherent emptiness — empty of
clinging to *this* and *that*. The third kind of experience is the
deluded, inauthentic experience of relative forms (*maya*)
which is the imputed reality (*parikalpita*) experienced by the
generality of mankind.

*Parinispanna*, or 'empty' consciousness, refracted, as it
were, through the individual mind, is revealed in the forms
and colours of the ten thousand things, the *maya* of patterned
reality. That experience will be a comparatively authentic
one (*paratantra*) at the higher levels of consciousness,
though its form will depend on the level of consciousness
(for example, gnostic monism, or theistic dualism), and also
on distinctive and differing cultural characteristics. These
more or less authentic expressions of reality have been
termed *dharmas* in Buddhism, for example the Christian
*dharma* (truth), and the *Buddhadharma*. (Though Buddhism
is usually known simply as 'the *Dharma*', and '*dharma*' is
anyway a compendious term with a variety of different
meanings.) But for all but the highest levels of consciousness
the mind-refractor is so distorted by egoic need as to produce a grotesque reality which gives rise, as we saw in Part
Three to much suffering.

This Yogacara epistemology is anticipated in the Pali
canon as follows: 'This consciousness (*citta*) is luminous, but
it is defiled by adventitious defilements. The uninstructed
average person does not understand this as it really is.

Therefore I say that for him there is no mental development.'[55] And the following refers to the construction of relative reality (*sammuti-sacca*) contrasted with absolute reality (*paramattha-sacca*). The Buddha is here rebuking a spiritually unsophisticated goddess who has just unsuccessfully tried to seduce one his monks with her 'effulgent beauty':

> Those who go by names, who go by concepts,
> Make their abode in names and concepts,
> Failing to discern the naming process,
> These are subject to the reign of death.

> He who has discerned the naming-process
> Does not suppose that one who names exists.
> No such case exists for him in truth,
> Whereby one could say 'He's this or that — '

> If you know what this means, tell me, fairy.[56]

In the remainder of this chapter the Madhayamika-Yogacara perspective is used to highlight certain social phenomena.

Faced with some question or problem we seek to relate it to our cognitive map, our field of existing knowledge. However, most of us 'take reality personally', even if only aware that we do in extreme cases when others remind us not to do so. Where the problem is seen as an 'issue', it enters our awareness as much as an opportunity for self-expression as for sharing other people's view of truth and seeking together. Our standpoint may carry a heavy emotional loading if it is experienced as a facet of a picture of reality in which there is strong self-investment. Opposing views are received as a threat to selfhood. Extreme, simple, highly coloured standpoints which are strongly polarized give a strong, gutsy sense of self over against other. The whole cognitive and emotional map may consist of highlighted antipathies, without any threatening blank spaces of allowed ignorance, or doubt, or ambiguity, and with a restless rancour not far beneath the socially attuned surface. Some practice of meditative awareness can bring such phenomena alarmingly to the attention of most of us, if we are not already aware of them. There is the same tendency to *weighted polarization* both within the self and in encounter with other 'selfs'. Its social expression is the *antithetical bonding* introduced in Chapter 3. Others are readily categorized as being either FOR or AGAINST, or, if they cannot be, are either ignored or else treated with even more hostility than the AGAINSTs (who at least collaborate in a shared and mutually confirming conventional antipathy). Indeed, the FORs and AGAINSTs are mutually obliging in providing indicators of dress, vocabulary and so on by way of self-categorization.

Weighted polarization and antithetical bonding tend to become progressively acute in situations of threat and disagreement, and acquire their own momentum even though the actors may complain of the 'painful pressures' and 'imperatives' of the situation. Professor David Martin calls this phenomenon 'aggregate behaviour' and argues that even a 'relatively open system has a specific, pre-existing tendency to closure, which sucks decisions forward faster and faster towards the whirlpool. Many industrial situations have narrowed and narrowed over time till the script becomes totally formulaic. . . . The process itself tends to grind conscience out of existence and to promote the amoral playing of set games.' Martin's example of the party political process is particularly graphic:

> The politician has made an initial judgement that the goals and policies of a party are closer, though perhaps only marginally closer, to his conception of the social good than other parties. Once he joins that party he must obey a set of group imperatives at least partly rooted in the brute need to survive. Thus, he must accept the leadership in crucial matters, and refrain from dissociating himself from policy except in extreme circumstances and in matters understood to be decisions of conscience alone. All this amounts to a severe circumspection on his

acts and expressions of opinion. He cannot speak the truth freely. Beyond that he has to contend in public that crucial differences turn on the election of his party and he has to present other parties in stereotypes and caricatures.... Above all, within his own party he will experience a strong impulsion to exert pressure against those who, in any way, ignore these constraints. He knows that survival depends on solidarity, and solidarity on threat and obloquy. Fear is the bond of fraternity as much as faith or love.[57]

To that it is necessary to add that, although a reluctant Cincinnatus may be found here and there in politics, the above process is both functional (as described) but also expressive, existential behaviour which affords massive self-reinforcement for the actors subject to this cumulative, kammaic conditioning.

Contending perspectives on controversial issues, from abortion to the 'Irish Question', are, typically, manifestations (and confirmations) of unconscious assumptions and stereotypes, cherished beliefs and myths. At the most intellectually sophisticated level, however, they become *ideological*. Ideology is another Janus phenomenon. As a relatively comprehensive explanation of social reality, it gives a stronger and more reassuring picture of reality to those who uphold it, and may legitimize their own place in the world. Marxian ideology, for example, did this for the proletariat by proclaiming the historical inevitability of their revolutionary emancipation, just as Calvinism did much the same for those who were predestined to be the Elect. Similarly, Lionel Trilling, in his *Liberal Imagination*, defined ideology as 'the habit or the ritual of showing respect for certain formulas to which, for various reasons having to do with emotional safety, we have very strong ties but of whose meaning and consequences in actuality we have no clear understanding.'[58]

On the other hand, ideology may be understood *functionally* and *instrumentally*, as a master-theory for making sense of, and perhaps changing the world. Although some ideologies have evidently been more expressive than objectively valuable (and may be powerfully wish-fulfilling, like Nazism), most, arguably, have an ambiguous quality in their conception and use and are typical Janus phenomena. The Madhayamika dialectic introduced earlier in this chapter is self-evidently a solvent of all dogmatic ideology, that is, of ideology proclaimed as absolute and ultimate truth. As its exponents have demonstrated,[59] it either nullifies the ideology or else enables it to be evolved as no more than a contingent master-theory or working hypothesis. This also implies a shift away from a polarized position which *expressively* confirms the identity and interests of a particular social group. An example of such a shift is the Critical Theory of Marxism evolved by the Frankfurt School (for example, Marcuse, Adorno, Habermas) which has been concerned with an open-ended and continuously self-critical development of Marxism, in contrast to the economic determinism and other dogmas of heavily ideological Marxism (with Stalinism as the extreme example). Interestingly, the Frankfurt School has been much influenced (as was Marx himself) by Hegelian philosophy, which has close affinities with the Madhyamika dialectic.

The Madhyamika critique of ideology is in one sense about lightening the historic shadow of self need which the investigator, through his culturally loaded theories, throws across the subject of his investigation. In recent years some social scientists have moved away from the positivist research tradition of strongly hypothetically structured, quantitative and objectivized investigation that has so often squeezed psycho-social reality dry of meaning in order to sustain meaning in an abstract academic playground. They have pioneered an alternative 'situationist', 'illuminative' approach in which people and situations have been left more open to 'speak for themselves', through case studies, participant-observation and other methods that have some resemblance to investigative journalism.[60] To a Buddhist, they appear to have 'discovered' a Buddhist research methodology much as Schumacher discovered a Buddhist economics (with the difference that Schumacher was directly influenced by Buddhist ideas).

Examples of dogmatic, 'expressive' ideology can be found in the many periodicals which are dedicated to some particular viewpoint in social affairs. Month by month a wide variety of issues are refracted through the same ideological prism with the same predictable conclusions backed by cheer-leading optimism. Such formula writing confirms loyal readers in their beliefs, and across each new window that opens up on the world the view is obscured by the hanging of much the same pictures as before. Even in periodicals which claim to eschew ideological dogmatism and to be dedicated to exploring and promoting open, alternative social phenomena, the medium usually contradicts the message. The following example is interesting not only because of Schumacher's 'Buddhist economics' but because it comes from an influential British journal of alternative culture which not infrequently denounces dogma.

In issue number 84 (January-February 1981) the magazine *Resurgence*, which is associated with the Schumacher Society, printed a Schumacher Lecture given by Gerald Leach which questioned whether 'small was always beautiful'. Leach confessed that he was 'unhappily convinced that most small renewable sources (of energy) will be extremely costly either in human skills or time or in capital investment'. Moreover, 'renewable energies have virtually nothing to offer the Third World countries yet'. Anticipating criticism, Leach concluded that in deciding the 'energy future' 'we have to go beyond either/or; it's going to be both/and. I am also sure that Fritz Schumacher would have agreed. In *Small is Beautiful* he carefully argued that there is no single answer to the question of what scale is appropriate. For different purposes people need different structures, both small ones and large ones, but often find it difficult to keep these seemingly opposed necessities in mind. They always tend to clamour for a final solution. He then added, significantly, "Today we suffer from an almost universal idolatry of giant-ism. It is therefore necessary to insist on the virtue of smallness — where this applies. If there were a prevailing idolatry of smallness...one would have to try and exercise influence in the opposite direction." That is all I have tried to do.'

Leach's apprehension was well founded, and his chastise-ment came from John Michell, one of those columnists whose particular job in journals of opinion seems to be patrolling as guardians of the faith. In the July-August number Michell declared that he had 'never read anything in *Resurgence* which I found so unsympathetic or disagree-able'. However, his only reply to Leach's 'dismal thoughts' was to reflect (yet again!) on the *ipso facto* virtues of decen-tralization, supported by a nostalgic reminder of the Saxon folk moot and a warning about 'intellectuals' scorn for peasants and common folk'. Michell's response thus con-tains all the classic ingredients for rebuttals of this kind: (a) A stricture against spoiling the monthly family outing by being 'disagreeable and unsympathetic'; (b) A ramble round to invoke the household gods, such as in this case, the universal applicability of the doings of our sturdy fore-bears in more idyllic times; and (c) Playing the populist card: in effect, a patronizing 'Not in front of the children'. As for Fritz Schumacher, it seems to be a common fate for creative, open and original thinkers to have their ideas polarized out and concreted in by their followers after their deaths. 'Well, thank God I am not a Marxist' was the death-bed confession attributed to Marx. (I should add that *even* in *Resurgence* dogmatic polarization can show its powerful magnetism, for in other respects it is a periodical that complements this book more fully than any other.)

Proposals for furthering the *explicit* aims of polarized, campaigning ideologies are likely to be rejected if they threaten established confrontational satisfactions. Indeed, the purity of the vision may be more valued than mundane ways of realizing it which give the campaigners little psychological reinforcement. The pragmatic American peace worker Gene Sharp was strongly criticized by fellow proponents of non-violent action for his conviction that 'we must talk with the military, government people, with the people who are convinced we need military weapons. These are the people whose judgements and actions can be potentially catastrophic.' Sharp remarked that he had 'more success in convincing those people than I do when talking with pacifists, who are really much more narrow minded and rigid than army officers are.'[61]

It is the *ownership* of ideology and its value as a weapon that brings up the strong feelings. However, the same telltale vehemence is aroused over much more prosaic issues. Clubs and magazines devoted to relaxed leisure-time pursuits can be the scene of terrible human convulsions about how to climb crags, keep honey bees, or run a backpacking club (or, it seems, a Buddhist group!). If we can get as far as laughing, much can be learnt from these more manageable storms in teacups about how to work with bigger and more intractable problems.

The most extreme chiaroscuro pictures which ego paints of the world are those of *super ideology*. This is commonly the preserve of certain religious and humanistic groups since it operates at the fundamental nature-of-human-experience level. It can be applied as vehemently by the proponents of Transactional Analysis (a humanistic psychotherapy) as by, say, the Salvation Army or similar evangelical Christian sects. Its character stems more from its proponents than from its intrinsic content. Self and group righteousness is here so total that adversaries far from exciting indignation, receive nothing but pity and sympathy for their sad condition. Overwhelmed by love and understanding, it is no good them trying to make themselves heard, since anything they may say is treated as further evidence not of how wrong they are but of how fallen/sick/insecure and — yes! — *deluded*, they are. (There is a sinister parallel here with the psychiatric confinement of political dissidents in the Soviet Union.) Super ideology tries to make Other feel like a person in need of *help* rather than an adversary or even just an enquirer. To the observer it may seem that it is the proselytizers, however, who *need* the self-confirmation that so commonly comes from being able to help others.

So, is Buddhism itself no more than another super ideology?

Buddhism is an ideology if we mean by that simply a means of understanding the world. However, the more usual sense of the word (and the one uppermost in this book) is that of an absolute and enduring body of knowledge. In that case, Buddhism is *ipso facto* the antithesis of ideology, for the insubstantiality and impermanence of all phenomena, and our delusion that they are otherwise, are the three Signs of Being which it invites us to explore. And Madhyamika dialectical relativism is a philosophical device to the same end. Ultimately these are propositions which depend upon meditative insight for their validation, not only in Buddhism but in other, culturally distinct, gnostic practices. But even without direct insight your own experience of life may incline you to accept them at their face value, at least provisionally. Buddhism is a religion of *ehipassika*, come and see, come and experiment for yourself, if you want to enquire further. In a much quoted and very variously translated passage from the *Kalama Sutta* the Buddha is said to have advised: 'Don't believe anyone. Don't believe me. Don't believe the teachers. Don't believe books and traditions. Rather, look to your own experience. Look within, and see what it is that is conducive to the growth of understanding, wisdom, compassion and love. Those things should be cultivated. And then look to your experience to see what it is that leads to greater greed, hatred and delusion. Those things should be abandoned.'[62]

Ego has need to read the solidity of ideology into any

body of interpretative ideas. Buddhists, however, practise Buddhism so as progressively to be liberated from that need. And this practice includes progressively more subtle 'skilful and expedient means' (*upaya*) for declutching from ideology and lightening polarization. And hence, 'He who is attached to anything, even to liberation, is not interested in the Dharma [Buddhist teaching] but is interested in the taint of desire. . . . The Dharma is not a secure refuge. He who enjoys a secure refuge is not interested in the Dharma but is interested in a secure refuge. . . . The Dharma is not a society. He who seeks to associate with the Dharma is not interested in the Dharma but is interested in association.' *Vimalakirti Nirdesa*[63]

The power of ideology is not in what is thought but in what is felt, whether by the wielder of it or by the outside observer who feels the hot breath of it, the heaviness of it. You will be impressed by its absence after spending a day in any mainstream Buddhist meditation and teaching centre. Even after an evening at my local Buddhist group I have been taken aback by the grateful relief of newcomers at the absence of 'heaviness' and at not being 'put upon'. Recently some Buddhist friends were amused and nonplussed to receive a questionnaire from a School of Theology in which they were asked to estimate the number of people they had 'converted' to Buddhism in the last two years. It is not easy to explain just why the notion of 'converting' somebody strikes the average Buddhist as so oddly amusing. Some visitors to Buddhist centres who *want* attention may even be disappointed by a certain sense of distancing which pushes them back to responsibility for themselves. The enquirer's autonomy − 'where you are at' − is respected; compassion, as much for self as for others, has quite a different feel from patronage.

In all the above versions of weighted polarization ego identifies with this and weights it against that. Finally, there is the inverted relativism of the quietist, the nihilist, the other-worldly, who is polarized around the Absolute which

thereby becomes idolatrously Relative. Here, since 'ten thousand things' have only a contingent, insubstantial and
ephemeral existence they are no more than a passing show,
and the difference between this and that, war and peace, is
insignificant — 'all is vanity'. The compassion that arises
through feeling deeply for, and with, other people is here
lost in meditative bliss.

There is an inherent danger of sinking into other-worldly
quietism in any meditative tradition, and it has arguably
been the Eastern Pole, in contrast to the Western Pole of self-
deluding activism. Teachers in all the main traditions of
Buddhism warn again and again about the dangers of this
'spiritual' slide down one side of the Middle Way. Thus Zen
Master Rinzai warns his monks that 'If you take a state of
immovable purity for what is required of you, this is to
recognize [the darkness of] Ignorance for your lordship!' To
drive the point home, D. T. Suzuki, the translator of this
passage, adds the footnote: 'Immovability, purity, serenity
or tranquillity — they all refer to a state of consciousness
where all thought waves of every kind uniformly subside.
This is also called the dark abyss of Ignorance or of the
Unconscious, and the Zen-man is told to avoid it by all
means and not to imagine it to be the ultimate object of Zen
discipline.'[64] The relativism of such a nihilistic quietism is
made clear in several passages in the Pali canon, of which
the following is typical. The Buddha observes that 'The
world in general grasps after systems and is imprisoned by
dogmas and ideologies,' though the wise do 'not go along
with that system-grasping, that mental obstinacy and dogmatic bias.' 'The world in general inclines to two views, to
existence or to non-existence. But for him who, with the
highest wisdom, sees the uprising of the world as it really is,
"non-existence of the world" does not apply, and for him
who, with the highest wisdom, sees the passing away of the
world as it really is, "existence of the world" does not
apply.... "Everything exists", this is one extreme [view];
"nothing exists", this is the other extreme. Avoiding both

extremes [the Buddha] teaches a doctrine of the middle.'[65] We have now reviewed several aspects of polarization, which are summarized below.

First, there is the unweighted polarization of authentic awareness, experiencing reality in its relative differentiation (*paratantra*) but informed by a sense of its 'emptiness', its insubstantial and contingent quality.

Secondly, there is the polarization weighted by the mortal need to affirm a fixed and solid reality out there, whose strong black-and-white contrasts reflect ego's aversions and desires.

Thirdly, this weighted polarization is socially amplified by antithetical bonding; I, us and ours weighted against you, them and theirs.

Fourthly, the ideas which confirm and distinguish us and ours coagulate into our comprehensive belief system and world view (*Weltanschauung*) intellectualized as ideology and underpinned by a more or less dualistic culture (a theme taken up in the next chapter).

Fifthly, with super ideology 'our' relative pole becomes absolute and 'they' are absolutely wrong/evil. This includes the fanatic ideologies of millennial movements in which the opposing race or creed is depressed to a subhuman level.

Finally there is the phenomenon of attempted spiritual withdrawal into the absolute which is thereby polarized from the relative and so itself becomes a delusively experienced relative.

The remainder of this chapter explores further the first of the above cases, in which the difference between this and that is experienced not as the separateness of two entities but instead as a relative (but very real) distinction which constitutes a single reality. In this mutual confirmation the distinction both joins and separates, or more correctly, it both makes one and makes two. It is because dictatorship can and does exist that we distinguish and prize democracy. This experience of relative and absolute truth as a single reality has been called 'the Higher Third', a rather clumsy term, but less misleading than its synonym 'the Middle

Way'. It follows from this definition that the Higher Third is also a Third because it is a perception which transcends this and that. In the logic of ordinary language it inevitably appears contradictory and paradoxical. However, as Jung reminds us, 'the paradox is one of our most valuable spiritual possessions...because only the paradox comes anywhere near to comprehending the fullness of life. Non-ambiguity and non-contradiction are one sided, and thus unsuited to expressing the incomprehensible.'[66] Poetry, together with music and art, do have the capacity, however, to spring us out of structure and into imagination. This is why the Mahayana scriptures carry us off in myth and metaphor as well as tumble us out of our everyday minds with paradox piled on paradox.

When self is less driven by fear to invest heavily in reality-out-there, all separateness begins to dissolve and distinctions are lightened. This enlightenment of conscious-ness is the fruit of meditative experience. The Higher Third is thus an inconceivably different way of experiencing reality and of sensing the possibilities in otherwise intractable situations. No longer filtered out by desire and aversion, reality is experienced more profoundly when there is a total opening to the beauty and the suffering of the world.

Weighted polarization distorts and filters reality and so, if its push is not too strong and refusing, admitting more of the light of reality can help dissolve some of the deeper contrasting shadows which bring ego temporary relief at the cost of truth. Suppose that I believe that (a) the Soviet and American people are fundamentally different kinds of people, and that (b) the American–Soviet conflict arises from aggressive Soviet paranoia (a typical double-weighted polarization). However, if I am able to talk with typical Russians or read accurate and open-minded accounts I shall come to appreciate that they have much the same hopes and fears as ordinary Americans and that they are equally likeable as people. I shall also be made more deeply aware of the terrible devastation and suffering of their country in the Second World War and conclude that their fears are understandable. My prejudices will have been lightened, and the Cold War will now appear more ambiguous and less of a black-and-white matter.

However, old Janus reminds us to make two important qualifications about the above mitigation. First, we would unfortunately be wrong to conclude that the Cold War is largely a misunderstanding which can be remedied by more personal contact and sympathetic reporting. While it is true that Americans and Russians are one in their common humanity, it is *that*, as we have seen earlier in this book, that also divides them. Humanity does indeed have an impulse to friendship and to one-ness (otherwise spiritual paths running thus could not exist at all). But it has still to learn to live without *needing* enemies, without antithetical bonding. And, secondly, as to letting in more of the light of reality, most of humanity is trying to get by with filtering out disturbing reality and shaping the rest to make life more tolerable. It is not easy to live with 'too much reality', which lets in ambiguity and insecurity. It can even provoke defensiveness and aggression, as when cherished myths are cornered by awkwardly inescapable facts. Nevertheless, letting in a little awkward reality may prompt some to become aware at least on a superficial level that their prejudices obscure the view. And those whose consciousness is freed and open enough for them to look into reality do need to be well informed, particularly in view of the ambiguous nature of most problem situations. (The sages of old who lived in more of a small, face-to-face world did not have such an information problem.)

In the nuclear Cold War the USA and USSR each casts the other in the role of evil doer. In other words, the world's affairs are experienced in terms of a relative ethic, the ethic of this and the ethic of that. But the Higher Third is the experience of the whole situation and has its own implicit ethic. For Buddhism evil is delusive separation, particularly of self from other people. In contrast to a good which is defined by separating off evil, the Higher Third implies a

GOOD which lies in ending the delusion of separation.

The above example, however, is misleading if it implies that the allocation of 'good' and 'evil' between two contending halves is a matter of indifference to those who can see whole and undivided. True, if the situation is factually and ethically ambiguous such a black-and-white distinction would be unacceptable. On the other hand, there is a minority of situations which *are* more clear cut. For example, there are several countries in the world in which the 'this' of an uncompromisingly dictatorial regime and the 'that' of a violent popular resistance are mutually defining. Confrontation has polarized the middle ground out of existence, as it tends to. Each side is denying the full humanity of the other. If there is any good in either it can clearly only be relative good. But the conflict and the suffering has been initiated and is maintained by the dictatorship which has thereby brought upon itself the violence of retaliation. So, if wisdom be informed by compassion, the Higher Third must ultimately take the part of the relative good, the part of the oppressed, though *without identifying with it*. This is exemplified by the following report in the (London) *Observer* of 30 March 1980 written a few days after Archbishop Oscar Romero of the Cental American republic of El Salvador had been shot dead on the steps of his chapel. Romero had roundly condemned the armed leftist rebel factions for their daily killings and extortions. However, he also emphasized that these were the reactions of the common people being used as 'a production force under the management of a privileged society....The gap between poverty and wealth is the main cause of our trouble....And sometimes it goes further: it is the hatred in the heart of the worker for his employer....If I did not denounce the killings and the way the army removes people and ransacks peasants' homes I should be acquiescing in the violence.'

Archbishop Tutu of South Africa, Cardinal Glemp of Poland, Cardinal Sin of the Philippines, as well as the Dalai Lama of Tibet, have all responded in more or less similar ways to comparatively similar situations. This kind of involvement arises wholly out of the human needs of the situation, and not out of the need to affirm *my* dignity, *my* rights, *my* self. There lies the difference between the good and the GOOD....Such 'engaged spirituality', declared Erich Fromm, is 'the strength and joy of people who have deep conviction without being fanatical, who are loving without being sentimental...imaginative without being unrealistic...disciplined without submission.'[67]

The following poem by *Thich* Nhat Hahn, Zen monk and Vietnamese peace worker, makes a fitting conclusion to this discussion of the Higher Third. In particular it reminds us that its essence is the transcendence of the 'this' of self and the 'that' of 'out there' — the most fundamental of all the loaded polarizations.

## *Please call me by my true names*

Do not say that I'll depart tomorrow
because even today I still arrive

Look deeply: I arrive in every second
to be a bud on a spring branch,
to be a tiny bird, with wings still fragile,
    learning to sing in my new nest,
to be a caterpillar in the heart of a flower,
to be a jewel hiding itself in a stone.

I still arrive, in order to laugh and to cry,
    in order to fear and to hope,
the rhythm of my heart is the birth and death
    of all that are alive.

I am the mayfly metamorphosing on the
    surface of the river,
and I am the bird which, when springs comes,
    arrives in time to eat the mayfly.

I am a frog swimming happily in the clear water
    of a pond,
and I am the grass-snake who, approaching
    in silence, feeds itself on the frog.

I am the child in Uganda, all skin and bones,
    my legs as thin as bamboo sticks,
and I am the arms merchant, selling deadly
    weapons to Uganda.

I am the twelve-year-old-girl, refugee on a
    small boat,
who throws herself into the ocean after being
    raped by a sea pirate,
and I am the pirate, my heart not yet capable
    of seeing and loving.

I am a member of the politburo, with plenty
    of power in my hands,
and I am the man who has to pay his 'debt
    of blood' to my people,
dying slowly in a forced labor camp.

My joy is like spring, so warm it makes
    flowers bloom in all walks of life.
My pain is like a river of tears, so full it fills
    all four oceans.

Please call me by my true names, so I can hear
    all my cries and laughs at once,
    so I can see that my joy and pain are one.

Please call me by my true names, so I can wake
    up and so the door of my heart can be left
    open, the door of compassion

# 9   The Two Mentalities

This chapter is about two historic mentalities or paradigms. At about the time these were coming clearly into public view, Thomas Kuhn coined 'paradigm' to mean 'the entire constellation of beliefs, values, techniques and so on shared by members of a given community.'[68] I have named these two mentalities *dualism* and *monism*, to draw attention to the differing modes of knowing in which each is rooted. Although none of the characteristics of the monist mentality discussed below is exclusively Buddhist, all lie within the Buddhist perspective; they amplify it and are amplified by it. As perhaps the most sophisticated expression of monist experience, Buddhism offers a useful interpretative context for the different facets of that paradigm. And the latter can be helpful in making Buddhist social theory and analysis more explicit. Moreover, versions of the two paradigms are to be found in most books heralding 'New Age' consciousness and 'Green' alternatives.[69] Their discussion here suggests Buddhist affinities with this movement which receives more attention in the second half of the book.

The Cartesian dualism which appeared in Wilber's 'high egoic' period of Western civilization (AD 1500 onwards) denotes the experience of the thinking self as separate from all that is other. *Cogito ergo sum* was Descartes' historic dictum — I think, therefore I am. The omnipotent and lonely thinking self was thus launched on its project of dealing with the feelings, the body, and the whole world 'out there', armed with the power of Reason and the scientific method. Thus there developed a scientism which assumes that the investigative model of reality developed in the physical sciences − logical, structured and linear − is *itself* an accurate picture of that reality, and not just a useful symbolic and diagrammatic investigative tool. Having created highly sophisticated systems human beings become dominated by them, not only objectively (as in the case of the nuclear arms drive) but also subjectively. Thus, from being a helpful analogy in the observer's mind, mechanism becomes dominant: phenomena *are* mechanisms. For example, by analogy with the computer, brain function is perceived entirely in mechanistic terms and the computer tends to be treated anthropomorphically. Man (for man it characteristically is) *becomes* the mechanistic mentality, which constructs a mechanistic world in its own image. In brief, as an American astronaut concluded: 'Science is a methodology. As a belief system it is disastrous.'[70]

Scientism and the underlying dualism is about individualism, material progress, the supremacy of science and technology, the power of rational, calculative planning, and the building of a 'better' society. It is the traditional cornerstone of Western physical and social science, philosophy and theology. It is the characteristic Western form of kammaic cultural delusion. It is the water in which we swim, but particularly if we are male. Even if we have exorcized it intellectually, it will still be ingrained in our feelings and responses. Instrumental Janus is left to solve all the problems, by changing 'reality'. (For behavioural psychology even the mind becomes a stimulus−response mechanism somehow 'out there'.) But, as we saw in Chapter 7, it is the old, fearsome existential Janus who unbeknowingly really sets the pace.

Pushed by the kammaic energy of human history, it seems that the dualistic mentality must either facilitate the destruction of humanity or, by being pushed to its self-evident absurdity, facilitate its salvation. Ken Wilber has drawn our attention to the inherent 'self-liquidating' potential of classical, dualistic science.[71] Its increasingly rigorous methods of investigation inevitably bring it to a point where the investigator himself has to be included as 'object'. If I am part of the reality which I experience, then consciousness must be reality and vice versa, for there can be no self separate from its consciousness of itself. More correctly, we must conclude that reality *is* itself a high level of consciousness. Consciousness at the monist level reveals subject and object, observer and observed, as being one reality. Below that level, consciousness is distorted by the pressure of self-affirming need, and splits dualistically. Different modes of knowing therefore correspond to different levels of consciousness. At its highest level monist consciousness is, in the Madhyamika sense of the previous chapter, 'empty'; resuming its forms it is the world of phenomena, 'the ten thousand things', experienced in the monist mode of knowing (*paratantra*).

The quantum revolution in physics occurred because the physicists were carried by the traditional dualistic scientific methodology to a point at which it became self-contradictory, and were pushed over the edge into an intuitive and creative understanding. Nils Bohr has written of 'the final harvest' of physics as being 'a sheaf of formulae [which] will never describe nature itself.'[72] Such mathematical formulae square with the equations but refer to phenomena which are *inconceivable*.

The highest level of monist consciousness is found in gnostic, 'esoteric' spirituality, that is, in Buddhism and in the mystical currents running through the other great world religions.

This is a total and all-pervading consciousness which has been *intellectually* confirmed by philosophers like Hegel and by the great subatomic physicists. Of sixty-two statements of 'how the world works' gathered by Lawrence Le Shan, the half gathered from mystics cannot be readily distinguished from those by physicists.[73] In the West, from Epicurus, Democritus, Heraclitus and Lucretius onwards, a monist awareness of reality has been witnessed, at various levels and in various forms, by an ignored or martyred or half lost-to-history succession of philosophers, mystics, scientists and artists. It has been dualism in its various manifestations that has been the paradigm of centralized political power, exoteric religion, prestigious rationality, patriarchy, high technology and the dominant educated élite.

In most contemporary subject fields there appears to have been in recent years a more or less pronounced shift towards a monist awareness both in the picturing of reality and the methodology of investigation. In 1970 Alan Dawe published a seminal paper in the *British Journal of Sociology* entitled 'The two sociologies'. In contrast to the dualistic sociology modelled on Newtonian science, the 'situationist' investigator immerses herself in social reality as participant—observer.[74] In Chapter 6 we saw how this phenomenological sociology sees the social landscape as being constructed by its inhabitants out of the shared meanings which they communicate. The situation has now been reached where fields such as organization theory are 'populated by people who do not share the same universe of discourse...and consequently are unable to speak to one another,' and, moreover, 'whose differences prescribe contrasting sets of methods and interpretive criteria and whose conflicts are philosophical rather than scientific.'[75] In the same collection of papers, Albert Cherns concludes that the 'social technologies' (for example, management, planning) are now 'in total disarray'.

This kind of evidence accumulating from different fields reinforces the arguments over the last two or three decades that a major paradigm shift is occurring in response to a changing cultural climate. However, it is taking place in a pragmatic, piecemeal and, literally, blind fashion, articulated in paradigm definitions which reflect a lower level of reality-awareness than the overarching monist/dualistic distinction. For example, a monist inclination represents organizations and other social entities as organisms rather than mechanisms.[76] In other words, it sees them as complex, self-determining unities rather than clockwork-like bits and pieces dependent for their operation on a hierarchial power-train. Organismic/mechanistic is, however, a low level representation of the two paradigms because, for example, an organismic perception can, arguably, accommodate such higher level dualistic forms of awareness as positivism and anthropocentrism (see below). It is part of the rationale of this book that Buddhism and other high level monist modes of knowing have a potentially important contribution to make to the paradigm shift at lower and more − in Buddhist terms − delusive, levels of perception. This shift in mentality extends beyond academic research and teaching through the 'social technologies' to the overall social consciousness wherein lies the real centre of gravity, as in the shift to new, grassroots, alternative perspectives of social change and to ecological awareness and protection.

We have seen that in various ways the scientistic push of dualistic delusion is paradoxical in effect. On the one hand it is pushing humanity towards global disaster. On the other hand, as we have seen in the case of first physics and now the social sciences, dualism is ultimately self-liquidating. This occurs at a fundamental cultural level in that human consciousness has, over the last hundred years, been stripped of historic layers of myth, belief, explanation and consolation down to its existential nakedness. I have quoted some examples from Don Cupitt in Chapter 2. In Britain the ending of the (coercive) Age of Deference, when everyone knew their correct social station, has arguably contributed to a growing sense of anomie and insecurity, with lower social standards seen in an increase in vandalism and violence for example. But it has also made possible the more effective assertion of human dignity and self-responsibility (what has been termed 'permissiveness'). It has long been known that, for the individual, exposure to existential reality can lead either to madness and despair or, if the way is prepared, acknowledged and actively cultivated, to positively welcoming that reality and to recognizing the delusive character of what has been lost. It is in these alternatives that, for a whole civilization, the dualist and monist modes of awareness have now culminated.

The second part of this chapter identifies characteristic features of the dualistic mentality and relates each to its monist counterpart. The latter, however, have been less elaborated, since they are treated in 'Indra's Net' in Chapter 12.

First, dualism is an expression of the ordinary, and therefore restrictive and delusive, level of consciousness. It assumes that this ordinary consciousness is optimal, controlled and rational. The contrary view is that higher consciousness states do exist, can be attained by training, but cannot except in limited ways be characterized verbally. 'I have no doubt whatever,' wrote William James, 'that most people live, whether physically, intellectually or morally, in a very restricted circle of their potential being. They make use of a very small portion of their possible consciousness...much like a man who, out of his whole bodily organism, should get into the habit of moving and using only his little finger.'[77] As to 'control', who or what is it that 'controls' consciousness? Consciousness appears controlled only on its own terms, and the narrowness of these is evident as soon as ordinary consciousness attempts meditative concentration. Such a meditator will discover within minutes that he or she has more control over their pocket handkerchief than over 'his' or 'her' restless consciousness. Again, rationality exists only on the restricted terms of that level of consciousness, and readily translates into the rationality, for example, of an economic system which has to warehouse and destroy 'excess' food in a world where millions starve. From the viewpoint of the mystic, the dualist's well-ordered world must appear as a blind, wilful and destructive fantasy.

Secondly, scientism, grounded in dualism, is positivist. It claims to be objective, detached and value free. Phenomena are believed to have objective character and to be capable of intellectual analysis which is verbally communicable. And all this is true and useful at a gross, symbolic level. To cook a dinner it is useful to have a recipe of ingredients, quantities and cooking times. Yet different cooks following the same formal recipe commonly produce different tasting dishes. The contrasting position of Madhyamika monism has already been noted in the previous chapter. The one reality will be experienced differently, depending on cultural and personal differences. Among those who do *really* experience it phenomenally there will be some phenomenal, formal differences of an ultimately superficial kind, as between, say, Buddhist meditators and Christian contemplatives. But for most of us that reality will be more or less distorted by our variously inherited and lifelong existential fear. To be aware of such a distortion is the beginning of wisdom. Some phenomenological, situationist social scientists begin their research reports by writing about their personal values and assumptions and the frailties of their research method. Readers can thus appreciate that they are reading about the investigator's reality. Such a reality will have a quality of factual reportage in contrast to scientistically reported social reality which, through much reliance on quantitative methods for example, will seek objectivity by maintaining a high level of abstraction. This does have its uses, but in general it tends to dessicate experienced reality so as to fit it into conceptual frame works.

Positivism helps sustain a strong sense of individualism. If there is a truly objective reality out there (and not just your version of it or mine or ours) then this better affirms a secure sense of self. Individualism is what 'high egoic' culture is really all about. The freedom of 'the individual' fully to develop all of his or her potential has been the ideal of virtually all the Western intellectual movements of modern times. This has both nourished a deep humanity and respect for individual dignity and has at the same time licensed some to develop their powers at the expense of the lives and dignity of the many. Professor Trevor Ling has frequently proclaimed Buddhism as the 'remedy for the disease of individualism',[78] and whilst this is fundamentally true, the underlying situation is more paradoxical. For example, as a Buddhist you must have a strong enough sense of self in order to lose it (to an 'awareness identity'), an argument to which I shall return in the last chapter of the book. Moreover, there must be a sufficient dualistic sense for the autonomy and uniqueness of another person to be fully experienced in its own light and without being compromised by 'my' needs. The humanity of the other can only be fully appreciated to the extent it is reflected in my perception without egoic distortion. This monist humanism, which awakens to oneness through the unobstructed awareness of the other, is the Higher Third beyond either a self-confirming and alienating dualism or a self-deceiving pseudo-spirituality in which I believe that I am 'at one' with the rest of humanity without in fact ever really being aware of other people in their own right.

The anthropocentrism of humankind as master and arbiter of all that lives and grows on planet Earth and beyond is a particularly deep-rooted expression of dualism. And here again, beyond delusive self-need, there is a paradoxical element of truth in that in (monist) deep ecology (Chapter 12) humans as the most evolved and powerful beings *do* have an outstanding responsibility. But this has to be informed by the needs of other living and growing things (bio-centrism), and not by a paternalism of 'environmental protection', which is no more than a reformed version of anthropocentrism.

The dualistic consciousness which splits reality into subject and object likewise experiences a universe of conflicting opposites, of a separate this against a separate that, good against evil, and so on. Its binary logic chops up 'reality' and orders the pieces into reassuringly comprehensible structures. These impose an apparent order where once there was what was experienced as chaos and confusion. Examples in this mechanistic paradigm are Aristotelian logic, Cartesian philosophy, Hobbesian political theory, Newtonian physics, Linnaean biology, Weberian bureaucracy and Parsonian functionalist sociology.

In the dualistic, scientistic mentality order is related to control — and ultimately to 'my' control — and loss of control is the root fear, whether it be losing control of my emotions, a descent into social anarchy (the underlying preoccupation of virtually all political theory until recent times), or, at bottom, the terror of falling into existential chaos, of self annihilation. The passion for control goes very deep, and is experienced daily in the workplace, where, for the most part, management remains the control of most people by some people, whether grossly or subtly. Parents experience much the same problem in 'bringing up' their children. Truly yielding up even some control and investing real trust in others goes against the grain of that compulsiveness that rises in the place where our fears are also our desires...

Order and control relate to hierarchy, the ordered system of control of the lower by the higher. This, again, is a picturing of reality which does have a certain symbolical validity appropriate to a gross and approximate level of comprehension and manipulation. Physiology, for example, can be usefully pictured in terms of hierarchies of control. But here again scientism identifies such schematic approximations with experience of reality itself.

The dualistic mentality of scientism is also reductionist. Having analysed a phenomenon into its constituent parts this tends to be seen as a sufficient definition. That *is* the phenomenon. But a heap of levers, pinions and springs only function as a clock when in a certain relationship to each other. And for that to happen between themselves they need to be in a wider environment, in the clockmaker's workshop. In this sense, the constituent parts do and do not constitute the whole. In the holistic perspective, most finely honed in the Madhyamika dialectic of the previous chapter, meaning is found in the relationship between the apparently separate parts. In contemporary natural and social sciences concern is increasingly with processes rather than entities, that is, it is the ongoing relationships between things rather than the static nature of each which is explicatory. As Fritjof Capra observes:

> Quantum Theory — the theoretical framework of atomic physics — shows that subatomic particles have no meaning as isolated entities; they can be understood only as interconnections between various agencies of observation and measurement. Particles are not things, but interconnections between things; and these things are interconnections between other things, and so on. Thus Quantum Theory reveals the basic oneness of the Universe.[79]

Buddhists, incidentally, will be familiar with the anecdote about King Milinda's chariot in the Theravada scriptures, where the parts of the chariot are analogous to the human faculties or 'aggregates' (*skandhas*). This kind of mechanistic logic may be seen as a kind of preliminary truth, opposed in this case to the logical alternative of a self, a 'soul' to be found other than in the contingent faculties that constitute the human being. But only the dialectic can accurately express the paradoxical nature of reality, and although this was fully developed in Mahayana Buddhism it does also sparkle out again and again in the Theravada scriptures.

Scientism reduces time as well as space to clearly definable and manageable entities, as a linear, monochronic time of minutes, hours, days and years. Prediction is needed, as well as control. Time greed and time starvation are characteristic forms of suffering arising from the linear delusion of our culture and afflict not least the burnt-out case, the overworked activist trying to paddle against the time-flowing current of nuclear and ecological escalation. This is a river in which there is no time left to go fishing; was there more of it when Thoreau went fishing in it?[80] Perhaps there

is no scientistic kind of awareness better than this monochronic one for meditation, on how mere chronometric
convenience, take it or leave it, can be appropriated and
made into a hard delusive reality by the fearful existential
lust for control which at the same time highlights the sense
of doomed finitude. As usual, there is no refuge in the
inverted delusion of clinging to 'timelessness'. Again, only
the paradox serves, of polychronic monism where time
exists out of time.

In short, scientism dualistically chops up reality 'out there'
into distinct, separate and manageable units in a structured
world of linear time, predicting, projecting, calculating and
planning, and invincible on its own terms. It is not so much
a level of consciousness as an insatiable, deluded and driven
compulsion, inspired by a vision of endless achievement
and progress, of ever-widening knowledge and control,
extending to worlds beyond after this planet has been burnt
out by it. It appears to imply a dangerously widening
alienation between self and 'out there' as we enter the
Information Society. Here pervasive, electronically generated
information becomes the new and even more distanced
surrogate reality anticipated by T. S. Eliot:

> Where is the Life we have lost in living?
> Where is the wisdom we have lost in knowledge?
> Where is the knowledge we have lost in
>    information?[81]

The next chapter examines one expression of scientism
which is especially relevant to this book, that of benevolent
social engineering. In conclusion, however, it will be helpful
to attempt some final clarification of the relationship between
the monist and dualist mentalities. In most of the previous
examples of the dualistic mode of knowing the qualification
has been made that the same forms also exist in the monist
mode of knowing. But in dualism they are informed by the
existential and cultural compulsion to impose order, control
and predictability, and to distance, protect, achieve and

dominate. On the other hand, in the monist paradigm the same forms have only a preliminary, provisional, superficial, symbolic and contingent character. For example, we earlier noted the need to open fully and unreservedly to the autonomy, the alarming separateness of another person so as to be *at one* with them without the distancing and distortion of any residual self need. Again, we do need to be able to work with the reality of this and that, of structure and logic, as a gross-level convenience without being deceived by apparent separateness. This is the Madhyamika *paratantra*, the monist relative reality informed by the 'emptying' of self. That this mode alone is capable of giving knowledge of reality is, in Wilber's view, the 'unmistakable and unanimous view. . . of the vast number of scientists, philosophers, psychologists and theologians that have fully and deeply understood these two modes of knowing.'[82]

Two examples may be helpful. At work the analysis of time-and-motion study may break down a manual job into its smallest constituent parts, eliminating some and re-designing others and reassembling in a different pattern. But the experience of the new job for the operative may be that it has become 'soul destroying', and his output may fall instead of increasing. Again, an architect may design a complex of apartments which appear to promise many conveniences to the future occupants as well as meeting various abstract social and psychological criteria. Yet in the event several such constructions have been experienced by the occupants as 'frightening', 'dreadful', 'lonely', 'depressing'. In both cases professional skills were employed objectively in every sense of that word. Dualism, by dessicating our own feared humanity and distancing that of others, creates inhuman realities for all of us. To try to use scientism, its action philosophy, in order to resolve our global crisis is a contradiction in terms. In Einstein's words, 'The world we have made as a result of the level of thinking we have done thus far creates problems that we cannot solve at the same level as the level we created them at.'

# 10  *The Social Fallacy and the Inconceivable Liberation Movement*

There is a commonplace dualistic mentality which has grown up over the past five hundred years with our increasing mastery over the 'objective world' and the decline in religious belief. This is the assumption that relief from affliction is obtained exclusively by adjusting reality 'out there' in order to meet our requirements. Both spiritual self-transcendence and the consolations of exoteric religion have receded, together with magic and fatalism, and the traditional range of objective adjustments noted in Chapter 3 (power over others, enjoying riches, belonging to something worth identifying with, and so on) has been vastly extended. It now ranges, for example, from the meaningfulness of actually building a new society to the peace of mind of life insurance, and from faith in the infinite power of modern medicine to the instant distraction offered by several television channels. And progress promises that what cannot be done now will certainly be done later. Even the self is thus objectified. In the world's richest country it is common to put the mind in for regular servicing by one's analyst much as the car is put in for servicing by one's garage, so that it will run more smoothly along the ways of 'normalcy'. Only old age, death and the diseases which medicine still cannot cure remain outside the mentality of everyman's and everywoman's quick-fix scientism. As far as possible they have therefore been variously ignored, devalued and tabooed. Recently, however, they have been subjected to the determined optimism of a world in which it is assumed that 'everybody wins'. This makes it more difficult for us truly to learn something from them. As newcomers to Buddhist groups have later explained, though they do indeed experience various forms of suffering, they were initially reluctant publicly to admit to such shameful personal failure.

It is in the above climate that the Social Fallacy flourishes. This is the belief that human well-being is to be achieved primarily or solely through social development. (A more modest version is that social and economic problems can be remedied solely by social change.) The social fallacy is a taken-for-granted assumption that is shared almost right across the political spectrum. It is shared by 'Dry Blues' who believe that through Free Enterprise private vice will become public virtue (the Adam Smith dictum that became the American Dream). It is shared by gradualist conservatives (Wet Blues) who argue that 'inherent market forces' should be modified by some welfarism and planning. Its Pink form is that of Social Democracy and the Welfare State. Its most absolute form is the Red or Social Revolutionary Fallacy, in its variants of Marxian ideal Socialism, hardened by bureaucratic Communism, and Third World People's Liberation Movements. Even a Green Social Fallacy is possible, when the grass roots are poisoned by ideology, as we shall see in Part Eight.

The modern high egoic age not only brought a sense of scientific, technological, commercial and industrial mastery. The old religious millennial beliefs and utopias gave way to a confident rationality, a social cohesiveness, a power of organization and communication, and a democratic firepower which brought whole new societies to birth at the end of the eighteenth century in America and France. In the nineteenth century the Radical Social Fallacy appeared in its socialist form, together with other less total forms of planned and benevolent social engineering (for example, universal elementary education as well as universal military conscription). The humanistic (and too-easily-forgotten) Marx predicted that the post-revolutionary satisfaction of men and

women's material wants would free them for the development of their full human potential. The 1917 Russian Revolution proclaimed that a new kind of human being,
Socialist Man, would shape and be shaped by Soviet society,
but what has in fact emerged is a consumer who has to
queue much longer than those who are trying to realize the
American Dream.

However mixed the motivation may be, the various forms
of the Social Fallacy overlie the great humane movement of
industrial materialist culture to relieve all the gross forms of
human affliction: to bring an end to war and the fear of war,
to ensure an adequate standard of living and welfare, health,
education and housing for all the world's peoples, and
freedom from the age-old exploitation and oppression by
the powerful and the wealthy. This is a cause which, in its
various expressions, has attracted the idealism and spirit of
self-sacrifice of some of the finest men and women of our
age. I believe that Buddhism and other ancient spiritual
teachings that are now attracting much interest must wholeheartedly come to terms with this movement by working
through its implications at all levels. The Dalai Lama, in
numerous statements like the following, has set an example
to Buddhists:

> It is quite obvious that without material progress
> we will lack many material comforts. In the mean-
> time, without inner peace material things alone
> are not sufficient. There are many signs which
> indicate that material progress alone is not suf-
> ficient for men. There is something lacking. There-
> fore, the only way is to combine the two.[83]

Notwithstanding its fallacious assumptions and its ultimate failure, the socialism of the Social Revolutionary Fallacy
has inspired and is inspiring some impressive achievements. It has shown what can be done. Social Democracy
has brought immense benefits to the Scandinavian and
other countries, including the British Welfare State. More-

over, the socialist revolutionary movements, under much more difficult conditions, have historic and honourable achievements to their credit. For example, in pre-revolutionary China the death of millions by famine and flood hardly rated a headline in the world's newspapers, so commonplace was it. Today this quarter of humanity has been freed from these afflictions. Again, whatever reservations there may be about the regimes in Cuba and Nicaragua, there can be no doubt about their clear moral superiority over the gangster dictatorships which they supplanted.

Nevertheless, Socialism, in all its variant forms, has substantially failed to live up to its promise.

In the first place, it has failed even to mitigate the historic drive to global crisis described in Chapter 4. In some ways it has strongly fuelled it, most notably through the aggressive and militarized industrial materialism of the Soviet Union.

Secondly, where it has fully established itself, revolutionary socialism's intellectual élites have only been able to consolidate their power through an oppressive collectivism. These inert bureaucratic societies have no resemblance to what Marx envisaged, with their massive hierarchies of power, their harsh restriction on political and religious liberty, their persecution of dissidents, their insistence on ideological conformity, and the persistence of patriarchal patterns of life. We shall have to find something better than revolutionary exultation, as Gary Snyder has insisted:

> The release of Demonic Energies in the name of
> the People
> must cease
> Messing with blood sacrifice in the name of
> Nature
> must cease
> The stifling self-indulgence in anger in the name of
> Freedom
> must cease
> this is death to clarity
> death to compassion.[84]

Thirdly, socialism today shares the same industrial materialist culture as capitalism, even if in more collectivized and less grossly egoic forms. The overriding social goal is here, also, production to satisfy higher and higher levels of consumer greed beyond the satisfaction of reasonable material needs. Environmentally, the record of the Soviet Union and China appears to be even worse than that of the capitalist countries. And variants like Hungary's market socialism and Yugoslavia's self-management socialism are less promising new departures than attempts to make the traditional orthodoxy more just and workable.

Huge resources have been accumulated by humanity, with a science and technology capable of controlling disease and famine, and with organizational, planning and communications systems capable of applying these benefits on a large scale. It has nevertheless proved impossible to provide each human being with the essential necessities for life and to free him or her from the grosser and remediable afflictions. On the contrary much of this wealth is being used for destructive ends. The Social Fallacy is exposed. Something fundamental appears to be missing...

Like other problems which face us the problem of creating a society free of war, poverty and tyranny is insoluble on its own terms. The Social Fallacy is a secular inversion with built-in failure unless it can somehow be flipped right side up, to a higher, monist level of consciousness which includes the self which makes social reality. Viewed from that perspective, the Social Fallacy can appear only as an heroic but grotesquely contradictory and superficial phenomenon — rather like trying to extinguish a fire with kerosene. W. H. Auden, after describing how superbly equipped for 'The Quest' was the human expedition, sadly concludes:

> In theory they were sound on Expectation,
> Had there been situations to be in;
> Unluckily they were their situation.[85]

For the social theorist and social activist alike 'human

nature' has long been relegated as a constant, background factor. Talk of changing it is still beyond the pale of serious political discussion, unless perhaps the change be in the crucible of a new society. As for religion as the key to social change, religion for the average activist is associated with ideological control, obscurantist authoritarianism, and the moral legitimization of an unjust social order. It is charged with preaching humility as a virtue and suffering as something to be borne with patience in expectation of reward in the hereafter. Indeed, nowadays matters are sufficiently reversed for Simone Weil to have claimed that, 'It is not religion but revolution which is the opium of the people.'[86]

As to personal spirituality, whether Eastern or Western, Buddhist or Quaker, in the secular social perspective this is irrelevant or marginal at best. At worst it is viewed as escapist, irresponsible and other-worldly. Since many of the spiritually inclined apparently believe that social phenomena have, at best, no immediate relevance (the Quietist Fallacy), the separation of spirituality from active social concern is mutually confirming. From *either* standpoint mysticism-and-militancy appears as bizarre hybrid, ready antithesis or suspect paradox. Whether it be weed or flower, however, it grows strongly on the margin between these two well-ordered gardens.

Buddhism implies that unless there is some significant personal and individual change in the ways we feel and think about ourselves and about others we shall try to go on evolving societies which express and reinforce the futile struggle of each of us to escape from our root fear into varieties of acquisitive and aggressive belongingness identity. In the second half of the book I maintain that only some spiritual kind of conviction and training have the strength to bring about the necessary radical shift. It is not an enlightened society of saints that I have in mind, but rather a significant number of people to create a social climate which will help everyone to be more human. That means relating to others positively and warmly and working with them unselfishly and fearlessly. It means discovering and diminishing the urge to secure ourselves, to put down others, to escape into negativity and passivity, to repress or to be carried off by our feelings, and to deceive ourselves and others in the multi-layered 'games' of trying to live a life. In place of clinging to every kind of quick-fix this implies the cultivation of a strong and fearless awareness identity. All this amounts to a veritable learning society, to learning alone and in interaction how, in the words of a Thai Buddhist activist, 'to grow spiritually'. 'First of all,' Sulak Sivaraksa writes, 'one has to be calm and impartial so that one can find out what sort of a person one is. On the whole, one does not know or admit that one is lustful or greedy, although one would like to become rich at the expense of others. If one lacks that negative quality, one is normally ambitious and would like to play with power — in the name of social justice or serving the poor. Beyond this one is fairly ignorant about oneself as well as about the world in which one would normally dare to be involved and claim that one would solve those worldly problems.'[87] The reader may know at least one or two truly good-hearted people who are both gentle and compassionate and yet strong and fearless enough in themselves as not to need to put their shadows over others. Imagine what it would be like if the average man and woman were thus; if there were enough of such people not just to modify the inhuman effects of so much in our structures and institutions but to evolve whole new lifestyles and forms of social organization arising from the kind of people we had become. And these new norms and institutions would in turn support and nurture personal change, instead of frustrating and distorting it.

However, we are still talking in terms of personal change being necessary to facilitate fundamental social change, as if spirituality were no more than the handmaiden of truly profound and human social revolution. We have still only tipped the secular mentality through ninety degrees.

Buddhism and other kinds of spiritual path are not about

social liberation but about human liberation, about release of human potential trapped in the delusive suffering which arises from the root human condition. Hence they are also about social liberation as an integral though dependent part of this process. The secular vision of liberation is, by contrast, both superficial in that it does not go down to the roots of human behaviour and also narrowly confined when set against the concerns of our lives. We can be bereaved as well as unemployed. We can be terminally ill as well as threatened by the Bomb. We can experience deep inner loneliness as well as being badly housed. We can suffer from self-hate and corrosive self-pity and bitterness as well as suffering from a pension that is insufficient. We are human beings before we are citizens; the inevitability of our death is still infinitely more significant to us (to the extent we can open to it) than whether it will be nuclear or not. It is not just that both these contrasting pairs afflict us, but that the 'remedy' for both lies ultimately in how we experience and live our lives. The tacit assumption that we have spirituality for the first of each pair and social action for the second blights the effectiveness of both and deludes us into supposing they are separate.

If social liberation — or even material liberation in its various forms — has become the hope of the world, then grotesque limits are set upon the potential of the mass of humanity. It is as if we were to inhabit the back of a terrace of houses, knowing only our back doors opening out to fenced-in back gardens. The existence of a grand front door opening out to a spacious high street is unimaginable. For human liberation is not just an extension of the field of social liberation; liberation from self-need implies liberation to a different level of consciousness which is inconceivable when imagined from the present one. And so, of the front door, R. D. Laing has written:

> Before one goes through the gate
> one may not be aware that there is a gate
> One may think there is a gate to go through

and look a long time for it
without finding it
One may find it and
it may not open
If it opens one may be through it
As one goes through it
one sees that the gate one went through
was the self that went through it.[88]

There is a Buddhist parable about the invention of leather. Long ago in the time of the birth of the world's great religions, there was a king who was delighted to learn of the invention of leather. He proposed to relieve the suffering of feet from stones and thorns by covering the whole kingdom with it. Fortunately in one sense, the wealth and technology of the realm was, as his ministers pointed out, much too limited to make this dream remotely practicable. The council was therefore obliged to be more imaginative and an insightful minister came up with the invention of the leather sandal, whereby each foot would carry everywhere its own protection.

We have now made, at least conceptually, the 180 degree flipover from the secular to the spiritual perspective. However, two further shifts must be made to complete our understanding of the matter.

At 180 degrees there appears to be only a personal liberation prospect; the social context has disappeared. As we saw in Chapters 5 and 6 only individuals can be (kammaically) deluded. But their social culture reinforces and confirms this delusive consciousness. Therefore the Way leading through a more complete humanity towards an inconceivable liberation from existential suffering can be made much easier or much harder for both self and others depending on whether the social climate helps us to become more human or whether it stokes up the Fires of delusion, acquisitiveness and ill will. Since human beings are social beings, the Way of Liberation does indeed have a social dimension, with relevant social change on the agenda. And, again, to the extent individuals change so will they inevitably effect social changes. No Buddhist judge, for example, will wish to administer laws which fortify ego against others. This is a further step in the argument, now a 270 degree turn from the original secular perspective.

However, there is one further logical step to complete the transformation from the Social Fallacy to a spiritual perspective of social change. For if delusion is separation and alienation from other beings and if, to the extent we are freed from an egocentric level of consciousness, we experience a greater sense of oneness with them, then we become compassionately at one with their suffering and their afflictions. And at this level of consciousness the notion of self-liberation has become delusive, because there is no longer a sense of a separate selfhood from which to be liberated. Liberation thus becomes the liberation of all beings from suffering; hence the first vow of the aspirant bodhisattva (Buddhist saint) is: 'Beings are innumerable, I vow to free them.' This, of course, means liberation from existential suffering. But since no bounds are put upon compassion, it also means liberation, so far as is practicable, from all gross affliction (the distinction between affliction and suffering is noted in Chapter 1). Now we do have the means to carpet over quite a lot of the realm of the parable and free it of poverty, war and curable disease.

Our circle has now spiralled up and round through 360 degrees, up from the militant to the bodhisattva. In place of the Social Fallacy, with its narrow vision and its inbuilt human spoiler, we now have the prospect of human liberation back in focus in terms of a higher level of consciousness. It may be ultimately inconceivable from our present vantage point, but the first steps are certainly clear enough and are the subject of the second half of this book.

In this chapter we have had our first encounter with the secular mentality, which will now be explored more fully in the chapter which follows.

# 11  *Secularization: The Life We have Lost in Living*

Today the secular humanist tradition finds much that is valuable and congenial in Buddhism, as we shall see in the final section of this book. It has even conceived it as a kind of transpersonal megatherapy. However, whatever future adaptations the perennial Buddhadharma may make, it is recognizably part of a *spiritual* tradition present also in the other great religions (Gnosticism in Christianity, Hasidism in Judaism, Sufism in Islam and Vedanta in Hinduism). As a new religious phenomenon in the West which will become increasingly visible, Buddhism will need to come to terms with the host religion. Around such shared concerns as social activism it will need to appreciate the contemporary situation of Christianity and learn from its experience in a culture of industrial materialism. That culture perceives and translates spirituality in terms of a secular mentality with which Buddhism, from an unreservedly spiritual perspective, must also come to terms.

This chapter examines the process of secularization in the West and the distinction between the esoteric spirituality and the exoteric religion which that process has more clearly exposed. This will prepare the ground for the discussion in Part Eight of the book on the possible role of Buddhism in the creation of a future 'Good Society'. This chapter will also throw some light on the secularization of Buddhism itself, though this is specifically examined in the oriental context of Part Six.

The terms 'secularization' and 'secularism' have been

used with many different meanings. Here secularism is the denial of validity to spiritual and transpersonal levels of consciousness and the implict assertion of the prevailing egoic level as the only acceptable reality. Characteristically it is a dualistic mentality and a typical phenomenon of Wilber's 'high egoic' era. Secularization is here the process by which spirituality is denied in a culture as well as the stripping down of formal, exoteric religion in society. As we saw in the previous chapter secularization also inverts and reduces spirituality to being a handmaiden and auxiliary in projects for social change, in psychotherapy and in other areas wherein a lower level of consciousness and a secular perspective prevail. Respectability can be borrowed by including a clergyman on the campaigning platform, a psychotherapy workshop can be spiced up by borrowing some techniques from an oriental religion, a priest can be borrowed for television to appear as the obvious specialist in morality. Spiritual witness is tamed to become a marginal attraction in the secular zoo. 'Reductive modernism' is the term used here for that movement in religion which in effect secularizes religion from within.

'Spirituality' comprises the consciousness, values and perspective revealed by mystical insight, perfected (more arguably) by living it out in the world. This higher transpersonal level of consciousness has already been characterized in various ways in this book, as for example, the 'Higher Third' of Chapter 8. Scholars and researchers are agreed that mystical insight reveals a profound sense of the unity of all phenomena, beyond past, present and future. This gnosis appears with the force of simple fact, and cannot be adequately communicated. The occurrence, frequency and profundity of such insights can be affected by established systems of training, preferably under a spiritual director (for example, roshi, guru, shaykh or staretz). The various documentations of mystical experience, together with supporting commentary by scholars such as Huxley[89] and Happold[90] suggest that although, in Happold's words, 'Mystical experience may take more than one form, it is (nevertheless) a quite definite and recognizable form of experience.' The general confirmation of the 'world view' of the mystics by developments in contemporary science has already been discussed in Chapter 9.

Although we all do, I suggest, have the potential for mystical insight, comparatively few, even with the benefit of training, appear to attain it in our present-day industrial culture. Whether they do or not, they may nevertheless affirm the validity of its view of reality by attempting to maintain a spiritual perspective themselves and, through meditative and other practice, may attempt to open themselves more to experience of it. As already emphasized, in all such practice what is important is not 'the Goal' (which is inconceivable anyway) but 'the Way' of training, values and relationships through which we do our best to live out the spiritual truth and so become more truly human as creators of a more truly human society.

The so-called esoteric part of religion is its gnostic or spiritual part. This comprises a diagnosis of the human disease and systems of psycho-physical training whereby individuals can realize their True Nature, 'the Kingdom of Heaven within you'. The exoteric part of religion comprises dogmas, moral codes, institutions, and other means for readily communicating, manifesting and sustaining religion in society. These will include some kind of economic base, charitable and educational activities, the affirmations of public worship and ritual and the exercise of political influence.

At this point we may note two levels of spiritual consciousness. The lower is theistic, dualistic and exoteric in character, the tradition of God the creator and law-giver of the Western religions in their orthodox and conventional aspect. The higher is the gnostic, monist and esoteric tradition of the Godhead as Void, Source, Dharmakaya, Tao which transcends the dual, the relative, and which receives most sophisticated expression in Buddhism, Taoism and

Vedanta Hinduism. But it has also flourished in the esoteric tradition of the Western religions, with the Gnostic Gospels of Christianity as a particularly eloquent witness.[91] However, as Wilber observes, 'in the orthodox religions of the West, the spheres of the Divine and the Human never evolved to the natural point where they become one ....Thus the *separation* of God and man, or Creator and creature, was never overcome in a higher synthesis and transformation, either in theory or practice.'[92]

From the start of Wilber's 'high egoic' period in Western civilization there has been a steady decline in the Christian mystical, esoteric tradition which has only recently shown signs of reversal. Even by the sixteenth century the extensive, living, esoteric tradition had largely disappeared and was subsequently sustained only in the margins of orthodoxy, by the Carmelites and the Quakers, for example. Institutional Catholicism and Protestantism both became almost wholly preoccupied with punitive morality, dogmatic orthodoxy and institutional and political power, a caricature of spirituality which reached its nadir in the bleak 'industrial Christianity' of the nineteenth century.

Jacob Needleman has drawn attention to this 'bizarre forgetting of the instrumental nature of religious forms' with the following analogy:

> It is as though millions of people suffering from a painful disease were to gather to hear someone reading a textbook of medical treatment in which the means necessary to cure their disease were carefully spelled out. It is as though they were all to take great comfort from that book and in what they heard, going through their lives knowing that their disease could be cured, quoting passages to their friends, preaching the wonders of this great book, and returning to their congregation from time to time to hear more of the inspiring diagnosis and treatment read to them....Perhaps for some a

troubling thought crosses their minds as their eyes
close for the last time: Haven't I forgotten something? Something important? Haven't I forgotten
actually to undergo treatment?[93]

The scientific revolution of the seventeenth century
undermined the authority of religion as an interpreter of an
otherwise inscrutable and divinely moved universe. Attention shifted to the moral authority of Christianity. But
whereas the old spiritual tradition was a training in opening
up to the will of God, the new, half-secularized morality
emphasized human reason and power to determine God's
will and then to go and do it. This was the Christianity
of muscular righteousness which still casts such a long
shadow — especially over any attempt to return to the very
different spiritual tradition of moral training, as outlined in
Part Four. For those who cannot, unlike the Calvinists,
obtain some massive self-assurance the Christian experience became what Thomas Merton described as 'one of
anxious hope — a struggle, with occasional doubt, with the
"right answers", a painful and constant attempt to meet the
severe demands of morality and law, and a somewhat
desperate recourse to the sacraments which are there to help
the weak who must constantly fall and rise again.'[94]
    With its loss of spiritual heart and its repressive and
obscurantist character in the nineteenth century, the exoteric
shell of Christianity increasingly lacked credibility and the
power to command allegiance. As an increasingly godless
society was seen not after all to collapse into moral chaos,
the churches, chapels and synagogues lost much of their
remaining authority as society's 'moral specialists'.
    However, from being privatized out to the wings, Chris-
tianity has latterly been moving back onto the secular stage
and involving itself in peace movements, opposition to
racial discrimination, inner city decay, unemployment and
Third World poverty. Surely the question here is less
whether to be involved or not than the underlying motive

for such involvement. Is there here an unconscious search for continuing relevance and updated legitimacy by involvement in these concerns on the secular terms which are approved and readily understood by society at large (the reductive modernism noted earlier)? Or is the light of a startlingly different and disconcerting level of consciousness brought to bear on increasingly worn-out secular ways of feeling and thinking about these concerns — what we might call a 'transcendental modernism'?

It would seem that the loss of a shared wisdom-gone-beyond has not for most people been filled by a positive and robust humanism. Industrial materialism seems rather to have left an aching void unrelieved by even the most subtle consumerism. Thus Kenneth Leech, a perceptive Christian activist, observes:

> That we live, in the West, in an atmosphere of spiritual deprivation and impoverishment is abundantly clear. For whatever reasons, conventional Western religion does not provide adequate nourishment for the souls of men and women...[but] while it is clear that both conventional religion and conventional theism are suffering major sicknesses in various places, it is equally clear that atheism remains a minority belief, and that widespread unbelief is marked more often than not by a sense of confusion and bafflement.[95]

There are, however, many parts of the world where Christianity has been less marginalized than is implied above, notably in the USA (where evidence of its strength can be found not least in its powerful social pressure groups) and in the Latin Catholic countries, where religion is still more or less culturally integral to society.

The results of secularization have been complex. On the one hand it is a part of the process by which humankind has driven itself into a destructive crisis whilst at the same time it has arguably made access more difficult to the levels of consciousness necessary for resolving that crisis successfully. On the other hand it has been associated with material progress which has rid the world of much gross affliction; and it has also put bracing questions to traditional quietistic spirituality, even at the risk of secularizing it. By stripping down exoteric Christianity, secularization has helped to expose its ancient spiritual roots — and also created a demand for oriental imports. Certainly there is now under way a revival of both Western and Eastern forms of spirituality in the West and a growing interest in what Don Cupitt calls 'post-dogmatic religion'.

Nevertheless, the spiritual search, whether in traditional forms or valid modernizations, requires a kind of intensive and sustained practice which has always made it a minority activity (though not necessarily confined to the cloister). This still seems to apply today. Many read the books and attend the groups but relatively few appear to commit themselves to an ongoing practice and of these some become discouraged, drop out or 'try something different'. For every one dedicated to the practice there seem to be a dozen who do at least value and continually affirm some explicit form of spiritual truth and wish to be associated with it.

Exotericism is therefore unlikely to be squeezed out between a still powerful secularism and a growing spiritual practice. However, it may be an exotericism less of religious dogma, ritual, myth and symbolism and more of moral values, ideology and social filiation in respect of specific spiritual traditions. These are exoteric phenomena in the sense that they are comparatively accessible from the prevailing culture. For example, Buddhism in the West is part of the personal cultural equipment of quite a lot of people who value it as a system of ideas and orientation, and this is an important fact in any discussion of Buddhist activism, as we shall see in Part Eight of the book, It is, however, something that has been appropriated and *used*, rather than something that has profoundly engaged the personality as in the case of the dedicated practitioner. The flavour is different.

As to more conventional forms of Buddhist exotericism, those in the East are, of course, long established, whereas in the West Buddhism is still preoccupied with finding its esoteric heart. But already, as it grows in strength, Western Buddhism is beginning to make a more public witness. In Britain it is perhaps significant that the London Peace Pagoda was raised by Japanese, and not by British Buddhists, as the first Buddhist statement encountered by the public without them having to go and look for one. However, homebred expressions of exoteric Buddhism are also beginning to appear in the UK, like the Angulimala organization of prison chaplains, and the Buddhist Peace Fellowship. On the big nuclear disarmament demonstrations a small group of British Buddhists is to be found behind their yellow BPF banner, preceded by a contingent of drum-beating, pagoda-building Japanese monks, and marching with the Christian peaceworkers. Amidst the slogan-shouting tumult, there is here a calm, silent spiritual statement being made which most of the bystanders clearly sense as something different, prompting a different kind of reflection. These are public reminders of a renewed and refreshingly relevant spirituality, appearing amidst the frustration and anger of an all-too-familiar secular milieu.

# 12  *Indra's Jewelled Net*

Indra's Net is a metaphor for the most fully developed Buddhist understanding of social and other phenomena. Central to the somewhat earlier Theravada Buddhism of the Pali scriptures is the doctrine of dependent co-arising (*paticca samuppada*) which maintains that all phenomena are mutually conditioning. On the basis of the Madhyamika and Yogacara philosophy of Mahayana Buddhism that was introduced in Chapter 8 this doctrine was dramatically developed from a mechanistic to a dialectical level in Avatamsaka Buddhism (Hua-yen in China; Kegon in Japan), which D. T. Suzuki believed to be the summation of oriental thought.[96] Its basis is the Avatamsaka Sutra (scripture) which appears to have been composed mainly in China, about the third century AD. The teaching was refined by Chinese sages from the sixth to the eighth centuries AD, and became a formative influence on Taoism as well as Buddhism. Suzuki maintained that 'Zen is the practical consummation of Buddhist thought in China and the Kegon (Avatamsaka) philosophy is its theoretical culmination.'[97]

Indra's Net was one of the favourite analogies of Avatamsaka scholars attempting to depict the interdependence and interpenetration of phenomena or, more precisely, their identity-in-separateness, in time as well as space. A comparatively superficial and preliminary resemblance to the Avatamsaka schema is found in modern systems theory, or Koestler's idea of 'holons' as entities which are both wholes and parts and in each of which there are opposed yet complementary tendencies, the one being a self-assertive

136

tendency to the maintenance of individual autonomy and the other an integrative tendency to support the functioning of the whole.[98] However, the Madhyamika doctrine of the Void and the insight of the Higher Third which springs from it gives Avatamsaka Buddhism a dialectical transcendence, so that it signifies a 'purified' level of consciousness as well as being a valuable intellectual tool.

At each intersection in Indra's Net is a light-reflecting jewel (that is, a phenomenon, entity, thing), and each jewel contains another Net, *ad infinitum*. The jewel at each intersection exists only as a reflection of all the others and hence it has no self-nature. Yet is also exists as a separate entity to sustain the others. Each and all exist in their mutuality. As Suzuki renders the Sutra, this is 'a world of lights not accompanied by any shade'.[99] None is denied by the shadow of another since none casts its light separately.

In other words, all phenomena are identifiable with the Whole, the One, *just as the phenomena which make up a specific phenomenon are identifiable with it*. Each has no existence except as a manifestation of all, the Whole, the One. Contrariwise, the One exists only through the many. The many are and are not the same as the One (or lesser wholes). For example, a chair is no more than its parts, yet it is more that its parts in the sense that they have been put together so that I can sit upon that assemblage. The arms, legs, seat and back thereby become a chair. This is the case of King Milinda's chariot again, quoted in Chapter 9, where further examples will be found in terms of individualism, anthropocentrism, hierarchy and holism.

Indra's Net exists not only in space but in the polychronic time identified in Chapter 9. The days and years, the experiences and episodes, which together constitute our lifespan is each experienced separately, one at a time, and each could be an infinity, an eternity out of time if our imagination were not continuously exercised to make a whole of them. Moreover in Indra's Net the warp of time and the weft of space are themselves not separate, but constitute the one reality-consciousness.

That Indra's Net expresses the monist consciousness of the Higher Third does not, unfortunately, make it ideology-proof, and it can be misappropriated to serve a dualistic *this* or *that*. This chapter will invoke it as a corrective to the excessive centralization and specialization in contemporary society, but it can be as readily and properly invoked against a 'Green' ideology which dogmatizes about decentralization and mistakes self-sufficiency for self-reliance. The 'Net' is another device to wean us away from investing ourselves in the one as against the other (the 'weighted polarization' of earlier chapters) and helping us to see more clearly what the situation requires rather than what we require of it.

For example, the network of autonomous groups is now regarded by many people as a more appropriate response to most or all task situations than the alternative model of hierarchical bureaucracy. But the network must be operationally effective and also give some long-term satisfactions to all its members rather than providing an opportunity for individuals and groups to pursue their own interests regardless of those of the whole. Such networks often give the strong and the charismatic a freedom to exert influence which overrides the wishes of others. Poorly managed, slack networks can also create high levels of anxiety arising from uncertainty and ambiguity, bringing nostalgia for the good old days of bureaucracy when everyone knew where they were. Networking should therefore be the freedom to work together which, beyond the excitements and frustrations of consensus seeking and conflict resolution, requires agreements on aims and purposes, checking on decision implementation, monitoring progress, keeping records, maintaining good communications and other business of joint management.

Weaving Indra's Net is likely to be hard for most of us, since it goes against ingrained behaviours, against *kamma*. So we must try to weave it both as a meditative learning exercise which increases our self-awareness *and* as a model of how to do things better; these are just opposite sides of the same weave.

Deep ecology, and derivations such as permaculture and bio-regionalism, are instructive exemplifications of Indra's Net and useful entry points for exploring its social implications. Developed by writers like Aldo Leopold, Rachel Carson and Arne Naess, deep ecology is a mentality in which all beings are seen as having equal rights to their own forms of unfolding and realization within their biosphere, whether it be a tract of woodland, human society, or the whole planet. Deep ecology is about the cultivation of a consciousness so that, in Arne Naess's words, 'with maturity, human beings will experience joy when other life forms experience joy, and sorrow when other life forms experience sorrow.' It contrasts with environmentalism, a benevolent form of anthropocentrism which casts humankind in the role of paternalistic lord of creation who protects and conserves nature only on his own terms and from his own standpoint.

Deep ecology requires us to be aware and responsible and yet at the same time a force of nature, a selfless phenomenon of the ecological process — we, who *have to think* about what we should do. Indra's Net is the undeceived reality-consciousness, whereas although the 'I' which rejects anthropocentrism (evil) and cleaves to the good of not 'interfering' with nature has indeed taken a step forward it may be only the romantic quietism of inverted anthropocentrism. When the 'I' has less need to confirm itself and less self-regard, then there is freedom for the Good of the Higher Third to come forth so that it acts as a 'responsible' force of nature, at once both the most evolved and powerful force of nature and yet no more than nature. As John Rodman explains:

> Acts of Ecological Resistance are not undertaken primarily in a spirit of calculated long-term self-interest (of the individual, the society, the species), or in obedience to a spirit of moral duty, or in the

spirit of preventing profanation. One resists because the threat to the land, the river or the biosphere is perceived *also* as a threat to the self, or,
rather, to the principle of diversity and spontaneity
that is *the endangered side of the balance* that defines
and sustains the very nature of things.[100](my italics)

A major application of the deep ecology wisdom
of Indra's Net is the design concept which in agriculture,
forestry and energy use is known as 'permaculture'. This is
the design of renewable life-support systems, embracing
food and raw materials production and processing, energy
use and waste disposal, so that full use is made of diversity
*and* the interdependence and interaction of the different
parts of the system, together with their recycling over time.
These are conditions for systems designed to be stable,
sustainable, self-reliant, waste-free, and producing more
energy than they consume. Permaculture is a response to
the ecological crisis of air and water pollution, deforestation
and soil exhaustion caused by the conventional ideal of
monoculture and other forms of extreme specialization, with
their prodigiously wasteful use of energy and uneconomic
discharge of waste products. Moreover, socially and politically this eco-economic model eliminates creative work for
the many, undermines the self-reliance of local communities,
and is associated with increasing concentrations of wealth
and power, whether in terms of agribusiness or of the whole
economic system.

The principles of permaculture are based on observation
of natural ecosystems and on traditional polycultures, and
hence of working with, rather than against nature, with
maximum understanding and minimum interference. For
example, battery farm chickens have to be fed, kept warm,
dosed with chemicals to stop them getting sick and their
wastes have to be disposed of, and all with an energy input
cost about six times greater than the output of comparatively
low quality eggs and meat. Free-range chickens forage for

themselves, keep down pests and weeds in gardens and orchards as well as manuring the ground, and need only a night shelter (where they can warm the adjacent greenhouse). The happier hens produce superior eggs at much lower energy costs.

The basic permaculture unit is a production system designed for a specific site and the group of people who are going to work it. It aims at basic food and energy self-reliance, plus some cash income from commercial crops, craft work or services. Many such sites have been established in the USA and Australia, and they are beginning to appear in Britain.[101] Such projects point towards a possible future society of self-reliant communities which have sufficient autonomy and inner strength to link up with others on a basis of equality and mutuality. (Self-reliance gives an acceptable measure of economic and political independence together with a margin for specialization, and should be distinguished from self-sufficiency.) Moreover, the permaculture principle, which so accurately expresses the reality signified by Indra's Net, clearly has applications for the design of larger and more complex systems of production and exchange, beyond agriculture and forestry, and with social and political implications of considerable significance for Buddhists. Bill Mollison, the principal originator of permaculture, writes:

> Permaculture both conserves and generates the fuel energies of transport systems, and would enable any community to exist comfortably on very restricted land areas. Supplemented with the appropriate and available technologies of methane and alcohol fuels, dry distillation processes, and wind, water and solar energies, it would provide the basis of a sustainable and regionalized society. Combined with community co-operation, permaculture promises freedom from many of the ills that plague us, and accepts all the organic wastes of the community it serves.[102]

In the last two hundred years in the West increased concentrations of wealth and power associated with high technology and elaborated bureaucracy have overriden the traditional bio-regions and communities upon whose ecological foundations distinctive human cultures had evolved over the centuries. A classic early example was the overlay of the ancient French *pays* and provinces by the *départements* established at the time of the French Revolution. All over the developed industrial world the sense of local place and home area is being undermined economically, socially, politically, administratively, and demographically. In the United States a grassroots countervailing movement has begun, emphasizing the ecological bio-regions and established communities that have grown up with the landscape. Local self-reliance, diversity and complexity on a rich and human scale are being nurtured, as indicated by Gary Snyder, a Buddhist who is active in this movement:

> Stewardship means, for most of us, find your place on the planet, dig in, and take responsibility from there — the tiresome but tangible work of school boards, county supervisors, local foresters — local politics. Even while holding in mind the largest scale of potential change. Get a sense of workable territory, learn about it, and start acting point by point. On all levels from national to local the need to move toward steady state economy — equilibrium, dynamic balance, inner-growth stressed — must be taught. Maturity/diversity/climax/creativity.[103]

This exploration of the ecological and social meaning of Indra's Net has led us from over-arching deep ecology through permaculture production systems to the politics of place. It suggests an alternative future to that of the over-centralized, over-specialized, and ultimately unsustainable kind of society that has cumulated from out of the historic power-and-wealth lusts. These themes will be developed further in the concluding section on the Good Society.

Indra's Net can prompt our understanding at several different possible levels, ranging from the basic level of intellectual analysis through moral precept and practice to fine-grained insight.

Thomas Cleary, the Hua-yen scholar, has emphasized its 'instrumental value' as 'a set of practical exercises in perspective -- new ways of looking at things from different points of view, of discovering harmony and complementarity underlying apparent disparity and contradiction. The value of this exercise is in the development of a round, holistic perspective which, while discovering unity, does not ignore diversity but overcomes mental barriers that create fragmentation and bias.'[104] This intellectual level of understanding and analysis is possible if we are well informed and are able to appreciate the complexity and *mutuality* of social and other phenomena, as between, for example, the nuclear arms peril, the destruction of the Amazonian rain forests, and unemployment in Britain. And understanding of these connections may be informed by awareness of their relatedness to bloody-minded trouble at one's workplace, and, going deeper, to depths of fear and resentment which we have meditatively plumbed within ourselves. All the world's striving and frustration seems to be in the big fly buzzing and beating itself against the inside of the window this morning, woken up by the winter sunshine.

> A dog starved at his master's gate
> Predicts the ruin of the State.[105]

William Blake's example is true at the coarse and explicit level that the quality of our relationship with other beings, even where seemingly trivial compared with matters of state, has a suggestive, pervasive, and cumulative social power. It is *kammaic* and accumulates a social fund of 'merit' (or otherwise) in the best sense of that traditional Buddhist term. But if we let the verse take us unaware, as it were, before the question and before intellection, it just informs us of what we already know (even if somewhat hidden), that goodness is seamless and undivided.

Ethically, Indra's Net suggests respect and gratitude for all things which reciprocally sustain our being, including respect for the things we must consume and destroy in order to live, and a lean, aware frugality in our use of resources. This is very much in both the Zen and the Franciscan traditions, with permaculture as an excellent contemporary example. In a single passage Francis Cook has nicely encapsulated the intellectual lure of Avatamsaka Buddhism, the ethical guidelines which it provides, and the ultimate experiential validation that is possible. The intellectual lure 'attracts the aspirant to the practice which will presumably culminate in an existential or experiential validation of what was before only theory. At the same time it guides the aspirant in actual relationships, serving as a kind of template by means of which the individual may gauge the extent to which his actions conform to the reality of identity and interdependence.'[106]

Like the other great Buddhist scriptures, the Avatamsaka is not the fruit of intellectual activity but of the kind of spiritual insight which enabled William Blake

> To see the World in a grain of Sand
> And Heaven in a wild Flower,
> Hold Infinity in the palm of your hand
> And Eternity in an hour.[107]

It is upon this insight that their validity really depends, and only to the extent that we share that insight can we fully enter into their meaning.

The Dharmadhatu, the true world of reality, is felt in the Avatamsaka as a tangible force, a power, like the sun, seeking to burst forth through the rational and emotional clouds of ego delusion, if only ego could open to it. It is a power which has a personal meaning, through the Buddhas and Bodhisattvas and other 'skilful and expedient' myths. Here Buddhism touches fingertips with theism. 'Owing to

its self-expanding and self-creating power a great loving
heart transforms this earthly world into one of splendour
and mutual fusion, and this is where the Buddha is always
abiding,' is Suzuki's free translation.[108] Such passages suggest something of the awakening which can transcend social
analysis and the ordinary experience of social action. And
they also suggest how understanding through Wisdom is at
the same time an active principle of Compassion. Only at a
superficial level is Indra's Net a concept for our use. More
profoundly, we are each within the Net, if only we could
allow ourselves to experience it.

# II   Action

*He who regards worldly affairs as an obstacle to his*
*training only knows there is no Way in worldly affairs,*
*not knowing that there is nothing such as worldly affairs*
*to be distinguished from the Way.*

Zen Master Dogen (*Shobogenzo* I)

*Part Four*
Training and Lifestyle

# 13 Just Letting it Rain in

This second section is about 'the first vow of Buddhists: to save all beings, to bring the truth of organic fundamental oneness into the clear light of day, and to practise it with everyone and everything.'[109]

That ordinary human experience of life is inauthentic and actively deluding was the theme of Part One and this was socially and historically elaborated in the remainder of the first section of the book. Just as the analysis of personal experience is seen as the foundation of social theory, so must social action and social change be firmly based upon a perspective of personal and individual transformation. If our perceptions are distorted through the prism of self-need and our actions are ultimately rooted in self-need then we contribute to, and are a part of, the problems we believe we are remedying.

The first Part of this section — *Action* — corresponds to the basic diagnosis of the human condition which opened the first section — *Understanding*. Here is presented an introduction to the traditional Buddhist system of training and lifestyle (*sila*) — the Way — designed to effect the progressive dissolution of self-centredness in an 'inconceivable liberation': reunion with all that was previously experienced as alien and other, and hence a spontaneous opening up to the compassionate service of others.

If this training is undertaken with the feeling that it is some kind of means of achievement, then it will strengthen the acquisitive ego instead of weakening it. It is therefore best seen simply as a way in which one has decided to live out one's life, bringing all possible attention to bear upon the practice itself. Personality change will then take place of its own accord; it cannot be willed. Far from detracting from the practice, a judicious involvement in social action may even help to draw the practitioner away from the danger of spiritual greed. The latter leads to a subtle spiritual arrogance in which, in Harvey Cox's eloquent description, 'all one's venalities grow more ethereal. Lust moves from the loins to the heart. Anger poses as patience and martyred condescension. Even pride no longer delights in its own possessions but in its humility. . . . If there is anything more unattractive than a self-righteous Pharisee boasting to God about his piety it is a self-righteous humble publican parading his lack of it.'[110]

There are two different ways in which ego can don the robes of spirituality. First, pietism makes repressive use of the will so that both self and others are deceived by the appearance of spirituality. This has to be hard won by prolonged wilful labour, which is why it tends to be cold, censorious and self-righteous, recalling W. B. Yeats' words (even if from a different context) that 'the fascination of what's difficult has dried the sap out of my veins and rent spontaneous joy and natural content out of my heart'. Contrasting with self-willed moral spirituality is self-willed amoral spirituality, a rarer perversion of which the 'beat Zen' of the 'Dharma bums' is the most memorable example. If someone believes himself 'enlightened', whether from drugs or meditation gone-to-the-head, he is inclined to believe that he operates in a higher spiritual realm beyond ordinary notions of right and wrong. The profane dictum of the 1960s that 'if it feels right, do it!' was thus given a spiritual lift. The problem is still with us.

Patience, humility and a mindful abstinence are fundamental to the Buddhist Way (though even they are not proof against pietism). Rilke has written beautifully — as a poet — of those strengths through which we are enabled to find the inner calm to go on working for the possible in a seemingly impossible world:

> Patience. To let each impression and each kernel of feeling come to completion wholly in itself, in the dark, in the inexpressible, the unconscious, beyond the grasp of your own intelligence, and to await with deep humility and patience the birth-hour of a new clarity....Be patient towards all that is unresolved in your heart and try to love the questions themselves, like locked rooms or books written in an unknown script. Do not seek the answers, which cannot be given to you now because you would not be able to live them. The point is to live everything. Live the *questions* now.[111]

In one of the most ancient Buddhist texts the Buddha explained the purpose of the training as follows:

> It rains through the thatch; it rains not through the open.
> So open up the thatch; thus will it not rain through.[112]

In contrast to our unavailing attempts to block the holes in our ever leaky roof, the training is a graduated system to enable us to open up bit by bit to the experience of suffering and the realization that in fact it arises delusively from our very attempts at evasion of reality. Let it rain through.

# 14   *Buddhist Morality*

The focal importance of morality in the cultivation of wisdom and compassion has been acknowledged in all the main Buddhist traditions. 'Refrain from evil; do good; do good for others' are the three 'Pure Precepts' of Mahayana Buddhism. 'Avoid evil; do as much good as possible; purify your intentions. This is the teaching of all the Buddhas' is one of the less well-known Zen fundamentals. And, recently, to the question 'What is a simple basic practice one should bear in mind if one finds it difficult to comprehend all the different levels of practice?' the Dalai Lama gave the following reply, 'I think in short that it's best, if you're able, to help others. If you're not able to do so, however, then at least do not harm others. This is the main practice.'[113] Moreover, since Buddhist social action is an expression of Buddhist morality, an understanding of the nature of Buddhist morality and how it is practised is the foundation of a Buddhist social activism.

It is not unusual for Buddhist centres to advertise meditation classes as a lure. We may surmise as to whether advertising an ancient technique for becoming a better person would attract more comers. Morality and its attendant themes of guilt and retribution remain powerful in the minds of 'secularized' people. It is still as if there were tangible standards of Good and Evil available somewhere 'out there', to be implemented by the will if only they can be discovered. The anxiety to appropriate them, or defy them, is also evident. Moral justification is an important prop in personal and collective identity building. Above all else, we have to be in the right. And the public moralities of both the establishment and its critics all too transparently mirror their respective interests. While the revolutionaries proclaim the Leninist dictum that all ethics must be subordinated to the class struggle, the government, 'for reasons of State' or 'in the interests of democracy' suspends basic civil liberties and often basic decencies also.

Literalist theology did provide God-and-the-Devil and other popular and idolatrous relativities-made-absolute. But our secular age has set itself adrift on a trackless ocean of relative truths of which, twitchily and unconsciously, it tries to make absolute values. Janus-like it is assumed that these values are read into the objective situation by free and objective actors. Rather are they *needed* to empower Me, Us and Ours – the absolute good of free enterprise, or feminism, or animal rights. These are the morally weighted polarities which we encountered in Chapter 8. How can we look deep into that clinging need to assert *our* good, and loosen the hold of our need for an opposed evil? How can we experience more clearly the underlying moral ambiguity in most social problems, and become free to act out Good (the ethical Higher Third described towards the end of Chapter 8), solely in the light of those problems and without the adulteration of personal and collective ego-need? 'Whatever's wrong, throw it out. If it's right, then take it and use it. But actually we practise in order to let go of both right and wrong. In the end we just throw everything out. If it's right, throw it out; wrong, throw it out! Usually if it's right we cling to rightness, if it's wrong we hold it to be wrong, and arguments follow. But the Dhamma is the place where there's nothing – nothing at all.' That incidentally, is not a quotation from some Zen Master but from a talk given by *Ajahn* Chah, an outstanding Thai teacher in the Theravada tradition; experientially, there is only one Buddhadharma.[114]

The threatening, freighted and confused character of morality in our culture and the fears and angers which it can arouse do appear to make it an appropriate starting point for understanding the Buddhadarma.

Evil doing arises from existential ignorance of our oneness with all that is other, from the deluded experience of separateness, of alienation. 'Evil,' wrote Aldous Huxley, 'is the accentuation of division; good, whatever makes for unity with other lives and other beings. Pride, hatred, anger — the essentially evil sentiments; and essentially evil because they are all intensifications of the given reality of separateness, because they insist upon division and uniqueness, because they reject and deny other lives and beings.'[115]

And my virtue is not only confirmed by putting down your evil but also by practising virtues upon you which confirm me at your expense. By becoming the recipient of my magnanimity you affirm your own weakness, inferiority and inabilty to help yourself. In this way also, others exist ultimately only for us and their own intrinsic humanity is denied, even if unknowingly and for the best of motives. 'Nobody has the right to manipulate anybody with his stronger personality, not even for the other's imagined good, for nobody can know what that good is. This,' writes Irmgard Schloegl, 'is courtesy, rather than callousness, for the other's dignity is thus acknowledged.'[116] Similarly another Buddhist teacher, David Brandon: 'Respect is seeing the Buddha Nature in another person. It means perceiving the superficiality of positions of moral superiority. The other person is as good as you. However untidy, unhygienic, poor, illiterate and bloody-minded he may seem, he is worthy of respect. He also has autonomy and purpose. He is another form of nature.'[117]

An important aspect of Buddhist activism is, therefore, the acceptance that our moral motivation is likely to be a mix of both authentic fellow-feeling, the Buddha Nature, and, at the same time an alienating self-need. The latter diminishes as we become more profoundly aware of it, aware not just intellectually but in the depths of our being. And, correspondingly, our objective effectiveness will increase to the extent it is purified of self-need.

The driven volitions that have evil effects on both self and others wither in the light of our growing sensitivity to their origins in our root fear, and to how they drive us and how we are embodied by them even when we feel most free. If we can open wholly to the sense of emptiness from which arises our existential dread and our fear of self-annihilation, reality will carry us, will bear us up, bringing relief, joy, peace, gratitude. There is no fear, no necessity for fear. This is an uncovering that has the force of factual revelation; it is not 'I' having thought it through. It is 'I' giving up. It is the experience of the 'emptiness' of 'I', the experience of the paradoxical nature of self.

This Wisdom is perfected in many years (and lives?) of practice of a lifestyle and system of training embracing morality, meditation, and mindfulness set in a 'form' or 'discipline'. The perfection of Wisdom, of clear seeing, is, in social terms, the perfection of morality through awakening to unity with all beings, expressed in a compassion total, unqualified and spontaneous in response to others' needs:

> Superior virtue is not intentionally virtuous,
>     and thus is virtue.
> Inferior virtue will not let go of being virtuous,
>     and thus is not virtue.
>
> Lao Tzu[118]

The emphasis in Buddhist morality is therefore on the cultivation of a personality which cannot but be moral, rather than focusing upon the morality of particular choices and acts. But, to repeat, it is not the will that can create such a personality, no more than I can pick myself up from the ground by my own collar. It is to the training that the will must be applied, from which virtue will naturally flow. 'Hit the horse, not the cart,' as the Zen saying puts it. Simone Weil elegantly extends the metaphor when she writes that, 'Action is the pointer which shows the balance; we must not touch the pointer but the weight.' She refers to the pietism which arises from spiritual greed as 'a kind of idolatry which comes from the fact that, while thirsting for absolute good, we do not possess the power of supernatural attention and do not have the power to let it develop.'[119] The exercise of the will is, of course, needed by all of us from time to time in order to avoid doing harm to others or ourselves; the impulse to act is blocked short of action, but, if possible, there should be an open, non-judgemental awareness of the feeling that has flared. This requires much practice, as we shall see below. Willing virtue into life is a notoriously unsatisfactory way of bringing about changes in behaviour. Whether we fail or succeed, either way we lose. The self and the superself live in fear of one another; when self is indulged there is guilt; when self is repressed there is a nagging feeling of self-deception arising from something not freely obtained. The saintliness achieved by will-power alone is obsessed by evil and depends for its existence on evil. Fiercely determine *not* to think of a rhinoceros and what then is the first thing to spring to mind? Consumed by *not* being angry or *not* having sexual feelings, we are tossed endlessly on a sea of mutually punishing relativities.

To resume the main argument, the moral *personality* emerges through the ripening of wisdom/compassion. The ripening takes place through a system of spiritual training which *includes the practice of morality as a part of the practice of mindful awareness*. Through trying to conform to the moral precepts we incite an emotional revolt. Without either suppressing that revolt or being possessed and carried away by it, we open ourselves in full awareness to containment of that upsurge. By thus willingly enduring it we contribute to our overall practice of mindfulness (Chapter 17) which is part of the training system through which fundamental personality change occurs. The same training practice is to be found in the writings of spiritual adepts quite independent of Buddhism. Thus, Simone Weil writes of the will as a 'principle of violence within us' which we must use 'in a violent way: we must compel ourselves by violence to act as though we had not a certain desire or aversion − without trying to persuade our sensibility − compelling it to obey. This causes it to revolt, and we have to endure this revolt passively, taste it, savour it. . .'[120]

But also in many cases our use of the will has direct and objective significance in enabling us to avoid hurting others or self, as noted earlier. In other words we may by no means have evolved to the stage of spontaneously feeling at one with other people who have harmed us, but in such situations we try to follow the moral precepts and to act as if we did, yet without trying to deceive ourselves as to our real feelings. We need as far as possible to find a middle way in this use of the will, lest it strengthen ego instead of being a means by which ego is gentled, becomes more pliant and less stiff necked and opinionated. After some time in the practice it becomes possible to take decisions which previously would have required a self-destructive exercise of will: the ripe fruit can be plucked whereas previously it was as if the whole tree would have to be uprooted.

In short, the cultivation of morality in Buddhism (and not least in decisions and behaviour to do with social action) will be seen as double-edged and paradoxical. By (subjectively) serving the extinguishment of the delusive self, in 'doing *my* practice', at the same time we serve others (objectively), and vice versa, until this supposed dualism merges in the unity of self and other. As found in the *Digha-nikaya*, 'From the observing of the moralities comes wisdom and from the observing of wisdom comes morality....It is just as if one should wash one hand with the other...exactly so is morality washed round with wisdom and wisdom with morality.'[121] Similarly, Simone Weil has likened moral precepts to music practice scales. 'One does not play Bach without having done scales. But neither does one does play a scale merely for the sake of a scale.'[122] In other words, one does not become a truly moral person without having practised being one. But neither does one practise morality solely out of a concern eventually to become a moral person.

# 15  Precepts and Bodhisattvas

The Buddhist precepts are general guidelines for the ethical behaviour and training described in the previous chapter. They are in no sense commandments, since there is no Other to make commands. What is expected is a sincere effort to uphold the precepts, but the power of *kammaic* momentum is appreciated, and the ripening of an intrinsically moral personality takes time. One does one's best; acknowledges and forgives failure; and resolves to try to do better in the future. Thus Christopher Titmuss, a British meditation teacher, prefers the term 'ethical foundations' rather than 'precepts,' and formulates each as in: '*I endeavour to practise to be free from killing and violence.*' The significance of the precepts in the light of the previous chapter has been explained by Philip Kapleau, an American Zen Master, as revealing 'how a deeply enlightened, fully perfected person, with no sense of self-and-other, behaves. Such a person doesn't imitate the precepts; they imitate him. Until you reach that point, however, you would do well to observe the precepts, for unless your mind is free of the disturbance that heedless behaviour produces, you will never come to awakening. That is why the precepts are the foundation of spiritual training.'[123] Nevertheless, it is recognized that literal interpretation may, in a particular situation, violate the spirit and intention of a precept. This *situational* character of ethical choice is examined in the next chapter.

On the face of it, Buddhist prescriptive morality may seem unremarkable; it is much like the moral codes offered by all the world's great religions. Various codifications exist, according to the different schools of Buddhism. Here it will be sufficient to examine the three strands which are concerned with morality in Theravada Buddhism's 'Noble Eightfold Path' of lifestyle and training.

The cultivation of 'Right Conduct' is generally assumed to refer to the Five Precepts examined below.

The First Precept is to cultivate freedom from the urge to violence and killing, 'to avoid the killing of living beings and abstain from it. Without stick or sword, conscientious, full of sympathy, [to be] anxious for the welfare of all living things.'[124] (This precept is so important in the formulation of a Buddhist social activism that I have given it a Part to itself (Part Seven) towards the end of the book.)

The Second Precept, which is sometimes rendered as 'not to take what is not given' is hardly less central to the theme of social action. Its original formulation refers to a much less complex society than the acquisitive industrial society about which Proudhon could argue that 'property is theft'. Some present-day Buddhists have maintained that this precept is about more than petty theft and good table manners, that the fact of possession does not necessarily imply any moral right to possession, and that the piling up of possessions well beyond modest personal needs is a denial of the precept. More controversially, it has been argued that the accumulation of personal wealth through the appropriation of the time and energy of others who work for us either directly or indirectly is also something that violates the Second Precept. This raises the important question of *kammaic* social conditioning. Should we try to do the best we can to make an intrinsically unethical society less grossly immoral by working in accordance with its conditions (and hence necessarily unethically), or should we instead dedicate ourselves to radical change so that those conditions support and encourage personal autonomy and co-operation rather than subjection of some to the wealth and power of others even if for benevolent ends?

The question is a very sharp one today when the human and ecological effects of acquisitive industrial materialism are much more profound and pervasive than any immediate, short-term benevolent intention. It is also sharpened as never before by the development of all the resources necessary for evolving to a non-acquisitive *danaparamita* ('perfection-of-giving') Good Society. Given a sufficient change of heart by a sufficient number of people, this ideal is now a practical possibility. This has formidable implications for all the Buddhist precepts which have any strong social bearing. However, although the question needs to be posed in the above sharp form for each of us to answer, in practical terms, for herself and himself, how positive the response can be will depend on our personal situation — ranging from our strength of character to the number of our personal dependents, for example. As with all the precepts, we can only keep gently but firmly pushing ourselves to do our best — even if it's only to shift our investments to an Ethical Unit Trust which will not fatten them on armaments manufacture and the grosser kinds of Third World exploitation, or even if it is only to seek employment in another, less mendacious advertising agency. It is best to weed even the edges and corners of a lifestyle as far as we are able, since weeds tend to spread. However, as William Blake reminded us in the chapter on Indra's Net, even our objectively modest decisions create ripples beyond our awareness, ripples which can become waves.

Following through the implications of the Second Precept has brought us to another of the precepts of the Eightfold Path, that of Right Livelihood. Specific reference is made in the scriptures to trading arms, living beings, flesh, intoxicating drinks (including drugs) and poisons.[125] Usury is specifically debarred, and the monk-scholar Dr Saddhatissa has offered the broad interpretation that the layperson 'should be free of acquisitiveness or any connection with money-making, legalized or otherwise.'[126] For further exploration of Right Livelihood, E. F. Schumacher's book *Good Work*[127] makes interesting reading.

Let us now return to explore further the implications of
the Second Precept about honesty. The following passage
from Zen Master Robert Aitken's book *The Mind of Clover:
essays in Zen Buddhist ethics* is worth quoting at length as a
pungent example of the way in which the social implications
of Buddhist morality are now being opened up:

> Stealing is a pervasive element of our lives, and is
> the nature of our economic system. 'The rich get
> richer and the poor get poorer.' To take an extreme
> example, a large American corporation raises veg-
> etables in the Sahel, near the Sahara Desert. These
> vegetables are flown to Europe, where they fill the
> salad bowls of the affluent. The African workers
> on this giant farm, whose families and friends live
> at the edge of starvation, are searched at the end of
> each day to be sure they are not smuggling veg-
> etables home. Yet the corporation land they culti-
> vate was once their own for gleaning and grazing.
>
> We don't notice similar examples nearer home
> because we are used to them, but our slums and
> skid rows are clear symptoms of an economy that
> is manipulated here and abroad to provide a base
> of unemployment so that competition for jobs will
> keep wages at a minimum, and stockholders will
> realize maximum profits. The natural world is
> exploited for short-term benefit to a 'fortunate'
> minority while other people, animals, plants and
> the earth organism itself suffer.
>
> At the same time, exploitation is not something
> outside my mind or yours. Just a few minutes of
> television is enough to show each of us how easily
> we are seduced by appeals for consumption.[128]

At a more fundamental level, then, the Second Precept
can be taken as a self-meditation on the 'Fire' of acquisitiveness, of greed, of the quiet, persistent lust for power and
possession for their own sakes, to make mine, to affirm me.

Unless this can be felt deep stirring within oneself effective and compassionate action about it in the world will ultimately be futile. For one of the most exalted delusions is the lust for power over others to be used in what we believe to be their best interests.

The Eightfold Path also enjoins Right Speech, as does the Fourth Precept to abstain from lies and abuse. The 'unrighteous practices' in speech are set out in the *Majjhima-nikaya*, 1.41. as lying, slander, spreading dissension, and idle and malicious gossip. The wise man speaks only at the right time and in accordance with known facts, 'accompanied by arguments moderate and full of sense'. There is more than folk homily here. In many organizations, whether families or large institutions, communication is warped by heavy-handed authority and consequent resentments; the climate becomes clouded by a restless ill will which feeds upon itself through petty slander, rumour and gossip. This becomes compulsive, and it is difficult to resist being drawn into an insidious and corrosive daily experience.

And here again an ancient moral precept has been hugely amplified by contemporary social developments. Increasingly we live in an 'information society' where it is now a commonplace that much information is withheld or else manipulated in their own interests by those who have the power to do so.

For Aitken, the Third Precept is about abstention from 'boorish misuse of sex' or, as Christopher Titmuss puts it, from 'sexually exploitive activities'. The last of the Five Precepts refers to abstention from drugs and intoxicants, since these reduce the level of awareness and self-responsibility and are mightily kammaic in their habit formation. Both these precepts are worthy of close examination in the contemporary social context but they go beyond the scope of this book.

A Buddhist morality that stops short — as it often does — at our personal circle of family, friends, acquaintances and workmates may be adequate for a bygone village society but if it is to be fully helpful today and command respect then it surely must go as far as the newspaper and the television screen. The Buddhist ethic is an ethic of *intention*. But the implications of what we do in our global society are complex and far reaching. To act responsibly we need to be well informed. About the precept to abstain from violence and killing, the Thai Buddhist activist Sulak Sivaraksa has argued that:

> Unless the monk knows how to deal with the first precept in the modern world, he simply loses his role. For the last 2500 years Buddhism has had a corpus of writings explaining what is meant by killing. You must have the intention to kill, you must use a weapon or you must order someone to kill, and that is called the act of killing. But now you have all the new machinery of killing, you have the multinational corporations dealing with killing, and they are linked to banks, and the first precept on killing relates to the second precept on stealing, and so on. Unless you understand the complexities you simply cannot apply Buddhism meaningfully as an example for the younger generation.[129]

The precepts are neither internal commandments nor external legislation to provide a Buddhist 'party line'; they are delicate instruments for subtle investigation within and without. Nevertheless, if this is kept in mind the formulation of the precepts in contemporary terms provides a valuable set of prompts for maintaining a fully open awareness. The fourteen which follow constitute the spiritual discipline of the Tiep Hien Order which was founded during the Vietnam war as an instrument of 'engaged Buddhism'. They grew out of the experience of the Order members − nuns, monks and laypeople − in cultivating an inner serenity which sustained their anti-war demonstrations, social projects and resistance to all forms of violence and repression, from whatever direction they came. Many of the Order members lost their lives and others, like *Thich* Nhat Hanh, were forced into exile. These precepts are among the best guidelines we have for a Buddhist social activism, and deserve close attention.[130]

1. One should not be idolatrous about or bound to any doctrine, any theory, any ideology, including Buddhist ones. Buddhist systems of thought must be guiding means and not absolute truth.

2. Do not think the knowledge you presently possess is changeless absolute truth. Avoid being narrow minded and bound to present views. One has to learn and practise the open way of non-attachment from views in order to be open to receive the viewpoints of others. Truth is to be found only in life and not in conceptual knowledge. One should be ready to learn during one's whole life and to observe life in oneself and in the world at all times.

3. Do not force others, including children, by any means whatsoever to adopt our view, whether by authority, threat, money, propaganda, and even education. However, one should, through compassionate dialogue, help others to renounce fanaticism and narrowness.

4. One should not avoid contact with sufferings or close one's eyes before sufferings. One should not lose awareness of the existence of suffering in the life of the world. Find ways to come to those who are suffering by all means such as personal contact and visits, images, sound. By such means one should awaken oneself and others to the reality of suffering in the world.

5. Do not accumulate wealth while millions are hungry. Do not take as the aim of your life fame,

profit, wealth or sensual pleasure. One should
live simply and share one's time, energy and
material resources with those who are in need.

6. Do not maintain anger or hatred. As soon as
anger and hatred arise, practise the meditation
on compassion in order to encompass with love
the persons who have caused anger and hatred.
Learn to look at other beings with the eyes of
compassion.

7. One should not lose oneself in dispersion and
in one's surroundings. Learn to practise breathing in order to regain control of body and mind,
to practise mindfulness and to develop concentration and wisdom.

8. Do not utter words that can create discord and
cause the community to break. All efforts should
be made to reconcile and resolve all conflicts
however small they may be.

9. Do not say untruthful things for the sake of
personal interest or to impress people. Do not
utter words that cause division and hatred. Do
not spread news that you do not know to be
certain. Do not criticize or condemn things that
you are unsure of. Always speak truthfully and
constructively. Have the courage to speak out
about situations of injustice, even when it may
threaten your own safety.

10. One should not use the Buddhist community
for personal gain or profit or transform one's
community into a political party. One's religious
community, however, should take a clear stand
against oppression and injustice and should
strive to change the situation without engaging
in partisan conflicts.

11. Do not live with a vocation that is harmful to
humans and nature. Do not invest in companies
which deprive others of their chance to life.

Select a vocation which helps to realize your
idea of compassion.

12. Do not kill. Do not let others kill. Find whatever
means possible to protect life and prevent war.

13. Possess nothing that should belong to others.
Respect the property of others but prevent others
from enriching themselves from human suffering.

14. Sexual expression should not happen without
love and commitment. In sexual relationships
one must be aware of future suffering it may
cause to others. To preserve the happiness of
others, respect the rights and commitments of
others.

In addition to the precepts Buddhist moral training and
behaviour is inspired and guided by various meditations,
myths, ideals and traditional practices.

Particularly noteworthy is *danaparamita*, the virtue, or perfection, of giving. At its narrowest, *dana* is the material
support given by laypeople to the *sangha* or monastic community (which has a teaching role). Its practice is double-
edged; outwardly beneficent, inwardly, giving till it hurts is
a potentially transformative meditation. Giving up something of mine is a self-diminution and preparation for the
time the delusion of self may itself be yielded up. D. T.
Suzuki has characterized *dana* as 'anything going out of
oneself, disseminating knowledge, helping people in difficulties of all kinds, creating arts, promoting industry or
social welfare, sacrificing one's life for a worthy cause, and
so on.'[131] The essence of *dana* is that it really is *giving* and not
a form of exchange through which 'merit' or a sense of
virtue is acquired. Giving up the relative comforts of the
'householder's' life to become a humble monkish ascetic is
the great traditional renunciation. However, our earlier discussion of the implications of the Second Precept and the
virtue of 'Right Livelihood' suggests that history has now

brought us all to a point where we have to choose between either, on the whole, confirming the values of the dominant culture or, on the whole, seeking to disconfirm them and transform them. The latter can only be effectively undertaken in a spirit of self-abnegation, and so donning the robe (which in Buddhism is not necessarily a lifetime vocation) remains one form of the latter choice. But it is no longer the only one, and forms of more actively and socially engaged spirituality are now also appropriate.

This brings us to the bodhisattva ideal. Bodhisattvas are the great moral exemplars of Mahayana Buddhism, mythical personifications of wisdom and compassion and selfless action, who inspire the trainee to faith, energy and patient endurance. They are transcendental activists whose infinite executive capacity makes it somehow misleading simply to translate them as saints. They take upon themselves the cares of suffering humanity: 'May all sorrows ripen in me,' exclaims Shantideva, the great ascetic and poet, in his *Guide to the Bodhisattva's Way of Life* (*Bodhicaryavatara*). His words are the less extravagant when set against the course of human history in the twelve hundred years since he wrote them:

> I take upon myself the burden of sorrow; I resolve to do so; I endure it all. I do not turn back or run away, I do not tremble...I am not afraid...nor do I despair. Assuredly I must bear the burden of all beings...for I have resolved to save them all. I must set them all free, I must save the whole world from the forest of birth, old age, disease and re-birth, from misfortune and sin, from the round of birth and death, from the toils of error....For all beings are caught in the net of craving, encompassed by ignorance, held by the desire of existence; they are doomed to destruction, shut in a cage of pain...they are ignorant, untrustworthy, full of doubts, always at loggerheads one with

another, always prone to see evil; they cannot find
a refuge in the ocean of existence; they are all on
the edge of the gulf of destruction. I work to
establish the kingdom of perfect wisdom for all
beings.[132]

Bodhisattvas strive to relieve human affliction by all possible means, as well as through the ultimate liberation of
existential awakening. Thus, in the Avatamsaka Sutra there
are revealed to the young pilgrim Sudhana 'innumerable
Bodhisattvas walking, sitting, engaged in all kinds of work,
doing charitable deeds out of a great compassionate heart,
writing various treatises whereby to benefit the world...
[and] praising worldly business and all forms of craftsman-
ship which would increase the happiness of all beings.'[133]
There is nothing here of the quietistic indifference commonly
imputed to Buddhism!

In order to relate more effectively to different kinds of
people and situations the bodhisattva makes use of 'skilful and expedient means' (*upaya-kausalya*).[134] Thus the lay
bodhisattva Vimalakirti 'in order to be in harmony with
people...engaged in all sorts of business yet had no interest
in profit or possessions....To demonstrate the evils of
desire he even entered the brothels....He was honoured as
the landlord among landlords because he renounced the
aggressiveness of ownership,' and so on.[135]

Vimalakirti explains that although the bodhisattva 'may
show the ways of sophistry and contention, yet he is always
conscious of ultimate meanings and has perfected the use
of liberative techniques....He may show the ways of
the passions, yet he is utterly dispassionate and naturally
pure....He follows the ways of all the world, yet he
reverses all states of existence. He follows the ways of
liberation without ever abandoning the progress of the
world.'[136]

With all those attractions there is clearly a danger of falling
into the error of 'Beat Zen' and projecting what are lower

spiritual and moral states onto higher ones. Nevertheless, the selfless commitment of the bodhisattva, and his or her ability to relate ideals to the needs of people and situations without compromising those ideals, can be suggestive and inspiring for Buddhist activists. Their patron bodhisattva is surely the millennial Maitreya, who is usually depicted holding a vessel containing the waters of awakening. These he will sprinkle upon humankind to bring it to awareness when it has reached the ultimate point of delusion and destructiveness.

# 16 *The Situational Morality of Ignorance, Humility and Courage*

At a personal level there appear to be three kinds of obstacle in practising the Buddhist moral precepts.

First, it is necessary to summon up the necessary will-power and determination in order to affirm the precepts in practice, always bearing in mind the previously discussed limitations on the use of the will. Without some strong moral commitment, some energy and determination, it is impossible to get started.

Secondly, there is the difficulty of cultivating full mindfulness of the kick-back of emotion, of resentment, which occurs when the will is used to thwart desire, as when we have to push ourselves to get on with unrewarding work in order to meet a commitment previously made to others. As we shall see in the next chapter, this mindfulness is a self-awareness, but it is also a related awareness of the feelings of others.

Thirdly, there is the difficulty of moral choice, of knowing how to apply the precepts in complex and ambiguous situations. Just as in keeping to them there is a danger of making too heavy a use of the will, so in interpreting their meanings there is a danger of clinging to a narrow and superficial literalism. In many situations the precepts provide the questions, not the answers. We may have too little information to make a realistic decision or even know what really is the problem, or what will be the outcome of this or that decision. And what if greater good may come from lesser evil? What if by upholding one precept in a small way we break another in a big way? Is that not a self-serving virtue which refuses to see the large and inconvenient evils which follow from it? What if the merits of alternative choices seem equally balanced? If I mislead the huntsman as to which way the fox ran, will the fox ravage another hen coop tonight? And is my animosity towards the foxhunting class masquerading as pity for foxes? And is that animosity itself something that arises as a sense of ill will at my discomfort at being me, inside my skin, which ill will needs to find a morally justifiable outlet? This is not to imply that cruelty to foxes is an irrelevant matter or that 'it's all in our heads', but just to recall that reality is inside—outside and we must not forget old two-faced Janus.

Moral perplexity is more commonly experienced now-adays not, I suggest, so much because moral precepts are less observed but because it is more difficult to see where they point in the ambiguous, obscure, and interconnected situations in which we increasingly find ourselves. And the very fact that we live in a 'high egoic' era of human conscious-ness has increased our sense of choice whilst making it more difficult to choose. The perplexity has the merit of honesty, and is less disturbing than the quick fix of instant righteousness which is the usual public response. The latter tends to give moral weight to self-affirming polarization of people, systems, and ideas — the antithetical bonding to which I referred in Chapter 3.

In my experience a question which commonly disturbs Buddhists interested in embarking on radical social action is how they can *know* that their decisions are authentic res-ponses to situations of need and how far they are motivated by delusive self-need? For it has already dawned upon them that they do not act out their lives with the clear, selfless objectivity which they once thought they did. They may have tasted that good, gutsy satisfaction of knowing where you stand, why you are right, and where your loyalties and antipathies are.

In the first place, it is necessary to work for as much

inner and outer clarity as possible. Inner clarity may be increased by awareness, meditation and retreat situations which encourage these. These tend to clear, cool and purify the view and give some space for it to show itself when it becomes less full of 'my' wanting:

> To carry the self forward and realize the ten thousand things is delusion;
> That the ten thousand things advance and realize the self is enlightenment.
> Zen Master Dogen: *Shobogenzo*

Another Zen Master, Rinzai, spells out the same explanation: 'Only because of our affective [emotional] hindrances, the intuition is intercepted; [only] because of our imaginations, Reality is subject to differentiation.'[137] With greater inner/ outer clarity it is a common experience that we begin to ask new questions and seek different information (that is, less clear-cut, partisan, self-confirming material).

For example, the great good of most peace activists, moved powerfully by a well-informed moral revulsion, is nuclear disarmament, unilateral if needs be, whereas the main concern of the majority of people in Britain is an adequate defence policy, preferably without nuclear weapons if that is not too risky. They see the simple renunciation of the Bomb as reckless idealism. It is, however, extremely difficult to persuade most peace workers to turn their attention to the sordid realities of conventional, alternative, non-nuclear defence policies and strategies and to uncomfortable open-ended dialogue with political and military pragmatists who had previously been shunned. (The similar experiences of American peace worker Gene Sharp have already been noted in Chapter 8.)

Over and beyond what additional inner and outer clarity may be found to bear upon our particular moral decision, it will be appreciated that the very fact of being a Buddhist is acknowledgement of ignorance of one's deepest motivations and the delusive nature of one's experience of the world.

The following words by philosopher and novelist Iris Murdoch could equally be those of Simone Weil, for both write out of the great tradition of inner morality in which Buddhism is so strongly represented:

> What we really are seems much more like an obscure system of energy out of which choices and visible acts of will emerge at intervals in ways which are often unclear and often dependent on the condition of the system in between the moments of choice.... The chief enemy of excellence in morality (and also in art) is personal fantasy: the tissue of self-aggrandizing and consoling wishes and dreams which prevents one from seeing what is there outside one. Rilke said of Cézanne that he did not paint 'I like it', he painted 'There it is.' This is not easy, and requires, in art or morals, a discipline.... What I have called fantasy, the proliferation of blinding, self-centred aims and images, is itself a powerful system of energy, and most of what is called 'will' or 'willing' belongs to this system. What counteracts the system is attention to reality, inspired by, consisting of, love.... Freedom is not strictly the exercise of the will, but rather the experience of accurate vision which, when this becomes appropriate, occasions action.[138]

Without making a virtue of ignorance, it is important to acknowledge it, and be open to the awareness that in a particular situation we may not be focusing even upon the real problem let alone the real question, let alone the real answer. Yet my ignorance is a threat to my need to know 'where I stand'. Zen trainees are urged to keep an unblocked, 'Don't know' mind, which resembles what Keats described in a letter as Shakespeare's 'negative capability' − 'being in uncertainties, mysteries, doubts, without any irritable searching after fact and reason.' Unfortunately the creative use of ignorance is no more understood in our society than is the humility and patience that go with it. And yet it is out of that place that it is so often necessary to act (or forbear) and to do our best, appropriately and morally, 'according to our lights'. Moreover, no one else can take responsibility for the consequences of our actions, and these may be endurable only if we have learnt to be truly kind and compassionate to ourselves.

It may be helpful to conclude this chapter with two examples of situational morality at work. The first is the case of abortion, around which strong opposing and defending ideologies are gathered, and which is no less of a dilemma for a religion which is both profoundly compassionate and which counsels against all killing. The three statements by Buddhists in the West which I have encountered on this topic all come to similar conclusions. After reviewing the pros and cons, they acknowledge the complexity of life and the difficulty of living as a human being without taking life in some form or another, and they accept that abortion is a profound moral dilemma to which there is no clear-cut solution. All three agree that, 'Although others may be involved in the decision-making, it is the woman carrying the fetus, and no one else, who must in the end make this most difficult decision and live with it for the rest of her life. As Buddhists we can only encourage her to make a decision that is both thoughtful and compassionate.' ([Shin] Buddhist Churches of American Social Issues Committee).[139] In response to the question of how such a decision can be made, Zen Master Philip Kapleau counsels: 'If your mind is free of fear and of narrow selfish concerns, you will know what course of action to take. Put yourself deeply into zazen [meditation] – look into your own heart-mind, reflecting carefully on all aspects of your life situation and on the repercussions your actions might have on your family and on society as a whole. Once the upper levels of mind, which weigh and analyse, have come to rest, the "right" course of action will become clear. And when such action is accompanied by a feeling of inner peace, you may be sure you have not gone astray.'[140] Our third testimony is from Zen Master Robert Aitken, who writes:

> Sitting in on sharing meetings in the Diamond Sangha, our Zen Buddhist society in Hawaii, I get the impression that when a woman is sensitive to her feelings, she is conscious that abortion is killing a part of herself and terminating the ancient process, begun anew within herself, of bringing life into being. Thus she is likely to feel acutely miserable after making a decision to have an abortion. This is a time for compassion for the woman, and for her to be compassionate with herself and for her unborn child. If I am consulted, and we explore the options carefully and I learn that the decision is definite, I encourage her to go through the act with the consciousness of a mother who holds her dying child in her arms, lovingly nurturing it as it passes from life. Sorrow and suffering from the nature of samsara [the transitory world of phenomena], the flow of life and death, and the decision to prevent birth is made on balance with other elements of suffering. Once the decision is made, there is no blame, but rather acknowledgement that sadness pervades the whole universe, and this bit of life goes with our deepest love.[141]

For those Buddhists who take a *kammaic* retributive view, and believe that through present suffering we discharge the price of past moral transgression, the moral dilemma still remains (unless a literalist ideology be made of Buddhism) since either course of action is likely to bring suffering.

An episode from the life of the Revd. Michael Scott provides a second example of this suffering through of one's own ignorance with the moral courage needed to respond positively to the demands of the situation. Scott was in many ways an outstanding exemplar of spiritual activism.

His early work was in South Africa, against tremendous odds and with negligible support and recognition. Bishop Trevor Huddleston subsequently acknowledged, 'How effective an instrument can one man be if he guards his integrity.' Early in life Scott had become convinced of the value of Gandhian nonviolent civil disobedience, and he later became a rigorous and effective practitioner of that discipline. However, when the Second World War broke out, he experienced a profound dilemma. David Astor, in his obituary, explains:

> He felt bound to resist the Nazis physically (unlike Gandhi who advised the Czechs against doing so); on the other hand, he did not feel able to kill in the name of Jesus. He resisted the usual compromise of being a non-combatant chaplain and joined the Royal Air Force to train as a rear-gunner. This does not mean any loss of devotion to Christianity; he simply could not see its application to stopping the Nazis. It was an example of his scrupulous self-questioning.[142]

Astor recalls that Scott once said that he 'belonged to the Religion of Doubt'. In this he had much in common with Dietrich Bonhoeffer whose pacifism was also put to the test by the Nazi movement. After much suffering through profound inner conflict and doubt, Bonhoeffer joined the plot to blow up Hitler and other Nazi leaders in hope of bringing the war to an early close. The attempt miscarried, Bonhoeffer was arrested and was eventually executed only a few days before the end of the war.

I suggest that to experience these kinds of situation as moral dilemmas, as spiritual paradoxes, to suffer them through in the humility of ignorance, helplessness and despair, and to find the moral courage to act, may be evidence of a riper spiritual maturity than a ready certitude of what's right and what's wrong.

# 17  *Mindfulness, Meditation and Retreat*

Since Buddhist social action is essentially an extension of the traditional practice of *sila* (morality), the latter has received the main share of attention in this section on Buddhist training and practice. The relatively small space given to the round-the-clock awareness called 'mindfulness' and to sitting meditation does not therefore reflect their relative importance.

The mindfulness practice walks, as it were, on two legs, and, ideally, when the trainee is not walking on one he or she is trying to walk on the other. One leg is the continual attempt to give total attention, moment by moment, to what is being done now. Thus, of mindful tea drinking, *Thich Nhat Hanh* writes as follows: 'Allow yourself a good length of time to do this. Don't drink your tea like someone who gulps down a cup of coffee during a workbreak. Drink your tea slowly and reverently as if it were the axis on which the earth revolves — slowly, evenly, without rushing towards the future. Live the actual moment. For only this actual moment is life.'[143] The other leg of mindfulness is that of a scrupulous awareness of the rising and falling of the emotions as a physical sensation. This has already been touched upon as part of the cultivation of morality (Chapter 14), and it is with this second leg of mindfulness that most of this chapter is concerned.

Mindfulness practice is learning to open up to the on-slaughts of raw emotional energy without either letting it discharge itself (in anger, or self-pity, for example), or suppressing it, trying to rationalize it or otherwise getting it under control. This is not easy to describe, and requires a lot of personal experimentation. John Welwood writes of this 'befriending emotion' which, 'by neither suppressing emotions nor exploring the meaning in them, teaches us a way to feel their naked aliveness and contain their energy ....This approach to emotion is called *transmutation* in Vajrayana Buddhism as well as in other traditions.'[144] Some further explanation from teachers in different Buddhist traditions may help the reader to get the measure of mindfulness practice. In the Theravada Buddhist tradition, Nyanaponika Mahathera writes that, 'by the methodical application of Bare Attention...all the latent powers of a non-coercive approach will gradually unfold themselves with their beneficial results and their wide and unexpected implications.'[145] 'Let yourself be in the emotion,' writes the Tibetan teacher, Chögyam Trungpa. 'Go through it, give in to it, experience it....Then the most powerful energies become absolutely workable rather than taking you over, because there is nothing to take over if you are not putting up any resistance.'[146] In Irmgard Schloegl's teaching this is a 'daily life practice' which slowly 'grinds down the spikiness of ego'[147] and Hubert Benoit, another Western teacher of Zen, writes as follows: 'If a humiliating circumstance turns up, offering me a marvellous chance of initiation, at once my imagination strives to conjure what appears to me to be in danger...it does everything to restore me to that habitual state of satisfied arrogance in which I find a transitory respite but also the certainty of further distress. In short, I constantly defend myself against that which offers to save me; I fight foot by foot to defend the very source of my unhappiness.'[148]

Mindfulness is thus a practice of attentive yielding and accepting in the body, in the emotions, which gradually dissolves our futile root habit of conducting a kind of emotional lawsuit with everything that balks us or threatens us in any way. Energy previously blocked in 'controlling' ourselves or wasted in negative, self-centred discharge is thus purified of the various colours of driven feeling; it becomes available for making appropriate and positive re-sponse (including warm, outgoing feelings) to situations we encounter. The reader will recall how it often is when work-ing on a project with a group of people, or when approach-ing an individual to try to resolve a problem, much time and energy goes into resolving the 'personality problems'. The problem itself may receive inadequate attention because all the ritual ego dances have to be enacted before the spikier and pricklier characters have been propitiated. It is only after this we can get down to the really valuable differences of opinion, arising from different perspectives and expertise, which can make for a high-quality solution.

The precepts provide only one kind of 'tethering post' through which we can experience more fully the pull of our emotions. Buddhist practice and lifestyle customarily uses a 'form' or discipline which is sufficient to put our feelings under load and so expose them strongly to awareness but not so weighty as to invoke heavy and insensitive control, with the danger of becoming a robot or a self-righteous ascetic. The self-denying, tightly ordered programme of a monastery is an obvious example, but the pressures and tight deadlines of the modern working day can provide for many people as much of the 'discipline' as they can handle, especially if combined with child rearing and housekeeping.

Social action typically provides plenty of opportunity for a disciplined awareness practice. We usually make a volun-tary commitment of time and energy to some project and to the other people who are working on it. It is likely that much of the work will be tedious and not immediately reward-ing − a round of fundraising, secretarial and committee work, leafleting on street corners, knocking on doors on dark, rainy nights to win support for a petition. Much indif-ference, hostility and even abuse may be experienced, creat-ing feelings of frustration, fear and defeat. Not least, social action requires us to work in close fellowship with others, whom we may find awkward or disagreeable, and often in an emotionally loaded atmosphere of dedication and commitment not usually found in the workplace.

Moreover, if we are to be effective in our social action we have to be able to learn from hard experience even when it contradicts our deeply held assumptions and even threatens that person who at the present time we feel we are. Peace work and similar kinds of campaigning are likely to feel most comfortable and self-confirming when we distance ourselves from those with whom we are trying to communicate. If we talk with them at all, then we talk *to* or *at* them, and make sure we do most of the talking so as to retain control of the situation. Listening can be more threatening than doing the talking; expressing our own feelings or receiving someone else's is more threatening than cool, rational discusssion. And yet closeness, real dialogue and shared feelings are the best ways of opening up genuine communication. And these are excellent opportunities if only we can handle them, for cultivating the mindfulness practice and hence slowly becoming the kind of person who can make effective, heartfelt response to the fear and resentment which can be invoked when people are reminded about the Bomb or some other threat.

And there are other ways, also, in which our awareness needs to be extended and informed. *Thich* Nhat Hanh reminds us that 'Society makes it difficult for us to be awake. I am sure you know this, but you keep forgetting: forty thousand children in the Third World every day die of hunger, forty thousand of them. We know, but we keep forgetting because the kind of society in which we live makes us forgetful. That is why we need some exercise for mindfulness, for awareness. A number of Buddhists practise this — they refrain from eating a few times a week in order to be in communion with the Third World.'[149]

How self-awareness of emotional states can help others as well as oneself is illustrated in the Buddhist scriptures by a story about two travelling acrobats who performed hazardous feats on the end of a long bamboo pole.[150] One said that their act would be accomplished safely if each watched and attended to the other. But the other and wiser one maintained that if each concentrated on doing his own part of the act safely and well he would thereby protect his friend as well as himself. Our concern to help others may conceal a need to affirm ourselves. The other person is commonly seen as 'the problem', unless we have a low sense of self-identity and confidence, so that invariably we see ourselves as 'the problem'. In either case increased awareness of self is the way to greater wisdom about self, and from which arises the compassion truly to help others.

Consider the situation in a stormy group meeting where an important but contentious decision has to be made. Would it not be helpful to pause, to shut up for a while, to look inward at the turbulence of one's own seething indignation and see how this — and the angry feelings of others — makes it more difficult to find a sound and acceptable solution to the problem at issue? Is that what each person does really want? And having looked inward, would not some fellow-feeling arise for one's gesticulating, red-faced adversaries? It is often at this point that someone suddenly sees the comedy of it all, and makes the joke that bursts everyone's inflated ego in the funniest and most undeniable way. Then the meeting can really get down to business.

Social action can throw up many 'white water' situations, when the emotional rapids become too turbulent for us to paddle our little mindfulness canoe skilfully enough and it capsizes. We 'go over the top' with our feelings, or screw them down with white-faced control, or slide into a wallow of self-pity, or otherwise forget where we are. Therefore it is best to learn in what is likely to be fairly calm water which does not toss us about too much. This means avoiding certain situations which cannot yet be ridden out without upset to self and without contributing negatively to what is happening. For example, some animal rights campaigning appears to have this kind of inflammatory power over certain people. All mass nonviolent demonstrations tend to arouse powerful emotions which may threaten the success of the action, as well as upsetting the mindfulness practice of any militant mystics who happen to be involved! In a British pamphlet entitled *Preparing for Non-violent Direct Action*[151] there is a section on 'Forestalling violence' in which demonstrators are advised: 'Deliberately calm yourself before an action, so that you feel centred; if you start to feel wound up, concentrate on your breathing for a time.' The pamphlet has warnings about doing anything which might further inflame 'an already frustrated, aggressive and abusive demonstrator'.

Organizations and campaigns which imply the absolute virtue and truth of their own cause and the unmitigated falsehood and evil of their opponents are probably too common to be avoided, but it is usually best to steer clear of those which go out of their way to foster their well-researched hates and which have built-in means of instilling conformity to such weighted polarization. Such is the case in many centralized, hierarchical and comparatively authoritarian organizations (including the authority of the majority), whose business it is — as with conventional political parties — to be adversarial at all costs. The seemingly inexorable process by which they squeeze out the middle ground and solidify a black-and-white conformity has already been examined in Chapter 8.

Mindfulness practice reinforces, and is reinforced by, daily periods of sitting and walking meditation together with meditation retreats of several days' duration. Mindfulness and meditation are both awareness exercises and are, in effect, interchangeable terms, but in sitting meditation a more strongly focused mindfulness is possible. Most commonly the meditator concentrates attention on some phenomenon such as the rise and fall of the breath. Power of concentration develops until all sense of self is swallowed up in it: the self loses the self (in trance) and comes back to a calmer, clearer less fear-driven reality.

A specific meditation directly related to social activism is the ancient *brahma-vihara* (sublime abidings) meditation. The meditator generates within themself a spirit of loving-kindness (*metta*) which is directed successively to themself, to a friend, to a stranger, and to an enemy. When he or she has become adept at this *metta-bhavana*, they extend their meditation successively to include the virtues of compassion (*karuna*), sympathetic joy (*mudita*), and equanimity (*upekkha*). On the face of it this meditation appears to be a kind of wish-fulfilment, a willing-of-virtue. Alexandra David-Neel offers some interesting discussion of differing opinions about it which she found among Buddhists.[152] One view was that the effect of the meditation could only be a superficial process of readily reversible auto-suggestion. However, it would be in the mainstream of Buddhist practice if it were undertaken as a simple acceptance, awareness and befriending of the negative emotions aroused by all this willed benevolence. This in itself has the effect, over the months and years, of exposing, softening and dissolving our deep-rooted capacity for ill will.

An American Buddhist, Joanna Macy, has developed many 'spiritual exercises for social activists' which she teaches in 'despair and empowerment workshops'. These facilitate 'the psychological and spiritual work of dealing with our knowledge and feelings about the present planetary crisis in ways that release energy and vision for creative response.' Macy's *Despair and Personal Power in the Nuclear Age* is a valuable resource book which describes forty-seven 'exercises' (including guided meditations, group interaction, dance and ritual), together with much useful advice. The book can be used by individuals as well as groups, and the material can be readily adapted and modified to a variety of situations, including traditional spiritual retreats.[153] Arising from Joanna Macy's visiting workshops a British 'Interhelp' network has been established. It publishes a newsletter, *Threads*, and has been active in organizing workshops and training facilitators.[154]

Daily meditation periods and periodic meditation retreats

are essential for spiritual activists, as many have testified. Thus Sulak Sivaraksa of Thailand writes:

> These meditation masters [and] monks who spend their lives in the forests, are very, very important for us and for our society. Even those of us who are in society must go back to these masters and look within. We must practise daily our meditation, our prayer. We must do it at least every morning, or every evening, or both. And those of us...who work in society and confront power and social injustice, we get beaten every now and again and we get tired often. At least annually we ought to retreat into the forests, into the monasteries, to sit at the feet of the masters, to gain our spiritual strength, in order to come out again to confront society.[155]

Without meditation and retreat it is difficult to remain steady and centred against the inherent ego-pull of social activism. Retreats, in particular, are laboratories for intensive spiritual practice, with a strong discipline and framework (including extra sensitivity to others' needs), freedom from everyday distractions, the support of other retreatants, and the inspiration and leadership of a teacher or facilitator.

# 18  *Monasticism and Social Activism*

Traditionally the *sangha* (fellowship, community) is of central importance in Buddhism. Its potential contribution to a Buddhist social activism is, I believe, unique and important even though indirect. However, the future role and significance of the sangha and particularly in the West, will probably be strongly affected by the changing character of the laity and their activities.

Monks and nuns are people who have dedicated themselves to spiritual training under conditions which are rigorous but also very supportive. Members of this *institutional* sangha (*bhikkhu-sangha*) serve to personify the ideal of spiritual dedication. In addition, monastics are likely to have evolved over the years as people of some considerable spiritual insight and compassionate awareness. Walpola Rahula reminds us, however, of the distinction between the institutional sangha and the *spiritual* sangha (*savaka-sangha*) as the fellowship of all spiritually evolved people, lay and monastic.[156]

In Mahayana Buddhism 'sangha' commonly denotes the whole community of Followers of the Way, lay and monastic, but in this book, if used without qualification, it means the monastic community only. Furthermore we may distinguish a smaller, *teaching* sangha of men and women who should be of the spiritual sangha, should normally have trained some years in the institutional sangha, and should also have a natural bent for teaching that has been developed by at least some formal training in that craft. I suggest that these distinctions, between spiritual, institutional and teaching sanghas can usefully clarify discussion in a rather foggy area in which there has been remarkably little discourse since Buddhism came to the West.

The monastic (or institutional) sangha provides experienced teachers of Buddhism, some of whom may subsequently disrobe and continue as lay teachers. Others teach at, and out of, a monastic community and certainly in the West the demand for their services is often so great that teaching appears to be the main activity of most senior monastics. Others, again, head a teaching and practice centre of their own, financially supported by their students some of whom may live in so as to form a communal household which may become the nucleus for a quasi-monastic community.

In South-East Asia and the Far East Buddhist monasticism is not necessarily a lifelong vocation as it is in the Christian tradition. In Thailand, for example, it is common for lay-people to ordain and train for periods ranging from a few weeks to a few years. There would be many advantages in retaining this flexibility in the West, where it is even more relevant, rather than following the Christian vocational tradition. The gap between sangha and laity is much narrower in many respects than it is in pre-industrial societies and both would benefit greatly from this and other kinds of cross-fertilization.

The historic role of lay people has been, and remains, to provide material support for the monastics, and to try to follow their example as best they are able. In return the laity received teachings and guidance appropriate to their generally ill-educated condition and their necessary preoccupation with winning a livelihood and bringing up their families. By contrast lay people in many countries today are as well educated or more so than typical monastics; they have leisure and other means for becoming knowledgeable about Buddhism through the extensive published literature; and many of them are dedicated practitioners of meditation, mindfulness and a Buddhist lifestyle.

In the East the growth of strong lay Buddhist movements of various kinds has perhaps been the most significant development in contemporary Buddhism. In the West there are the beginnings of lay social action organizations which cut across and complement the established practice centres, as we shall see in Part Five. Stephen Batchelor, a writer with considerable sangha experience himself, confirms the validity of Buddhist monasticism today, but at the same time he concludes that 'it can no longer be taken for granted that as a monk one will automatically be serving a more valuable role [than as a lay person] in the preservation of Buddhism and its sangha. Likewise the traditional notion that a monk is somehow intellectually and morally superior to the laity can no longer be accepted....Whatever form it takes, an alternative sangha structure needs to arise in correlation with the present situation that is able to replace the traditional model of monastic domination and lay-monk polarity....In the face of the new laity actively assuming many of the tasks which were traditionally his, more and more (the monk) may come to feel the burden of being, in the words of Thomas Merton, a "guilty by-stander".'[157]

Without necessarily subscribing to the latter view, a new kind of partnership between sangha and laity seems certain to develop in the future and to be both necessary and welcome. In addition to their traditional support role, the laity now have more knowledge, experience and expertise to contribute in their relations with the sangha, as well as furthering the Buddhadharma through predominantly lay organizations in various fields. Particularly urgent is the need to find ways of ending sex discrimination and the admission of women on equal terms with men to all monastic sanghas. On the other hand, the absolutely vital training and guidance role of the sangha remains more important than ever. As Batchelor puts it, even at the simplest level, and 'irrespective of one's intellectual opinions about monasticism, to actually encounter a monk has a definite psychological impact: in a believer he acts as a concrete affirmation of one's faith; in a non-believer he challenges an exclusive preoccupation with secular affairs and stirs unconscious tendencies to spirituality.'

In my view the relationship between sangha and laity will develop pragmatically, under pressure of circumstance, and concern should rather be directed towards some danger of secularization and spiritual dilution in the organizations and projects of an over-confident laity. The vital support function of monasticism in social activism needs particularly to be appreciated. Sulak Sivaraksa has stressed that 'the important thing in an individual who acts is not his action but his personality. In the Thai context, a monk like Bhikkhu Buddhadasa is so important, although he hardly does anything outside his community except preaching and writing, and he lives far away from anywhere.'[158] 'In the night of our technological barbarism,' wrote Thomas Merton, 'monks must be as trees which exist silently in the dark and purify the air.' One of a group of American peace workers who had participated in a retreat led by Merton on 'the spiritual roots of protest', testified that:

> Many activists, those of us who were in the streets...could not have done what we did without dedicated souls in monasteries to back us up. Merton was anchored in reality, and we looked to him to help us keep our balance and sense of reality. Many of us could vouch that, when desperate times came, when we seemed to be accomplishing nothing, when we were calumniated and tempted to give up, Father Louis and others like him salvaged us. We were not salvaged by the strategies and sociologists, but by men and women of highly advanced spiritual dimensions.[159]

Monasticism is evidently not only vital for the personal training in Dharma, in lived-out truth, upon which a Buddhist social activism depends but it also provides direct support and inspiration.

## Part Five

The Rationale and the Forms of
Buddhist Social Activism

# 19   The Grounding of Buddhist Activism

Sulak Sivaraksa recalls how, as a Buddhist activist from Thailand, he was warned by the Venerable Dr Saddhatissa, a senior monk long resident in Britain, that 'most Westerners embrace Buddhism out of private spiritual need and not for social responsibility. He advised me to contact [instead] Western Christians who were sympathetic to Buddhism and to social justice.'[160] In 1985, some five years later, the same writer was forced to conclude that 'the Western Buddhist concept of non-action in society has already crept into my country, expecially among the Western-trained intellectual élites.'[161] However, it was just at this time that a shift of opinion became evident in the North American and British Buddhist communities. Thus the editor of the influential journal of the (London) Buddhist Society, *The Middle Way*, reported in the November 1984 issue that 'a striking new feature of our daily postbag in recent months has been the volume of incoming letters and literature on matters not strictly spiritual but rather of a social or political complexion.' He goes on to observe that it would be 'understandable if [lay Buddhists] began to grow a little restive on their meditation cushions; if internal work upon themselves failed to allay growing frustration entirely − if, in short, they began to feel the need to act.'[162]

Chapter 21 reviews the beginnings of a Buddhist activism in the West. First, however, this present chapter will summarize the rationale for a Buddhist activism and will argue the merits of founding it on Dharma fundamentals rather than relying primarily on direct scriptural exegesis. And in Chapter 20 some objections and problems that have been raised in connection with Buddhist activism will be discussed.

A socially engaged Buddhism needs no other rationale than that of being an amplification of traditional Buddhist morality, a social ethic brought forth by the needs and potentialities of present-day society. And, as we have seen in Part Four, doing our honest best to help others can be a part of the mindfulness training through which we are enabled to help others selflessly.

The argument for a contemporary Buddhist social ethic is given particular strength by the identification of 'social kamma' (Chapter 6) or, more precisely, the socio-historical contribution to individual kammaic conditioning. The great bodhisattva vow to 'liberate all beings' now also implies a concern for changing the social conditions which in every sense discomfit us, whether through gross affliction or through supercharging the existential folly through which we make what William Blake called our 'mind-forged manacles'. These are surely among the conditions which the Buddha declared 'lead to passion, not release therefrom; to bondage, not release therefrom; and to the piling up of rebirths; these to wanting much, not wanting little; to discontent, not to contentment; these to sociability, not to solitude; these to indolence, not to exertion; these to luxury, not to frugality; of these things know with certainty, this is not the Dhamma, this is not the Discipline, this is not the word of the Teacher.'[163]

The argument for social activism which follows from the acknowledgement of kammaic social conditioning may be stepped out as follows:

1. We cannot work selflessly and fully effectively to change society so long as we are driven by divisive and delusive self-need;

2. The latter is the ordinary root response to the predicament of being human;

3. But that individual response is compounded in socio-historical conditions which *institutionalize* alienation, ill will, aggressiveness, defensiveness, and acquisitiveness;

4. In turn, those social conditions are kammaically inherited by each new generation, whose delusive personal struggle for identity and meaning is socialized and supercharged by previously mentioned norms and institutions;

5. Therefore out of *wisdom* we need to create different social conditions of a kind which nurture positive personality change, and out of *compassion* we need to create those conditions because the present ones give rise to so much gross physical and mental affliction; 'Reason not the need...';

6. If our work to effect these social changes is at the same time undertaken as a meditative training which ripens inner awareness then we shall at the same time contribute to our own eventual 'inconceivable liberation' from self-need — or at least become a little more human!;

7. Thus we shall be more free to see clearly and act effectively so as to meet the material and spiritual needs of others, facilitating both personal and social change.

The above dialectic constitutes the Higher Third of a Middle Way which transcends the polarities of the Social and Quietist Fallacies introduced in Chapter 10. The argument has been summarized as follows by Charles Upton:

> To say that a revolution in consciousness can have a direct transformative effect on social conditions, that social conditions are an automatic expression of mind, is to fall into the utopian error and its fantasies of magic; but to say than social change is the necessary prerequisite for all psychic transformation, that mind is no more than a reflex of social conditions, is to fall into the error of mechanistic materialism, and to deny humanity any standpoint outside historical conditions from which to creatively engage those conditions. Thus

it is wrong to say that psychic transformation must precede social change, or that social change must first create the ideal society which will then be conducive to psychic growth.[164]

The history of Buddhism affords many examples of the influence of specific social conditions. The Buddha-dharma itself emerged at a momentous time when patriarchal tribal institutions were breaking up amidst cultural disorientation and reorientation. Gotama, the future Buddha, who was the son of one of the clan chiefs, himself joined the many socially and culturally displaced seekers and wanderers. His subsequent ministry was very much associated with the eruption of a mercantile urban culture which favoured an open-minded self-reliance and was critical of the traditional Brahmana and Vedic cults. *Sutta* analysis shows that most of the Buddha's preaching was in urban centres, even outside the periods of Rains Retreats. The judgement of Dr B.G. Gokhale, an authority in this field, is that, 'It is now generally accepted that early Buddhism rose to popular acceptance on the crest of an urban revolution... [which] did not create Buddhism, but was certainly vital for its early popularity and material support.'[165]

Associated with the above rationale for a Buddhist activism is the question of *validation*. That is to say, on what basis, on what foundation, is Buddhist social analysis, and the activism derived from it, to be grounded?

It will be evident by now that this book draws directly on the social implications of fundamental Buddhist teaching (Dharma), which I have taken to mean the Four Noble Truths, the Eightfold Path of training and practice, and the root insights of Mahayana Buddhism arising from these. In this I share the view of Edward Conze when he wrote that:

> The cornerstone of my interpretation of Buddhism is the conviction, shared by nearly everyone, that it is essentially a doctrine of salvation,

and that all its philosophical statements are subordinate to its soteriological purpose [its goal of salvation]. This implies...that each and every proposition must be considered with reference to its spiritual intention, and as a formulation of meditational experiences acquired in the process of winning salvation.[166]

My method of validation can be characterized by terms such as primary, existential, perennial, epistemological. It contrasts with the other method of validating Buddhist social analysis and justifying social activism, which is secondary, exegetical, culture-bound and contingent in character, relying on specific scriptural evidence and historic Buddhist practice to give direct and prescriptive guidance. These primary and secondary methods of validation approximate to the distinction emphasized by *Ajahn* Buddhadhasa between *patipatti-dhamma* (the teaching of the Way, the practice) and *pariyatta-dhamma* (scriptural teaching).[167] The two methods are not exclusive, of course, but complementary. However, I believe that the main weight must be put upon the first, with the second only supplementary, suggestive and confirmatory. There are two reasons for this.

In the first place, even where scriptural and historical evidence apparently does carry some spiritual authority, it is, notwithstanding, more or less the application of Buddhadharma within the specific conditions of a bygone culture. Meaning must therefore be scrupulously teased out of that context and translated back into primary Dharma before it can be related to present-day conditions. Further, as Conze reminds us, 'much of what has been handed down as "Buddhism" is due not to the exercise of wisdom but [solely] to the social conditions in which the Buddhist community existed, to the language employed, and to the science and mythology in vogue among the people who adopted it.'[168] In particular it is not legitimate to find instant scriptural and historical authority for contemporary secular ideas and ideologies (like democracy or Marxism) by *reading them back* into the evidence from scripture and history, whilst ignoring both the spiritual significance of that evidence and/or its culture-bound meaning. This is a common device of the reductive modernism which was introduced in Chapter 11, and which will be much encountered in Part Six to come.

Secondly, Buddhism is not a 'religion of the book', and its relationship to its scriptural record is highly ambiguous. Scripture is intended only to signpost the way to direct experience of reality and not to be a sufficient substitute for that realization. As emphasized in the celebrated Kalama scripture (Chapter 8) Buddhism enjoins seekers to rely first and foremost upon their own experience, whilst working all the while to deepen this and so make it a more reliable guide.

All that having been said, since much of scripture *is* the expression of a high level of spiritual consciousness, then it must carry considerable weight in validations of social theory and action. What is really at issue here is not the legitimate guidance of scripture as understood within its spiritual context and in terms of its soteriological purpose. What is being contested is the secularization of both scriptural meaning and engaged spirituality by annexing both to contemporary social categories and perspectives confined within a superficial and secular consciousness. And, of course, the fundamental and perennial Dharma on which I have tried to base this book does itself necessarily go back to scriptural record, though only at the most fundamental and generalizable level.

Let us illustrate the above with the example of the egalitarianism which I believe to be implicit in Buddhism (as in all great mystical traditions).

Men and women of all races tend to be afflicted by the same delusive human condition, yet share the same Buddha Nature and the same sacred potential. To harm, reject or use other beings as inferior or alien is delusive denial of that shared nature and of a common humanity. It is to deny both wisdom and compassion.

The above root Dharma receives *confirmatory expression* in scriptures which refer directly to the social contexts of early Buddhism, such as the Sonadanda *sutta* on the indefensibility of brahminic supremacy. It is also evidenced by egalitarian and decentralized monastic practices which went against the current of an increasingly centralized and hierarchical society at that time. Thus, when members of the four castes 'begin to follow the doctrine and the discipline as propounded by the Buddha, they renounce different names of caste and rank and become members of one and the same society.'[169] The authority of each monk, for example, depended solely on his years of sangha membership, all important questions had to be resolved unanimously, and the Buddha emphasized the importance of working openly and patiently to resolve differences and disagreements (see also Chapter 31). Much of this egalitarian tradition has been preserved in the contemporary Theravada Buddhist sanghas. (The inclusion of women in the sangha was as socially scandalous then as is their continued exclusion today.)

So, it does seem reasonable to argue that gross social inequality and the oppression and exploitation of the poor and the powerless by the wealthy and powerful, economically, politically, racially, sexually and militarily, do violate the whole spirit of Dharma. There are indeed implications here for a Buddhist activism, but these must be understood in terms of the underlying spiritual significance of this egalitarianism, *from which* contemporary political implications flow. To read into the above meanings which spring from a blinkered contemporary secular awareness of values such as human equality is a secular reduction of Dharma. It is sometimes motivated by the belief that even in a secular age a little extra, 'spiritual', throw-weight can still be useful. But the truth is that the Buddha's revolutionary analysis of the *human* condition does carry *social* implications, and that the latter are immensely more radical than anything imaginable within the secular mentality.

Two subsidiary points need to be made about the above example of egalitarianism. The monastic practices were devised solely to be supportive of the spiritual search; they are no more than 'skilful and expedient means' (*upaya*) to that end. Typically, the secular mentality reads foreground importance into them; they portend a social revolution which has arguably only been postponed....In the second place, some people's spiritual potential is more readily realizable than others.' Spiritual maturity, authority and charisma will differ between individuals, and the ripening, whether fast or slow, is the precise opposite of that ego achievement through which equal secular social rights are made real for a person. The unequal burdens of kammaic conditioning are compassionately recognized as well as the sacred individual freedom to work to relinquish them. Spiritual egalitarianism therefore honours individual differences and the importance of each person being able to develop their potential in their own unique way and at the pace proper to them. Its emphasis is different from the populist egalitarianism of the contemporary mass society, with noteworthy social implications to be examined in Chapter 32.

# 20  *Objections and Problems*

The following objections and problems have been identified from scattered references in contemporary Buddhist writing and from points made at meetings and discusssions when the subject of Buddhist activism has come up. All of them have sufficient truth in them as to be useful reminders to Buddhists who have committed themselves to social activism. Moreover, differences of this kind among Buddhists should be seen as a potential source of strength rather than regretted. Discussion conducted in the right spirit can, at the least, keep differences open rather than closed off and give a strong sense of fellowship in the midst of diversity.

## 'MANYANA BUDDHISM'

This is the Buddhism of *mañana* − tomorrow. The term is altogether too dismissive for my liking, but too memorable to be discarded. It has been coined to describe the belief that a Buddhist should postpone all overt social action until such time as he or she may have fully opened to the wisdom and compassion without which truly selfless and effective intervention is impossible. Otherwise he or she will be caught up in the delusiveness of the social process and will themselves become part of the problem they set out to resolve. Thus, Milarepa, the eleventh-century Tibetan sage, warned that 'even without seeking to benefit others, it is with difficulty that works done even in one's own interest are successful. It is as if a man helplessly drowning were to try to save another man in the same predicament. One should not be over-anxious and hasty in setting out to serve others before one has oneself realized Truth in its fullness; to be so, would be like the blind leading the blind. As long as the sky endureth, so long will there be no end of sentient beings for one to serve; and to every one cometh the opportunity for such service. Till the opportunity come, I exhort each of you to have but the one resolve, namely to attain Buddhahood for the good of all living beings.'[170]

Therefore, according to this view, effort should be directed to 'dissolving the root of social evil within each individual'[171] instead of cutting back its branches by social action. This is to be effected by the quiet, radiant example and spiritual teaching of all sincere followers of the Way.

Underlying the 'manyana' position is the Quietist Fallacy noted in the previous chapter, which fails to take account of the historical institutionalization of delusion and the power of social kamma. Society is assumed to be no more than the aggregate of individuals comprising it. Manyana Buddhism seems to belong to a static and simple social order in which tomorrow will be much the same as today and in which any constructive social change other than through the occasional benevolence of the wealthy is inconceivable.

Most Buddhist activists do acknowledge the dangers in strong social engagement, of being pulled off-centre by headstrong partisanship and swept along by heartwarming idealisms. It is noteworthy, however, that there are fewer warnings from the traditionalists about the no less dangerous spiritual hazards of business enterprise, of professional ambition, and, of course, falling in love! Even the hazards of everyday morality in the mainstream of traditional Buddhist practice are common enough: helping other people can be very self-deceiving. A trenchant rebuttal of this 'perfectionist' position comes from Zen Master Robert Aitken, who does not believe that 'before one can work for the protection of animals, forests and small family farms − or for world peace − one must be completely realized, compassionate and peaceful. There is no end to the process of perfection, and so the perfectionist cannot begin Bodhisattva work. Compassion and peace are a practice, on cushions in the meditation hall, within the family, on the job, and at political forums. Do your best with what you have, and you will mature in the pocess.'[172]

For the person who has dedicated their life to the cultivation of spiritual awakening the possible seductions of, say, working in the peace movement are surely less than the dangers of becoming spiritually self-obsessed; some extrovert social action could even be a useful safeguard. Strongly associated with the ethereal egoism of pietism is that quietism which Zen Master Rinzai described as 'the darkest abyss of tranquillity, purity, serenity — this is indeed what one has to shudder at.'[173] It would seem that the Westerner approaching Buddhism has more need of that warning than had Master Rinzai's monks. There is the popular association of Buddhism with an other-worldly nirvana that lies beyond the sufferings of this illusory world. There is the highly developed individualism in the West and the poor sense of social solidarity; each individual is left to work out their 'salvation' in their own way (and to take up Buddhism does require considerable private enterprise). Buddhism as an intensely personal quietism has been emphasized by scholars like Max Weber: 'Salvation is an absolutely personal performance of the self-reliant individual. No one, and particularly no social community, can help him. The specific asocial character of genuine mysticism is here [in Buddhism] carried to its maximum.'[174] More recently in the West there is the growing need to shut off from an increasingly unbearable world. The American Catholic activist, Daniel Berrigan, warns that 'in the derangement of our culture, we see that people move towards contemplation *in despair*, even though unrecognized. They meditate as a way of becoming neutral — to put a ground between them and the horror about them....We have a terrible kind of drug called contemplation' (in Buddhist terminology, 'meditation').[175]

For the anxious, the introverted and the withdrawn, Buddhist practice may work as a veritable self-legitimization. By cutting off 'worldliness' and withdrawing from external commitments and emotionally demanding relations with others, they come to believe that they have 'transcended attachments' whereas in fact they have simply retreated from particular objects of attachment. All the unlived desire and attachment thus is transferred onto their 'spirituality', which is further exalted by a virtuous sense of 'self-renunciation'. Their 'spirituality' becomes very powerful: the traditional religious discipline is welcomed as a secure and orderly framework. A compulsive and meticulous neurosis performs 'religiously' all the exacting rules and prescriptions of a monastic or quasi-monastic practice, mistaking this for mindfulness practice. Thus in its extreme form quietism may extend to a whole neurotic syndrome of inverted spirituality, exemplified in a recognizable type of 'religious personality'.

It will be evident that what we have called 'manyana' Buddhism can have even more insidious snares and delusions than a socially engaged Buddhism, and especially when carried from its traditional settings into contemporary society. For a variety of legitimate reasons social activism will have little appeal for many Buddhists, but for those for whom it does it can provide a useful means of holding to the Middle Way in practice and of maintaining firm anchorage in a robust reality beyond the 'inner self' and its 'spiritual' preoccupations.

The activist/quietist polarization has caused concern also within Christian spirituality. Kenneth Leech argues that today 'part of the pathology of Western Christian life is the destruction of the essential unity of the mystical and the socio-political, the contemplative and the prophetic. Mysticism and politics are at best seen as alternative modes of discipleship, at worst as incompatible and ideological opposites.'[176] To the 'either/or' mentality militant mysticism appears confused, confusing, muddy and disconcerting –

in fact, a typically paradoxical reality that can either be delusively tidied up into 'this' or 'that' but not both, or truly suffered through and lived out. Simone Weil, whose intensely engaged spirituality makes her a mystic for all faiths and all seasons, characteristically declared that 'the contradictions the mind comes up against — these are the only realities — they are the criterion of the real. There is no contradiction in what is imaginary. Contradiction is the test of necessity. Contradiction experienced to the very depths of the being tears us heart and soul: it is the cross. When the attention has revealed the contradiction in something on which it has been fixed, a kind of loosening takes place. By persevering in this course we attain detachment.'[177]

The Satipatthana dictum that 'by serving others, I serve myself; by serving myself, I serve others' is the paradoxical beginning of a process in which self and other become increasingly indistinguishable — the dialectic of social activism that leads to the very heart of the Buddhadharma.

## HUMILITY

The importance of cultivating a spirit of humility in Buddhist training has been strongly emphasized in this book. It means opening up to situations and the grain of them so that they can speak for themselves, and softening up spiky self-opinionation. Problems that have balked us thus become more workable. 'Surrender yourself to what is, and be mindful of ego's craving to take hold of what is not' is a sound dictum of spiritual training which, however, has been confused and misappropriated by politicians and pietists down the ages. For it is a humility which is to be practised inside, not outside, the moral precepts, and as part of them. Humility is sharp-eyed and alert, and not to be confused with humiliation. The humility of mindfulness lives out the sufferings of humanity and shares them. Without evasion to left or right, it accepts the helplessness to relieve that whole ocean of suffering and yet accepts the unrefusable need to do so. When we have thoroughly suffered through our sense of helplessness and unclenched to our ultimate uselessness, from this comes the energy and faith to be of some real use. For a socially engaged spirituality, inner acceptance is the way to outer effectiveness. This paradox is explored further in the Epilogue.


DIVISIVENESS

There appear to be some who fear that any discussion of social activism within the Buddhist community could prove divisive and contentious and could create an atmosphere which would detract from the common spiritual pursuit. However, to insist that members concerned about the social engagement of Buddhism should keep quiet about it, or to proscribe their activity, would only create problems of another kind. On the contrary, working through these differences together can in many ways be beneficial to all, as was suggested at the beginning of this chapter. It would, however, be divisive for a Buddhist teaching and practice group or community to take up an official position on social activism or on controversial social issues, thereby formally committing its members to that viewpoint. Members who wish to organize themselves round some social commitment can form a group for that purpose (such as the Buddhist Peace Fellowships). The practice or other Dharma group or 'umbrella' organization thus remains open to all sincere practitioners of Buddhadharma, however they may interpret its social significance. Gary Snyder, when a Board Member of the American Buddhist Peace Fellowship, urged that 'Nothing should be done within any sangha to give any invidious feelings either way. Not only should it be possible for some members to be peace activists and some not to be, but there should be no feeling that one group feels superior to the other. They should be very open and accepted either way.'[178]

## SECULARIZATION

There is the apprehension lest social engagement should lead to some spiritual dilution, some secularization, of Buddhism. In the West the small beginnings so far in Buddhist activism do not support this view. In the East, however, where various forms of activism are well established, there do indeed appear to be some circles in which meditation flourishes in inverse ratio to vulgar Marxism. (There are others, on the other hand, where a strong emphasis is placed on balancing social activism with spiritual practice.)

Generally speaking I believe that the fear of secularization is not unfounded and that Buddhist activists need to be alert to it. Although this book was written primarily out of a wish to see Buddhism more socially engaged there is also in it a frequently expressed concern about activism opening the way to secularization. Secularization is a danger that has to be accepted and guarded against, but the alternative is a quietism which has nothing to say about much of the common experience of humanity and which is indifferent alike to its tragic social predicament and to its nobler social aspirations.

### HISTORICAL WARRANTY

It may further be claimed that the present-day interest in Buddhist activism has little warranty in scripture, history and tradition and is in effect a covert form of twentieth-century secularization grafted onto the traditional Dharma. Much of the evidence bearing upon this question — and particularly the scriptural evidence — will be found in Part Six, on the Asian experience. However, it will be useful to examine here certain phenomena which relate more directly to the question of historical warranty.

A good starting point is the following statement from Gary Snyder:

> Historically, Buddhist philosophers have failed to analyse out the degree to which ignorance and

suffering are caused or encouraged by social factors, considering fear-and-desire to be given facts
of the human condition. Consequently the major
concern of Buddhist philosophy is epistemology
and 'psychology' with no attention paid to historical or sociological problems.[179]

Although factually correct, statements like the above can be
misleading and they prompt clarification of two very
fundamental points.

In the first place, it is worth repeating that social analysis
and reconstruction were, and always will be, necessarily of
only secondary (though still important) significance in Buddhism. Buddhism's fundamental concern is existential: it is
about *human* liberation through entry into a higher level of
reality-consciousness. Ultimately successful social reconstruction remains dependent upon and secondary to this
'inconceivable liberation', though I believe it best proceeds
in parallel with it. A similar Snyder statement that 'The
mercy of the West has been social revolution; the mercy
of the East has been individual insight into the basic self/
void.'[180] is also worth saying but it could be taken as meaning
that what East and West are offering is equal and complementary. This is not so, and could tilt the understanding
towards secular inversion.

In the second place there are good *historical* reasons for the
sages' neglect of history and sociology.

Until the nineteenth century the social order in the Orient
evidently presented for many people much the same kind of
inevitability as the natural order. Oppressive rulers and
their wars and exactions together with periodic flood, pes-
tilence and famine were experienced along with the cycle of
birth, child rearing, old age and death as all part of the same
inevitable order of things, within which good and bad
fortune alternated. This has, however, probably been over-
stated by the 'Quietistic-Orient' school of thought; historically the rice-based societies have experienced much social

struggle and social criticism. The point is that the scale, character and pace of economic and technical change and of social conflict were not such as to stimulate profound societal enquiry or strongly to suggest the possibility of radical and volitional social transformation. The great question now for our global culture is how the insights and perspectives of Eastern spirituality can be disseminated and evolved so that wise and benevolent use can be made of the socio-technical capacity inherited from the Western industrial revolution.

Further to the above, Gary Snyder makes the well-founded suggestion that 'in the Occident, as early as the Greeks, the tradition of historical analysis began, and I think that Judaism and Christianity as history-centred religions contributed to this, a combination of Judaic and Hellinistic thought which came up with a tremendously important insight, and that is that societies are arbitrary and that history can be changed.'[181]

Within these limits there has certainly been in the Theravada Buddhism of South-East Asia a keen awareness of the importance of the social milieu, as we shall see in Part Six. Referring to the scriptural evidence, Robert Aitken reminds us that:

> The Buddha did condemn the caste system, and we find implicit in his teachings the futility of suppressing crime through punishment, the link between poverty and crime, and the importance of economic well-being for everyone. He did not live in a time like ours, when dangerous competition between various nations threatens to blow up the world. He was not faced with the probability of biological holocaust. He did not encounter the righteous imperatives of a feminist movement. I wonder what he would say today.[182]

The Mahayana Buddhism of the Far East remained a guest religion without deep and ancient popular roots to nourish a measure of political and economic autonomy, in contrast to

Taoism and Shintoism. It tended to make a virtue of its fidelity to government in order to survive politically and conserve its economic base.[183] Contrariwise, those rulers who did espouse Buddhism tended to associate religious faith with secular fealty. For example, the Seventeen Article Constitution of Shotoku Taishi (AD 604) demands both reverence to the Three Treasures of Buddhism *and* loyalty to the emperor: 'When you receive the imperial commands, fail not to carry them out scrupulously. Let there be a want of care in this matter, and ruin is the natural consequence.'[184] Both rich and poor patrons supported monks in order that their ascetic purity, rituals, devotion and religious orthodoxy should accumulate merit to the benefit of the laity. Interfering in such secular matters as political and economic morality would sully this purity and violate the contract; it was not what the laity paid for. Thus Buddhism in the Far East tended to be morally and politically dependent upon government and the patronage of the wealthy. It lacked the well-rooted countervailing power of the Theravada sangha, which could give or withhold the social legitimization which the secular ruler needed.

In the case of Zen Buddhism in Japan there has been a long history not of mere dependence and accommodation but of very active political and military support and complicity in the concerns of the secular establishment.

From the end of the thirteenth century to the Meiji Restoration in 1868 Rinzai Zen Buddhism in particular was closely associated with the martial arts of the samurai warrior class and absorbed its feudal values. The virtues of humility and self-renunciation became entangled and confused with those of feudal loyalty. Training in the finer points of killing became a 'skilful means' for teaching warriors mindfulness (or was mindful-ness a skilful means for improving their professional efficiency?). Thus Master Takuan Soho instructs a samurai:

> The uplifted sword has no will of its own, it is all of emptiness.... The man who is about to be struck

down is also of emptiness, as is the one who wields
the sword. . . . Do not get your mind stopped with
the sword you raise; forget about what you are
doing and strike the enemy. Do not keep your
mind on the person before you.[185]

This is not to detract from the meditative value of the martial
arts, but it is a long way from the First Precept and from the
unity of absolute and relative that is stressed in Zen. If this
mindful mayhem be a legitimate training then why not also,
say, the art of burglary?

There were, however, notable exceptions, including two
of the greatest Zen Masters. Although Zen Master Dogen
initially supported the feudal rulers of his time he was
subsequently disappointed by their behaviour, criticized
them for their lack of virtue, and sought to avoid dependence
upon them. He appears to have been exceptional in banning
weapons from his temple. Some six hundred years later,
Hakuin, one of the greatest of Zen Masters, was celebrated
not least for his manifold concern for the common people, at
a time when Zen was generally shifting its emphasis away
from the warrior class. Hakuin's forthright advice to various
feudal lords on the virtues of humane government are as
much Confucian as Buddhist in tone, but are nevertheless in
the historic mainstream of the Buddhist ideal of the Benevolent Ruler. Thus,'the Kingly Way is nothing more than to
give priority to dispensing benevolence, to rescue the common people with compassion, and thus to govern your
domain. In the world of today dispensing benevolence and
succouring the common people require no methods other
than to forbid luxury, regulate excessive expenditures and,
to touch upon a rather difficult subject these days, to reduce
the number of women in the inner chambers, and to simplify
all matters in general.' In the same letter the wealthy young
lord of Okayama Castle was told to abandon his income of a
million *koku* and his luxurious style of life. 'When the mind-
as-master is fixed with certainty, do not even for a moment
adopt the airs of a great ruler. . . . Clean up the garden,

change the water in the basins, and with a laughing face
wash the feet of the retainers' horses. Even if it be the work
of the most debased menial, practise and learn it.'[186]

After the Meiji Restoration feudalism was replaced by a
State dedicated to overseas expansion, and the Zen establishment found a new role in nurturing absolute obedience
to it and supporting imperial wars of conquest. In the 1930s
Zen Masters occupied themselves more and more with
giving military men Zen training, and during the Second
World War a large meditation hall was built in the heart of
Tokyo and used exclusively for that purpose. That the great
D. T. Suzuki himself was a strong supporter of Japanese
aggression on the mainland is evidence of the power of this
intoxication. The events of this military epoch in the history
of Zen have been chronicled by Ichikawa Hakugen, a Zen
priest and professor at Kyoto's Hanazono University, who,
in books like *The War Responsibility of Buddhists*, condemned
Zen's (and his own) collaboration with Japanese fascism. I
am indebted to Daizen Victoria for a paper which summar-
izes Hakugen's findings.[187] The following injunction by the
abbot of Hosshin-ji, Harada Sogaku (1870–1961) recalls that
of Takuan some three hundred years earlier:

> Forgetting [the difference between] self and others
> in every situation, you should always become
> completely one with your work. [When ordered to]
> march — tramp, tramp; [when ordered to] fire —
> bang, bang; this is the clear expression of the
> highest Bodhi-wisdom, the unity of Zen and
> war.[188]

The third phase of Zen's long social engagement with the
establishment is the extensive use of Zen training to instil
loyalty and disciplined efficiency into the employees of big
Japanese industrial corporations. This has been documented
by Daizen Victoria (above), with some bizarre examples of
spiritual training discipline used explicitly to serve the
needs of senior industrial management.

The emergence of a humanistic Zen in post-war Japan will be noted in Part Six. It is also interesting that in the American Buddhist community it is the Zen centres, with Masters like Robert Aitken and Philip Kapleau, which have been foremost in peace and human rights movements.

Tracing the long-drawn-out social engagement of Japanese Zen Buddhism through its successive phases has carried us well into the subject of Part Six on the Asian experience of Buddhist social activism. It is the most striking reminder in the history of Buddhism of the dangers of being drawn into active participation in morally corrupt secular concerns. In this case the involvement was with a conservative political and military establishment, but there have been examples in South-East Asia of equally unfortunate associations with revolutionary movements. In general, however, the vulnerable dependence of the oriental sangha on the political and economic establishment for patronage and protection forces it, at best, into a kind of 'apolitical' conservatism. This is the kind of situation that has developed in Thailand over the last fifty years.

Traditionally in Thailand rulers and governments have sought the blessing and support of the sangha in order to ensure legitimization in the eyes of the people. Sangha and government have been mutually dependent. However, the development of a sophisticated bureaucratic state has tipped the balance in favour of government, to which the sangha establishment is now subordinate at every level.[189,190,191] Hence the sangha has either kept silent on social and political matters or else its pronouncements have been pro-establishment. 'Consequently Buddhist teachings in Thai society have generally been contained at an individual level. Significant social messages such as the issue of peace and war lose their visibility in the eyes of Thai Buddhists.'[192] The Buddhist establishment is thus unprepared and unable to make effective and explicit response to the controversial pressures of multinational capitalism, communism, militarization, Western cultural infiltration and so on.

The whole of this chapter needs to be read in the light of the essential concern and priority of the sangha (or core of Buddhist teachers and practitioners) to maintain and disseminate intact the Buddhadharma at its fundamental, root-human level, and hence to make such unavoidable economic and political accommodations as may be necessary to support that end without too much compromising it. Having made such accommodation, an apolitical quietism or even seclusion behind monastery walls would be preferable to the moral corruption attendant on embracing wholeheartedly compulsive movements outside, whether conservative or radical. But sometimes it *has* been possible to give strong and positive social expression of the Dharma, most notably in the great Asokan tradition of Buddhist polity in South-East Asia, acting through the ideal of the benevolent ruler. And even in less favourable times and places individuals and small groups have borne public witness to the Dharma and spoken out against social injustice and military aggression. However, as we saw in Chapter 4, history has now moved into a new era, with previously unimaginable social imperatives and opportunities requiring a socially engaged spirituality as never before.

Since the end of the Second World War new currents of radical Buddhist activism have begun to flow in the East and there have been small but significant beginnings in the West. The remainder of Part Five and the whole of Part Six will be taken up with these developments, and from there we shall move on to perspectives for radical social reconstruction in the light of the Buddhadharma.

# 21 The Different Kinds of Engaged Buddhism

The accompanying diagram distinguishes the different kinds of social activism within the context of Buddhist practice.

The diagram cannot show how the different kinds of practice flow together. In particular what I have termed 'Inner' and 'Outer' Buddhism can no more be separated than the two sides of this page. Even a silent meditation retreat, for example, draws strength from the relationship with the teacher and from fellowship with the other retreatants.

In the West, so-called 'Inner Buddhism' is usually practised in a group or at a teaching centre within some specific Buddhist 'tradition', like Theravada, Zen or Tibetan Buddhism. Whether or not such groups or centres exist locally, there are many advantages in having an 'umbrella' Buddhist group in a specific town or district which can bring together people who are practising in the different traditions (perhaps by periodically travelling elsewhere), others who are unaffiliated, and also enquirers and beginners. Such a group will provide talks, discussions, meditation sessions and instruction in basic meditation, and general fellowship and support. It will present basic Dharma, will introduce the range of traditions represented in its membership, and will periodically host sangha and other outside speakers. A small lending library of printed materials and audiocassettes is a valuable adjunct to the work of such a group. Unlike a closely focused practice group in a specific Buddhist tradition, the town umbrella group provides a natural forum for discussion on the relevance of Buddhism to everyday

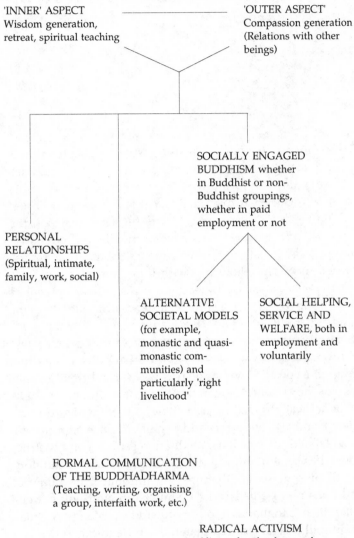

# BUDDHISM

'INNER' ASPECT
Wisdom generation,
retreat, spiritual teaching

'OUTER ASPECT'
Compassion generation
(Relations with other
beings)

SOCIALLY ENGAGED
BUDDHISM whether
in Buddhist or non-
Buddhist groupings,
whether in paid
employment or not

PERSONAL
RELATIONSHIPS
(Spiritual, intimate,
family, work, social)

ALTERNATIVE
SOCIETAL MODELS
(for example,
monastic and quasi-
monastic com-
munities) and
particularly 'right
livelihood'

SOCIAL HELPING,
SERVICE AND
WELFARE, both in
employment and
voluntarily

FORMAL COMMUNICATION
OF THE BUDDHADHARMA
(Teaching, writing, organising
a group, interfaith work, etc.)

RADICAL ACTIVISM
(directed to fundamental
institutional and social
changes, culminating in
societal metamorphosis)

Diagram to illustrate the context of Buddhist social activism situations at work, in the family and other relationships, and in the local community, as well as wider social issues. It can bring together people who want to undertake social action projects (particularly with Christian groups) and can introduce a Buddhist presence into local projects. The group provides a channel of representation for the small but growing Buddhist community in the town or district, in terms of interfaith activity, religious teaching in schools, town peace committee, hospital and hospice visiting, prison chaplaincy, displays and stalls at community events and in the public libraries, local press and radio and other demands made on a recognized local religious group that has come of age. The above is based on practical experience in such a group. It may suggest evangelical endeavour but in fact this is not so. Good publicity advertises what is on offer and if that is what is really needed then the effect is cumulative. In my experience the local community in due course makes its various demands on the Buddhist group, but it is not for the group to struggle for local prominence. To do so would negate the spirit of Dharma.

Socially engaged Buddhism is best practised if possible in some degree of association with fellow Buddhists who are working to the same ends, possibly through a loose organizational network. Such networks can provide support and increase effectiveness in conventional organizational terms (pooling of experience and knowledge, division of labour and specialization in publicity, research, co-ordination, education, lobbying). And as specifically Buddhist networks they can, through retreats, affinity groups, workshops and co-counselling, help individuals to remain centred amidst the pressures and distractions attendant on campaigning, lobbying and other social action.

Such social action networks and affinity groups are also, incidentally, valuable in dissolving any 'holier than thou' inclinations among Buddhists who had previously confined themselves to their own particular Dharma 'traditions'. Such networks may also include some of the many people of

Buddhistic persuasion who nevertheless do not regard themselves as formal 'card carrying' Buddhists. The presence
of such 'Buddhist Humanists', 'Buddhist Christians' and
'Buddhist Greens' makes for valuable fellowship and mutual
learning, as well as providing links with other social action
networks.

The Right Livelihood enterprises in the diagram are
Buddhist business enterprises (preferably co-operative)
which demonstrate positive, non-harmful ways of making a
living, and which may be based on a spiritual, live-in
community. Arguably such a community cannot generate
the spiritual concentration of a more cloistered kind of
community. On the other hand it does give financial autonomy and offers a socially integrated, economically working
model of Buddhism in action.

The outstanding examples are the Right Livelihood Co-
operatives of the Friends of the Western Buddhist Order,
mainly in Britain but with beginnings elsewhere.[193] Together
with the Communities of Order members and Friends, and
the teaching Centres, these co-operative businesses are intended both to be, and to prefigure, the 'New Society'.
Members of the teams which work each of these co-
operatives each have an equal share in the company and
equal voting rights. The success of the enterprise is the
responsibility of each member but he or she cannot sell up
or extract their share. There are over half a dozen such co-
operatives in the UK, and the movement is growing. Each
averages eight or nine members and is engaged in one or
more businesses, such as a vegetarian restaurant, a whole-
food store, building and gardening services, printing,
graphic design and candle-making.

In the FWBO making a living and working together are
seen as means of spiritual development, with time built in
for retreats, seminars and meditation. A senior Order member, *Dharmachari* Subhuti, argues that 'the self-sufficiency of
the spiritual community is vital. If it is not there is a danger
that it degenerates into a priesthood or has to compromise

with those who do support it as has happened in many cases in the East....Economics is power. The greater the economic independence of the New Society, the greater its ability to avoid compromise and to stand out fearlessly in its true colours.' The FWBO is critical of a Buddhism 'relegated to the status of an interesting hobby at the periphery of an otherwise "normal" life.'[194] It offers its members the opportunity to develop an all-inclusive Buddhist 'alternative culture'. 'The FWBO is seeking to bring about a "quiet revolution" by encouraging more and more people to set up for themselves a real alternative within the existing society. The more extensive and successful the alternative is the more beneficial will be its influence on the whole world. For Buddhists this is the only political programme which has any chance of success.'[195]

In the West, outside the FWBO, a common arrangement is for a group of lay Buddhists to install an ordained teacher in a large house which becomes also the residence for at least some of them and a Buddhist teaching centre both for them and the general public. Financial support comes from fees for classes, fund raising, and the pledged donations of supporters who are either in employment or receiving social security benefits. At least some of these live-in communities have, to my knowledge, examined the possibility of launching a co-operative or similar small business enterprise after the FWBO pattern. However, with limited capital (and credit-worthiness) such an undertaking can be very labour intensive, reducing the time and energy available both for servicing the teaching centre and for the group's own practice.

Right Livelihood communities of this kind in the USA appear, from the scattered evidence, to have had mixed experiences in this respect. The strong traditional vertical relationship between teacher and students can presumably detract from focusing energy horizontally in the work team, though I do not think this should necessarily be so. It is significant, however, that the FWBO relies on the low-key 'spiritual friendship' of its special brand of ordinands at local level, in lieu of the traditional teacher and student roles. The question of the spiritual Right Livelihood community evidently has quite widespread ramifications. The argument for such a community perhaps ultimately depends on whether there is sufficient commitment — and hence perhaps sufficient spiritual commitment — for people each to give up their own livelihood and concentrate their energies co-operatively, believing that this can be a strong form of spiritual practice and a living, public demonstration of a Buddhist alternative way of life. Certainly the idea of the Right Livelihood Community opens up the possibility of variant forms of 'monasticism' and could influence the changing relationship between laity and sangha examined in Chapter 18.

A second kind of social activism is helping in various ways people who are beyond our circle of family and friends (where help presumably comes more readily and informally). Such help may be given through paid employment in one of the caring professions and services, through work in a voluntary organization, or just through opportunities which can occur readily enough if we are open to them.

In some areas of helping it may be appropriate to develop a specifically Buddhist project or network, maybe because Buddhism has something distinctive to offer in that field. For example, help through official channels sometimes appears to be offered to social 'deviants' so as to enable them to conform to dominant (and by no means unquestionable) social values, regardless of real need and real respect for individual autonomy. It is a kind of social tidying up, 'dealing with a problem'. And some voluntary helping still has a patronizing smell about it.

An outstanding example is the Hanuman Foundation Dying Project in the USA. Founded by Ram Dass, its Buddhist director, Stephen Levine, writes that 'the purpose of the project is to create a context for the process of dying in which the work on oneself would be the central process for all involved — be they healers, helpers, families or the individuals approaching death. This collaborative endeavour is proving to be of immense benefit in transforming the dying process into one of spacious, living growth.'[196] In Britain the first steps to a Buddhist hospice project were being taken at the time of writing.

'Angulimala' was founded in Britain in 1985 as a Buddhist prison chaplaincy organization, to make available 'facilities for the teaching and practice of Buddhism in Her Majesty's Prisons'. A team of officially accredited 'Visiting Ministers' is being built up, and Angulimala liaises with government prison chaplaincy officials and advises on Buddhist matters. Quarterly day retreats are held for members and projects include after-care services, an internal newsletter for and by interested prisoners, a pen-friend scheme, and the provision of appropriate reading matter. Angulimala has a monk as spiritual director and is broadly based across the different Buddhist traditions and schools.

To the extent it can be an authentic giving of self, helping is very much the prime Buddhist virtue of *dana*, of giving of emotional, mental and physical energy, of time and of money. When Prince Gotama, the future Buddha, escaped from his father's palace for a day in order to experience what the world outside was like he was deeply moved by the sight of death and disease. Today we live in societies which are so complex and compartmented that many people are insulated from direct awareness of much of the affliction that is experienced in them, and some special effort has to be made to get in touch with that reality. Moreover these are societies in which it is possible to undertake much valuable social action at arm's length, by writing, publicizing, debating, petitioning, lobbying, demonstrating and so on. Such activity is necessary, is often valuable, and may be highly effective. It does, however, have the disadvantage that because it is insulated in one's head, one's group, one's project or movement, it may not pull the self out of the self as does the real, alien *taste* of affliction (or hatred or violence).

William Blake put it more bluntly: 'He who would do good must do it in minute particulars. General good is the plea of the hypocrite, scoundrel and flatterer.' Coming into close personal contact with human affliction can be a disturbing yet valuable experience if we can truly open to it. It is important, therefore, for Buddhist activists to go out and get their hands dirty, their equanimity ruffled, and their tacit judgements upset. It can be helpful to other people, too.

It will be evident that helping is rich in its opportunities for self-deception. When you are helping me, who are you really helping most, you or me? Are you not perhaps helping me at my expense, since you need me to affirm your own tacit superiority and virtue? In David Brandon's experience 'the greed of giving' (as D. H. Lawrence called it) can become a form of 'restless energy', 'a drug whose victims need the continuing contact with recipients to give added meaning to their lives'. Hence 'we have continually to examine the sources of our caring energy. In particular, the beginning of compassion both to oneself and to others is in decreasing the number of judgements that are made on others — if only I could throw away my urge to trace patterns on your heart, I could really see you.'[197]

The 'radical activism' identified in the diagram forms the main subject of this book. Radical activism is concerned with fundamental changes in social policies, practices and institutions in areas such as disarmament and defence policy, Third World poverty, environmental protection, women's rights, prisoners of conscience and the persecution of ethnic minorities. It is noteworthy that issues such as mass unemployment, cuts in social services, extensive poverty and severe pressures on civil rights which are increasingly prominent in the industrialized countries have not received much attention from Western Buddhists (nor from the Green movement with which they tend to associate themselves). They seem at present to be more concerned about the future of the Amazonian rain forests than the plight of the people of their inner cities, though the two are linked and equally significant. Dislike of the party-political associations may account for this strong preference, though this has not inhibited Christian leaders from speaking out loud and clear on these issues, and being widely respected for doing so. Radical activism must inevitably be to some extent involved in the questions of power and conflict, confrontation and partisanship, and the *antithetical bondings* and *weighted polarizations* discussed in the first half of this book. Buddhist activists have to find ways of coming to terms with these phenomena without being taken over by them and adding to the problems they set out to resolve.

Ultimately Buddhist radical activism is about the total socio-spiritual metamorphosis discussed in Part Eight. It is concerned with the creation of a global society free of war, poverty, curable disease and the many forms of oppression and exploitation, through the evolution of a compassionate and co-operative common-wealth. Above all, such a Good Society will aim to provide conditions of freedom and responsibility favourable to the evolution of consciousness towards the Great Liberation.

Buddhist Peace Fellowships have been established in the USA,[198] Britain and Australia[199] and are affiliated to the International Fellowship of Reconciliation. They are concerned not only with contributing to the peace movement but also with the other kinds of radical peacemaking. Typical are the aims of the British Buddhist Peace Fellowship, adopted in April 1984:

1. To make clear public witness to the Buddha way as a way of peace and protection of all beings; to be actively concerned with the roots of violence arising from greed, pride and ignorance; and to work towards ending the exploitation of all beings everywhere.
2. To raise peace and ecological concerns among Buddhists and to promote projects which express those concerns.

3. To share the Buddhist perspective of peace-making and the Buddhist way of peace in the wider peace movement and with the general public.

4. To develop a distinctive Buddhist way of non-violence, relating the rich traditional Buddhist teachings to our present global situation; to develop forms of activity which bear witness to this; and to awaken ourselves to our own nature, and that of others, in respect of personal and social violence.

5. To serve as liaison to, and enlist support for, existing national and international Buddhist peace and ecology movements, and to provide Buddhist fellowship in action.

6. To work to end the persecution of Buddhism and Buddhists.

The Buddhist Peace Fellowships are decentralized networks; the nine local 'chapters' of the American BPF, for example, can take on particular local, national or global concerns quite independently, co-ordinating through a national Board, office and newsletter.

The total number of Buddhists in the West is, of course, quite small (though remarkably difficult to estimate), and the number interested in social activism in the USA and Britain could probably only be counted in hundreds. Nevertheless an encouraging start has been made and it seems certain that socially engaged Buddhism will gather momentum in the West.

# 22   The 'Politics of Enlightenment' of Asoka and Nagarjuna

Part Six, on the Asian experience, has to serve two specific purposes beyond what its general title might suggest.

In the first place it identifies some characteristics of a Buddhist radical activism (itemized at the start of Chapter 24). These are particularly derived from the political philosophy of the ideal benevolent Buddhist monarch, as examined in this chapter, and from the experience of Buddhist grass-roots activism in contemporary South-East Asia.

Secondly, Part Six enlarges on the theme of Buddhist modernism — of updated interpretations of Buddhism, and especially engaged Buddhism — which was introduced in Chapter 19. First the background of post-colonial revolutionary nationalism in South-East Asia is introduced in Chapter 23, with some notes on developments in the Mahayana countries of Japan, Tibet and China (Chapter 25). Then, in Chapter 26, there is a critique of what is argued to be a secularized and reductive Buddhist modernism which has appeared in certain quarters. This is contrasted with the 'transcendantal modernism' which characterizes the present book.

This book has been written by a Westerner out of a Western social and cultural context. Eastern Buddhism has a different flavour, which cannot easily be distinguished from the different cultures in which it has grown over the centuries. And in this century it has been shaped by, and has interacted with, the phenomena of colonialism, nationalism, Western cultural influences, neo-colonial industrialization and 'development', communist power and American-inspired militarization.

Today the Theravada Buddhism of South-East Asia continues to exercise great public influence in Thailand and Sri Lanka. In Burma, which struggles to maintain an economic and social self-reliance, the political influence of the sangha appears now to be marginal. Vietnam, Laos and Kampuchea (Cambodia) are under Communist control and Buddhism exists there only on sufferance and in a much reduced state.

Theravada Buddhism has a long and enduring tradition of political and social involvement stemming from the social teachings of its Pali scriptures (Chapter 23). In particular, the achievements and pronouncements of the great Indian Buddhist emperor Asoka (third century BC), who was perhaps in his time the world's most powerful ruler, have been influential up to the present day. These 'politics of enlightenment' were amplified by Nagarjuna, greatest of the monk-scholars of Indian Mahayana Buddhism, whose 'counsels' are summarized in the second part of this chapter.

Asoka's policies and exhortations to his subjects are carved in rock as a series of edicts. In these Professor Robert Thurman has identified the 'operative principles of the politics of enlightenment' (using that word in the transcendental sense rather than with the eighteenth-century European meaning). He groups the Edicts under the following principles:

1. Individual transcendentalism;
2. Nonviolence (*ahimsa*);
3. Emphasis on education and on religious pluralism;
4. Compassionate welfare policies;
5. Political decentralization.[200]

1. The first of these principles is that both personal and public well-being depends on the personally undertaken transformation of one's own personality. This is the foundation of the politics of enlightenment. Thus Rock Edict XIII proclaims that 'It is difficult to achieve happiness, either in this world or the next, except by intense love of Dharma

[that is, spiritual truth], intense self-examination, intense obedience, intense fear of sin and intense enthusiasm.' Therefore Rock Edict VII declares that 'My officials act in accord with (these) rules: to govern according to the Dharma, to administer justice according to the Dharma, to advance the people's happiness according to the Dharma, and to protect them according to the Dharma.'

2. As to nonviolence, after his conversion to Buddhism Asoka renounced war as an instrument of policy and called upon his neighbours to follow his example. Rock Edict IV claimed that the emperor's inculcation of the spirit of non-violence amongst his subjects 'has increased beyond anything observed in many hundreds of years [with] abstention from killing animals and from cruelty to living beings.' Asoka did, however, find it necessary to retain the death penalty in extreme cases, though he also introduced an appeals procedure.

3. In working for the spread of the Dharma, Asoka distinguished between Dharma as transcendent truth and universal morality on the one hand and on the other the several specific religions (*sasana*) through which it was variously expressed in his realm. These included that of the sangha (Buddhism) to which he was personally dedicated. (But note that 'the Dharma' usually denotes Buddhism, as it normally does in this book.) So, in Rock Edicts VII and XII Asoka 'wishes members of all faiths to live everywhere in his kingdom. For they all seek mastery of the senses and purity of mind.... Growth in the qualities essential to religion in men of all faiths may take many forms, but its root is in guarding one's speech to avoid extolling one's own faith and disparaging the faith of others improperly, or, when the occasion is appropriate, immoderately. The faiths of others all deserve to be honoured for one reason or another. By honouring them, one exalts one's own faith and at the same time performs a service to the faith of others.... The objective of these measures is the promotion of each man's particular faith and the glorification of the Dharma.

4. In pursuance of Buddhist ethics Asoka established medi-

cal and veterinary services, built rest houses and hospices for the poor and sick, introduced programmes of public works and agricultural improvement, and appointed public welfare officers (Commissioners of Dharma). In Rock Edict II he states that these services have been inaugurated not only among his own subjects but also in the Tamil kingdoms of the south and in the lands of the Greek King Antiochus.

5. Whilst exercising strong personal authority Asoka nevertheless delegated considerable autonomy to his provincial governors, relying on the loyalty of his subjects to check any misuse of such local power.

Asoka's policies are very much in the spirit of the social teachings of the Theravada scriptures and have been strongly presented — but out of their transcendental context — by reductive modernists like Professor N.V. Banerjee, for whom it is 'evident that Buddhism was full of suggestions the implementation of which could transform even a kingdom into a sort of socialist state with a more or less humanistic foundation.'[201]

In a totally different vein is the sober though not unsympathetic conclusion of Professor A. L. Basham that 'Carried away by his new faith, [Asoka] increasingly lost touch with reality, until ultimately he was dethroned and the great Mauryan empire broke up, largely as the result of his intensely moral but thoroughly unrealistic convictions.' Nevertheless, whereas Buddhism was 'comparatively insignificant' in the two centuries before Asoka, after his reign it began to flourish extensively. Basham also suggests that the urbane humanity of the Gupta era in Indian history owed something to Asoka. Whatever substance his policies achieved however, it is certain that Asoka created a powerful myth which is still influential for a socially engaged Buddhism.[202]

Asoka has misleadingly been called the Constantine of Buddhism because he is assumed to have established Buddhism as a state religion. With him begins the long enduring tradition of the *cakkavatti* or enlightened ruler.

According to this notion the chariot of state should run upon the two wheels of power (*anacakka*) and righteousness (*dhamma cakka*), with the authority of the ruler, the *dhamma-raja*, legitimized by the monastic sangha. The latter were the king's influential advisers and, in a sense, were power sharers. Church and State were separate authorities sustained by separate hierarchies, and although Buddhism was the paramount religion it was traditional to recognize and tolerate others. Just as rulers sometimes intervened to purge the sangha of malpractices and even of heresies, so also was the sangha sometimes instrumental in the deposition of unrighteous monarchs. On this pattern great Buddhist civilizations were established in Sri Lanka, Siam, Burma, Cambodia and Indonesia.

It is noteworthy in passing that although the Theravada social theorists have made Asoka their own, in Basham's opinion it was unclear what form of Buddhism he practised, though it was evidently 'different from any form existing nowadays'.

A less well-known Buddhist social model is to be found in the advice given by Nagarjuna, greatest of the Indian Mahayana sages and scholars, to his friend King Udayi of south central India, some five centuries after Asoka. Nagarjuna's *Jewel Garland of Royal Counsels* is arguably more significant for engaged Buddhism than Asoka's reign, in that Nagarjuna's social perspectives are those of one of the most insightful personalities of world religions. Moreover, Nagarjuna writes out of the supposedly 'mystical', apolitical Mahayana tradition of Buddhism. Nagarjuna's *Counsels* are also valuable in that some two-thirds of the text are taken up with clarifying what Robert Thurman calls 'the first principle of Buddhist social ethics: individualist transcendentalism'. The work of personal transformation as the basis of social change was similarly emphasized in Asoka's Rock Edicts, and it is noteworthy that in his paper 'Guidelines for Buddhist social activism based on Nagarjuna's *Jewel Garland of Royal Counsels*', Thurman is able to distinguish much the same basic principles as are evident in the Edicts.[203] I am obliged to Professor Thurman for his presentation of the *Counsels*, from which the following notes are taken.

'Individualist transcendentalism' is emphasized by Thurman in contrast to the structural and collectivist perspective on purposive social change which is currently dominant. The ruler and his officials are urged by Nagarjuna to strive to awaken to a selfless understanding of society and its needs. 'The bodhisattva man of action can and must be responsible for intuitive wisdom, and so Nagarjuna presents the king with a quintessence of the methods for developing the wisdom basis of effective social action.'

Next Nagarjuna introduces the nonviolent principle in social activism, namely, in Thurman's paraphrase, 'revulsion from lusts, restraint of aggressions, vanity of possessions and power'. Violence begets violence, so Nagarjuna condemns capital punishment and advocates the rehabilitative treatment of prisoners. 'Just as unworthy sons are punished out of a wish to make them worthy, so punishment should be enforced with compassion and not from hatred or concern with wealth. Once you have examined the fierce murderers and judged them correctly, you should banish them without killing or torturing them.'

Since the goal of society is to provide favourable conditions for each person to evolve towards awakening to his or her true nature, education to that end must be the most important function of government. This is not, however, a call for mass Buddhist indoctrination. Nagarjuna, like Asoka, recognizes the validity of different routes to selfless enlightenment and he, also, used Dharma to signify spiritual truth in general, and not the specifically Buddhist path to its realization. He repeatedly argues that 'belief systems', 'dogmatic views', 'closed convictions' and 'fanatic ideologies', far from being the answer to anything are themselves the sicknesses that require to be remedied.

Fourthly, Nagarjuna advocates much the same kind of welfare state as did Asoka, and with the same concern for animals as for human beings. 'Cause the blind, the sick, the humble, the unprotected, the destitute, and the crippled, all equally to attain food and drink without omission.'

The ideal of a Buddhist political ruler concerned purposively, but without coercion, to establish a Buddhist culture in his realm in conjunction with the sangha, and with various institutions for the public welfare, was persistent and widespread. Thus, in Japan, four centuries after Nagarjuna and almost a millennium after Asoka, when Prince Shotoka proclaimed Buddhism as the state religion he not only made provision for a monastic sangha but also established a hospital, a dispensary, and an asylum for orphans and old people.

# 23 Post-Colonial Nationalism and Buddhist Modernism

Just as the Buddhist culture of South-East Asia was oppressed and denied by the military, religious and commercial powers of Western colonialism, so did Buddhism come to be strongly identified with the national struggle against colonialism. And in the post-colonial period Buddhism helped to restore national self-confidence and to impart a sense of identity. It provided a distinctive countervailing force against the infiltration of a prestigious Western culture and, later, against the pressures and attractions of communism. However, to some extent it did this by adopting Western secular and rationalist perspectives and thus undercutting its own spiritual roots.

Under U Nu in Burma and S.W.R.D. Bandaranaike in Sri Lanka Buddhism came near to being established as the state religion and it seemed for a brief period that the Asoka tradition would be updated in the building of a Buddhist socialist society. The highwater mark was the Sixth Great [Theravadin] Buddhist Council in 1954 which, it was believed, would inaugurate an historic Buddhist revival. With the collapse of empire, Christianity and Western culture were assumed to be on the wane and Buddhism, with its humanistic and scientific temper, was seen as the prospective religion of a new global era.

In the event, both the U Nu and Bandaranaike regimes came to an abrupt end. In Burma, provoked by a termagant (and even riotous) section of the sangha, the military regime in effect excluded all explicit Buddhist influence from the

political scene. However, in Sri Lanka, and even more so in
Thailand (which had escaped the trauma of colonialism),
Buddhism remains a major unifying and stabilizing influence in national life. In both countries the sangha hierarchy
is, in effect, part of the political establishment, implicitly in
Sri Lanka and explicitly in Thailand. In Sri Lanka it has,
arguably, been compromised politically through a tendency
to identify Buddhism exclusively with the interests of the
Sinhalese community against the Hindu Tamils. It has also
failed to offer any national and cultural alternative to government commitment to a particularly gross kind of neo-colonial
'development'. In Thailand the sangha, from being one
wheel of the chariot of traditional Buddhist polity, has come
more to resemble a cog in the state machine, as has been
explained in Chapter 20. In recent years the Thai government has attempted, not altogether successfully, to exploit the
traditional popular prestige of the monks by involving them
in government community development projects, counter-
insurgency, and questionable national and cultural integration schemes for ethnic minorities. Research into the
effect of these policies suggests that 'the presupposition that
the monks are the best agents for national development and
integration with consequent political modernization seems
unjustified. On the contrary, the use of Buddhism and the
sangha to serve political ends...may in fact bring undesir-
able consequences for the sangha's position and for
Buddhism.'[204]

In the heady post-colonial period, Buddhist intellectuals
were concerned to present the Dharma as a national, humanistic, democratic, and even socialist ideology for today.
Whilst having all the authority and tradition of a great world
religion, and a distinctively oriental one at that, Buddhism
was at the same time claimed to be no less rational, scientific
and 'modern' (and therefore *relevant*) than either the technological capitalism or the Marxian scientific socialism which
challenged it. Thus Venerable Walpola Rahula, a celebrated
Sri Lankan scholar-monk, proclaims that 'Buddhism arose in

India as a spiritual force against social injustices, against degrading superstitious rites, ceremonies and sacrifices; it denounced the tyranny of the caste system and advocated the equality of all men; it emancipated woman and gave her complete spiritual freedom.'[205]

This modernism is well illustrated in the syncretic 'Buddhist socialism' set out below, whose major ingredients are ideas associated with the classical Asokan era combined and synthesized with those deriving from Marxism and European socialism. Their origins are post-colonial Burmese, but they could equally have been Sri Lankan. Neither are they now merely of historic interest. They exemplify a secularly inclined Buddhist activism which still has a following among both monks and laypeople, particularly in Sri Lanka, and which contrasts with the activism of engaged spirituality introduced in the next chapter. The six 'ingredients' are, however, a very mixed bag; for example, (a), (c) and to some extent (f) are free of the secular inversion affecting the other paragraphs.

(a) The political objective of Asokan polity was that the populace be ensured material satisfaction and prosperity in order that Buddhist morality and religion may flourish.

(b) The organization of the sangha is democratic, particularly the rule that property belongs to the sangha as a collectivity. The sangha is thus a microcosm of an egalitarian socialist society, and provides a model for the larger society.

(c) The 'illusion of self' which is the greatest bar to the attainment of salvation feeds on private property which in turn encourages greed, acquisitiveness, domination and exploitation. Socialism, in so far as it does away with private property helps the elimination of the illusion of self.

(d) [This paragraph refers to the social contract found in the *Agganna Sutta* as a 'theory of govern-

ment consistent with socialism and democracy'.
KJ]
(e) Buddhism espouses 'materialism' (together with
the notion of 'process' and 'flux' and impermanence) just as Marxism does and just as modern
science does. These three systems are consonant
whereas Christianity in espousing totalitarian
theism is unscientific, and antagonistic to Marxism
and to democracy.
(f) Socialism in so far as it leads to deliverance from
economic suffering is the 'lower truth'; Buddhism
in delivering man from spiritual suffering is the
higher truth. Both are related, for Buddhism en-
compasses socialist truth. Escape from economic
want is a prior condition for spiritual illusion ['enlightenment'? KJ]. Thus socialism and Buddhism
are complementary and stand in an hierarchical
relation.[206]

This kind of reductive modernism in my view overem-
phasizes and misinterprets the significance of the social
teachings of the Pali canon, as we shall see further in
Chapter 26. Concerned to make Buddhism manifestly relevant to the social and political requirements of the post-
colonial era, these modernists tend to read the scriptures in
terms of certain dominant contemporary ideas, as if they
were originally a programme for social reform; their over-
arching spiritual and existential context and significance is
lost beneath a burgeoning humanistic rationalism. Meanings
are read into them which are at best arguable and at worst
extravagant and tendentious.

Buddhist texts which appear to have a strong social significance have conveniently been brought together and interpreted by Dr Siddhi Butr-Indr of Chiang Mai University,
Thailand. Thus, for him, *metta*, which traditionally means
loving-kindness, amity and harmony, becomes 'the development of sound pacific relationships in society'.[207] Quoting

several examples of this kind of exegesis, David Gosling concludes that they are 'bound to create the overall impression of arbitrariness. However, the important point. . .is that modern ideas are influencing both what people believe and the manner in which they interpret the historical texts.'[208]

Similarly, *A Green Buddhist Declaration* issued in 1984 by 'sixty Buddhist scholars, monks and laypeople' claims that 'the *Aggañña Sutta* denies a racial basis for social hierarchy, pointing to the role of private property and differences between the sexes in the co-evolution of delusion and deluding social structures.'[209] If the twentieth-century radical looks hard enough and needs hard enough to find all that in this fanciful and ingenious Buddhist book of genesis then I suppose he will succeed in doing so.

None of this is to deny that there are many unequivocal passages in the scriptures which do provide legitimate pointers to a socially engaged Buddhism, always provided that they are not read out of their historical context and they are seen in relation to the overall soteriological purport of the scriptures. There are, for instance, numerous passages (for example, in the *Mahavagga* and *Catukkanipata* of the *Anguttara-nikaya*) urging followers of the Buddha to 'live for the welfare of the many.' There is also some keen awareness of the effects of economic conditions upon social behaviour, as in the *Cakkavatti Sihanada Sutta* (*Digha-nikaya*): 'Thus, from provision not being made for the poor, poverty, stealing, violence, murder, lying, evil-speaking and immorality become widespread.'[210] Similarly, the *Kutadanta Sutta* warns that punitive treatment of such criminality is unlikely to be effective in the long run and that measures to promote social well-being are to be preferred:

> Now there is one method to adopt to put a thorough end to this disorder. Whoever there may be in this royal realm who devote themselves to keeping cattle and cultivating the soil, to them let His Majesty give food and seed corn. Whoever there may be in

this royal realm who devote themselves to trade, to them let His Majesty give capital. Whoever there may be in this realm who devote themselves to government service, to them let His Majesty give wages and food. Then those men, each following his own business, will no longer harass the realm; His Majesty's revenue will go up; the country will be quiet and at peace; and the people will be pleased and happy, and with their children in their arms will dwell with open doors.[211]

It will be recalled that in Chapter 19 reservations were expressed about the legitimacy of using scriptural exegesis at its face value to carry the entire weight of the rationale for a socially engaged Buddhism. The further discussion here is carried forward to Chapter 26, which deals more specifically with the problem of Buddhist modernism.

# 24    *Grass-Roots Activism in Sri Lanka, Thailand and Vietnam*

By the end of the 1960s it was clear that the Buddhist socialist modernism of the previous chapter had failed to engage effectively with the political and social process, notwithstanding the promise it had shown at the high noon of post-colonialism. However, by the 1960s another and very different kind of Buddhist activism was evident in South-East Asia, which may aptly be described as a *transcendental radicalism*. Although it took different forms in Sri Lanka, Thailand and Vietnam it does nevertheless display certain common characteristics, and these suggest the following working principles for a Buddhist radical activism. These will be exemplified in the remainder of this chapter, and will be carried forward, together with the Asoka and Nagarjuna principles, to Part Eight of the book as input to a Buddhist strategy for social transformation towards a 'Good Society'.

In the first place, this radicalism is *transcendental* in that radical social change is necessarily and explicitly based on personal development within a spiritual context, that is, through mindfulness, meditation and retreat, but also through trying to make a work of art of personal and group relations and following a lifestyle of the kind suggested, for example, by the Tiep Hien precepts quoted in Chapter 15. Conventional political radicalism is *transcended* in that radical personal change is also included as an essential part of the process of fundamental social change. For most people and in the short term this development may in spiritual terms be quite modest: just becoming a little more human. But this is nonetheless significant, as is also the overarching spiritual perspective within which it takes place. This engaged spirituality is concerned with creating at the same time social conditions which will both relieve affliction and also support and foster personal growth.

In the second place, transcendental radicalism achieves social change through grass-roots initiatives of individuals and groups working in a spirit of community self-help and self-reliance. This reflects the tradition of self-reliance in Buddhist practice to which we referred in Chapter 8. Emphasis is upon the development of networks of such groups and communities and the avoidance of hierarchical élites. Those who do the thinking also implement the decisions and those who implement the decisions also do the spade-work and take responsibility for it.

In the third place it follows that there is much emphasis on many different kinds of active learning, particularly from practical experience, and in a group, and through open dialogue, both for personal development and community and social development.

In the fourth place, transcendental radicalism is marked by its use of positive and active nonviolent strategies, which recognize the common humanity of the adversary and his dignity and autonomy. Change can only come through creative interaction (both inside and outside the movement) and the avoidance of negative forms of coercion even if they stop short of physical violence. These ideas are exemplified below, but are more fully examined in Part Seven. In particular, to appropriate the Buddhadharma to fortify one's own racial or national identity is grievously to pervert the Buddhadharma.

Fifthly, this is a conservative radicalism which seeks to foster all that is best in traditional culture and practice, and particularly the sense of community, regional and ethnic identity. Change has to be authentic and organic in character, from the roots, rather than imposed, mechanistic and manipulative. The old way of doing things, or some adaptation or evolution of it, may still be the best way. There is a particular concern to pioneer a Third Way of social and cultural development alternative to either Western capitalist-style 'development' or communist-style socialism.

Sixthly, transcendental radicalism is pluralist, nonsectarian, fraternal and open-minded in its relations with other belief systems, whether secular or religious, which share the same broad human values and concerns.

Seventhly, this engaged spirituality thinks globally as well as acting locally, and is particularly concerned with communication and co-operation between people of the First and Third Worlds.

## SRI LANKA

Sarvodaya, which means 'the awakening and welfare of all', refers to spiritually inspired, rural self-development movements in India and Sri Lanka. The Sarvodaya movement of post-colonial India attempted unsuccessfully to implement the Gandhian ideal of a network of autonomous village commonwealths, and Gandhi's heir, Jayaprakash Narayan followed his example of mass civil disobedience when the Congress government frustrated that ideal. By contrast, the Sri Lanka movement evolved in the Asokan tradition of a just relationship between village communities on the one hand and on the other a State which was perceived to be comparatively benevolent.[212]

Sarvodaya began in Sri Lanka in 1958, when a young teacher, A.Y. Ariyaratne, encouraged his students to organize a fortnight 'holiday work camp' in a destitute village. The students worked closely with the villagers and were concerned to learn what they themselves perceived as their needs and problems. Other schools and colleges followed this example, and a village self-help movement emerged, outside the official rural development programme. During the 1970s training centres for community co-ordinators and specialists were established with help from overseas aid agencies. These schemes included a programme for the systematic training and involvement of Buddhist monks, who traditionally are highly influential in village life. Over two and a half million people, living in 7000 of Sri Lanka's 23,000 village communities are now involved in Sarvodaya, aided by some 2000 monks. The Village Awakening Councils enjoy programme and budget autonomy, but receive much specialist support from area and regional centres backed by extensive training programmes. Projects include roads, irrigation works, preschool facilities, community kitchens, retail co-operatives and the promotion of village handicrafts (though impact on agriculture appears to have been disappointing). Joanna Macy describes the typical *shramadana* or voluntary co-operative work project as being 'like a combination of road gang, town meeting, vaudeville show and revival service — and these many facets build people's trust and enjoyment of each other.'[213]

Ariyaratne, now the movement's President, emphasizes that 'The chief objective of Sarvodaya is personality awakening.'[214] The root problem of poverty is seen as being a sense of personal and collective powerlessness. And 'awakening' is to take place not in isolation but through social, economic and political interaction. Personal awakening is seen as being interdependent with the awakening of one's local community, and both play a part in the awakening of one's nation and of the whole world.

The spiritual precondition for all-round social development is kept in the forefront through Sarvodaya's creative interpretation of traditional Buddhist teachings in forms which can be understood and experienced by people collectively and in social terms. Thus, the shared suffering of a community, the poverty, disease, exploitation, conflict and stagnation, is explored together by the members as is also the suffering experienced by each one of them. But, crucially, this suffering is shown to have its origins in individual egocentricity, distrust, greed and competitiveness, which demoralizes and divides the community and wastes its potential. In place of the corrupted traditional meaning of kamma as 'fate', Ariyaratne emphasizes the original Buddhist teaching. 'It is one's own doing that reacts on one's own self, so it is possible to divert the course of our lives.... [Once we understand that] inactivity or lethargy suddenly transforms into activity leading to social and economic development.'[215]

Similarly, each of the practices comprising the traditional Buddhist Eightfold Path is amplified socially. For example, Macy quotes a Sarvodaya trainer:

> Right Mindfulness — that means stay open and alert to the needs of the village.... Look to see what is needed — latrines, water, road.... Try to enter the minds of the people, to listen behind their words. Practise mindfulness in the shramadana camp: is the food enough? are people getting wet? are the tools in order? is anyone being exploited?[216]

The traditional Buddhist virtues and precepts provide guidelines for joint endeavour and a significant vocabulary in the open discussions which are the lifeblood of the movement. Thus, *dana* had come to be identified with monastic almsgiving, but Sarvodaya extends it back to its original wider meaning of sharing time, skills, goods and energy with one's community and demonstrates the liberating power of sincere and spontaneous generosity to dissolve barriers between individuals and groups. Similarly, the meaning of the 'Four Sublime Abodes' has been extended socially without, however, losing their original spirit. So, *metta* (loving-kindness) refers also to the active concern for others and refraining from any kind of coercion. *Karuna* (compassion) refers to active and selfless giving of energy in the service of others. *Mudita* (rejoicing in others' good fortune) refers to the feeling of well-being experienced when one has been able to make a tangible contribution to one's community.

*Upekkha* (equanimity) refers to independence from the need to achieve results and obtain recognition. It is the Buddhist remedy against burn-out of campaigning energies. Macy quotes a District Co-ordinator: '*Upekkha* is dynamite. It is surprising the energy that is released when you stop being so attached. . . . You discover how much you can accomplish when nothing is expected in return.'[217]

All these inspirational guidelines are presented in symbols, slogans, posters, murals, songs and stories, not as catechisms and commandments but as pointers and as tools of analysis. Above all, they are made fully meaningful through the practice of meditation, which is incorporated into Sarvodaya meetings and training sessions.

Sarvodaya aims at an economy of modest sufficiency, employing appropriate low and middle techonology, with equitable distribution of wealth and concern for the quality of the environment. Local and national cultural identities and diversity are respected and nurtured, and it does in fact seem that the movement makes its strongest impact in the more traditional kinds of community.

The local knowledge and influence of the sangha and the respect in which it is held at all levels of society enable the monks to make an extensive and significant contribution to Sarvodaya. Of the fifty-one members of the movement's executive committee no fewer than fifteen are monks. Macy writes that:

> The relationship between Sarvodaya and the Sangha is a symbiotic one, in that each benefits the other. As the monks serve as extension agents for the Movement's development program so do the Movement's ideology and expectations serve to revitalize their Order and their sense of vocation, restoring the wider social responsibilities they carried in precolonial days. This effect on the Sangha is not incidental or just a 'spin-off', but an acknowledged goal of Sarvodaya.[218]

# 246 *Action*

The Buddhist tradition of religious pluralism noted in the previous chapter is also present in Sarvodaya. Ariyaratne claims that 'the Sarvodaya Movement, while originally inspired by the Buddhist tradition, is active throughout our multi-ethnic society, working with Hindu, Muslim and Christian communities and involving scores of thousands of Hindu, Muslim and Christian co-workers. Our message of awakening transcends any effort to categorize it as the teaching of a particular creed.'[219]

As to Sarvodaya's relations with the State, Ariyaratne claims that 'when some aspects of the established order conform with the righteous principles of the Movement, the Movement co-operates with those aspects. When they become unrighteous, in those areas the Movement does not co-operate and may even extend non-violent non-co-operation [though so far it has never done so — KJ]. In between these two extremes there is a vast area...in which establishments like the government and the Sarvodaya Movement can co-operate.'[220] In fact, since there is virtually a national consensus about the desirability of rural self-help schemes Sarvodaya has been able to operate over politically neutral ground. Whilst co-operating with relevant government policies and accommodating to the national and local power structure, the Sarvodaya leadership's ambivalent and non-committal pragmatism has, arguably, so far enabled it to avoid compromising the movement's integrity.

Since the late 1970s Sarvodaya has been subjected to new pressures which have raised controversial questions about its character and its future.[221]

In the first place, the growth in size and complexity of Sarvodaya has led to what Kantowsky calls 'the routinization of charisma' in a bureaucracy, arising not least from the need to channel large amounts of foreign aid (which amounted at one time to eighty per cent of income). Although problems of bureaucracy, paternalism and communication undoubtedly persist, they have arguably been reduced by organizational decentralization (since 1980) and by the effects of cutbacks in foreign aid. At the same time Sarvo-daya's self-reliance has been increased by initiating a number of local projects.

In the second place, the increasing scale of Sarvodaya's support and activities and the growth of its influence have made it more difficult for it to continue to confine itself to relatively uncontroversial areas. New and pressing questions about the future direction of the movement have also arisen as a consequence of two major developments.

First, as from 1978 the government of Sri Lanka embarked on a classic capitalistic development policy, on the grounds that the economy would have broken down and social services would have become unsustainable had the island remained closed to foreign investment.

The only alternative, it was claimed, would have been some kind of austere totalitarian socialism. However, the social values implicit in the government's modernization projects are the antithesis of Sarvodaya's. International capital is now co-operating with the Sri Lankan élite in the creation of a competitive consumer society promoting a secular, materialist and Westernized culture. All the characteristics of this kind of Third World development are implicitly on the agenda: urbanization, centralization and bureaucratization; the erosion of local economic, social and political self-reliance; the progressive impoverishment of the rural population; and heavy reliance on huge infrastructural projects (like the Mahaveli hydro programme) which emphasize centralized, top-down development and mainly benefit those already in control of land and marketing. Also predictable is a substantial loss of economic and even political autonomy to international financial institutions.[222]

Hence Kantowsky could argue that 'Sarvodaya is now, at the end of 1978, probably just on the brink of being corrupted....The United National Party (UNP), now in power, tries to use Sarvodaya's image of traditional righteousness to camouflage modernization strategies which obviously run counter to basic tendencies of the Movement.'

Already, Kantowsky claimed, 'some of the really devoted workers and some of the younger monks have begun to question the Movement's co-operation with the government.'[223]

The foregoing developments have led researchers like James J. Hughes[224] to distinguish betwen the present 'social service' model of Sarvodaya and the 'social change' mission towards which it is now under pressure to move. Under the social service scenario Sarvodaya would remain a predominantly village self-help movement, avoiding political controversy and continuing as an independent partner of government in social welfare policies. In this case Sarvodaya would, in Goulet's opinion, actually need to make 'drastic reductions in size and membership'. In other words it would need to withdraw from its presently potentially compromising high profile in order to retain its original 'integrity and purity'.[225]

The other way in which that integrity can be maintained is through the alternative line of development strongly argued by Hughes: 'Sarvodaya must begin, as Goulet suggests, to work towards a macro-, long-term analysis and strategy, working to build a new society from the grassroots, while giving critical support to parties and governments that will at least allow such work to be done.' This would extend Sarvodaya's concerns from the rural to the qualitatively different urban and national levels. Its self-help welfare perspective would be extended to the creation of alternative institutions and social structural change to the extent necessary and practicable to defend and promote the movement's system of values. This would sooner or later require Sarvodaya to come to terms with the existing governmental and private, national and local, power structures. Hughes refers to a 1978 survey by Hans Wismeijer which indicated that 'seventy-six per cent of all Sarvodaya organizers favour the use of non-violent direct action (*satyagraha*) to attack entrenched power in the village. . . . But the upper classes and central bureaucratic clique in Sarvodaya were found to be

significantly less in favour of this idea than the lower
leadership, and Sarvodaya has never used these militant
tactics which Ariyaratne sees as an extreme last resort.'[226]

More conservative Sarvodayans would maintain that Sarvodaya always has had a social change perspective, through
influence and example. But this view fails to take account of
the changing economic and political climate in the country
and the dynamics of the movement's own growth. Its challenge to the industrial materialist model of economic and
social development is at present latent and potential rather
than active and significant. As the largest of the rural self-
help movements in the world today, involving directly or
indirectly one million out of Sri Lanka's fourteen million
population, Sarvodaya's wholehearted and explicit commitment to a comprehensive alternative development strategy
would be an event of enormous significance in the history of
the Third World.

The inclination to carry on making the best of the present
pragmatic accommodations with government and other
powers is an understandable one. So far Sarvodaya's urban
impact has been muted, and its success has been greatest in
the poorer, more isolated and traditional villages. Would
enough people find their true strength in Sarvodaya's socio-
spiritual values, as against the hard push and the seductive
pull of the acquisitive consumer society? Could Sarvodaya
retain its integrity as a spiritually inspired, independent,
nonviolent movement in a climate of increasingly polarized
partisan violence? If Sarvodaya were to fail in such a new
initiative it would become, as Goulet observes, an irrelevant,
nostalgic counter-culture. But if it were to continue in its
present restricted character, 'modernization' would doubtless consign it anyway to much the same fate.

Another factor which could push Sarvodaya towards the
radical alternative is the eruption in recent years of inter-
racial conflict which already, at the time of writing, was
beginning to overshadow all other issues.

At the time of the 1983 riots Sarvodaya acted promptly to

give what security it could to Tamils fleeing from Sinhalese mobs, and it subsequently provided refugee camps for many thousands. In a Declaration on National Peace and Harmony Ariyaratne blamed the conflict on the destruction of the Sri Lankan value system 'founded on the ancient Hindu–Buddhist Code of Ethics', and he outspokenly maintained that the Sinhalese community had the 'onus of responsibility' for redeeming the situation.[227]

One result of the crisis was to give Sarvodaya a higher and more controversial public profile. It earned the respect and support of a significant number of people in both communities who might previously have been inclined to dismiss it as just an innocuous movement of dogooders (as Macy remarks). And it has remained the only voluntary national organization in which Sinhalese and Tamils continue to work together. Elsewhere, however, the Sarvodaya response has aroused anger and suspicion from the emergent current of Sinhalese racist nationalism (which includes many highly placed monks). And 'Tamil separatists, as well as some foreign observers and even donors to the Movement have charged the Movement with not giving adequate attention to Tamil claims and grievances. They point to the clear allegiance, expressed in Ariyaratne's Declaration of Peace and Harmony, to the concept of a "unitary state", thereby rejecting any serious consideration of secession. Subsequent statements by the Sarvodaya leadership, they also point out, refrain from specifically denouncing oppressive government policies or indiscriminate acts of retaliation by Sinhalese police and military forces.'[228]

The polarizing and destabilizing effects of the ongoing communal conflict have thus to some extent obliged Sarvodaya to bear public witness to its beliefs, even at the risk of antagonizing powerful forces in Sri Lankan society. The future direction of the movement, however, is still in question. It remains arguably the largest and most comprehensive example of socially engaged Buddhism in the world today, although the mass Buddhist movements of Japan described in the next chapter have a comparable claim. For Buddhists Sarvodaya offers a still promising democratic updating of the Asokan ideal of a pluralist society, founded on a spiritual perspective of self-cultivation through open learning and dedication to radical social change. Even for spiritually inspired radicals working in different kinds of social situation, Sarvodaya offers a case study in the many problems and dilemmas which have to be worked through. Furthermore, both Kantowsky and Macy argue for Sarvodaya action on a global scale, 'uniting and empowering people in both under-developed and mal-developed (i.e. industrial) countries.'[229] For Sarvodaya principles 'cannot be expected to work in a few backward regions of the Third World while the industrialized countries continue their aggressive expansion.'[230]

Sarvodaya groups have, in fact, existed for some years in the Netherlands, Belgium and West Germany, and in 1981 a Sarvodaya Shramadana International was founded. This is concerned not only with questions of Third World development policy and funding but also with affirming the relevance of Sarvodaya principles to the problems of 'mal-developed' industrial societies. However, Kantowsky quotes the opinion of one Western Sarvodayan, David Radcliffe, that it would be a mistake 'for the Sri Lankan organization to attempt to create another distinct organization, competing for membership with those who are travelling the same road. It would be more appropriate to demonstrate its practical concern by identifying and working out ways to interact with Western groups that are already in harmony with the Sarvodaya analysis of the human condition. To their work Sarvodaya could add its own perspective, while in turn receiving encouragement that others are working towards the same converging objective.'[231]

As we shall see in Part Eight a 'Green', grass-roots, alternative culture or movement of diverse and complex character now flourishes in the West, and shares much the same perspectives as Sarvodaya. Kantowsky fears lest in the

West Sarvodaya principles be 'enshrined in some frugal ashram in sunny California or foggy Holland' (or 'alternative' enclaves tucked away in rural Devon and Wales), for there is no doubt that an alternative, self-help, community-based movement is highly relevant to the needs of the industrial inner cities and to whole communities devastated by high unemployment. Thus David Radcliffe has suggested that 'Sarvodaya's role in Western society would be to promote community development within an urban-industrial situation, by asserting that community is defined by conscious will, not by organization or sanction. For this purpose it could work through small clusters of associates working together to influence the large and impersonal institutions of society towards social, environmental and cultural sensitivity.'[232]

Years of low pay, unemployment, bad housing, inadequate health care and education, in ugly, worn out and often polluted urban environments tend to breed apathy, vandalism, crime, drug addiction and racism. The response of 'the authorities' is customarily very much in the instrumental—rational mentality described in Chapter 9, and is uncannily reminiscent of many Third World development projects. Data is collected and processed by the various agencies, to analyse 'needs', and programmes and services are 'put in' in order to 'improve conditions'. Fashionable top-down attempts at consultation and community involvement tend to founder (or at best remain superficial) because consultation is confused with public relations, because bureaucratic constraints frustrate good intentions, because of the paternalistic streak in much professionalism, and because, on the other hand, of the ingrained resentment, alienation, disbelief and defensiveness with which 'improvement projects' are commonly met. And the problems are sometimes compounded by an authoritarian need to 'contain' anti-social situations by strong intrusive policing which alienates whole communities.

Sarvodaya's Buddhistic approach is no different from the

approach of any intuitive worker in situations like the above. It involves establishing trust and mutual respect, helping people to identify their needs and to develop self-confidence and skills, so that they can begin to use such resources as are available. The true goal is self-reliance and self-determination through personal and group development. People involved in this kind of work have remarked that what eventually proved most important to them was not instrumental achievement (or failure) but the way in which they themselves had changed and the experience of fellowship in a common endeavour. As the Sarvodaya slogan has it, 'We build the road and the road builds us.'

Finally, the Sarvodaya experience underlines at least two hazards of which radical movements – spiritually inclined or otherwise – need to be aware. On the one hand, they need to maintain with official bodies, the media and other parts of the establishment an informative and educative dialogue, leading hopefully to some level of understanding and co-operation. On the other, they need to avoid being co-opted and used, even to the extent of assimilating values at odds with their own expressed orientation. Such a middle way is potentially much more creative than mere compromise, and finding it requires considerable sensitivity and insight.

Secondly there is the related danger of sliding into bureaucratic and authoritarian habits and mentalities. This is easily done, since these reflect the typical organizational culture in our society and are implicit in much professional training, as well as offering attractive short cuts and quick fixes. As it has grown in size Sarvodaya has taken deliberate steps to minimize these harmful tendencies. Power, for example, has been decentralized by giving the hundreds of Village Awakening Councils (*samhitis*) legally incorporated autonomy to administer their own budgets and devise their own programmes. In 1984 Macy testified that the decentralization policies introduced four years previously had proved substantially successful. Although considerable friction undoubtedly existed between headquarters and the field workers, there had been an evident shift towards the field in Sarvodaya's internal power structure.[233]


## THAILAND

In Thailand there are networks of Buddhist-inspired organizations which have much the same outlook and methods of working as Sarvodaya. They are, however, more fragmented and limited in scale and achievement.

Particularly noteworthy is the Asian Cultural Forum on Development (ACFOD) which aims to unite individuals and groups 'in all countries of the Asian and Pacific Region into a movement which participates in integral development'. ACFOD headquarters are in Bangkok. Its co-ordinator, Sulak Sivaraksa, writes of ACFOD objectives 'being achieved through the aid of different groups and individuals in both Europe and North America'.[234] The Thailand Development Support Committee liaises the activities of the smaller Thai Non-Government Organizations in the development field, with overseas support from the Thailand Development Information Service in London. *Thai Development Newsletter* provides information on various grass-roots development projects in health care, education, women's rights and other areas. Other bodies sharing what I have called the transcendental radical perspective are the Thai Inter-Religious Commission for Development (which publishes a well-produced periodical, *Seeds of Peace*) and the Co-ordinating Group for Religion in Society.

Several of the local development projects in Thailand have been initiated by members of the sangha. For example, Lung Poh Nah, abbot of a monastery situated in an impoverished province, successfully encouraged and assisted the local farmers to develop coconut and, later, palm tree cultivation in order to supplement their income from their unreliable rice crops.

The different facets of transcendental radicalism are well exemplified in the writing and work of Sulak Sivaraksa, a tireless organizer and prolific publicist. Typically, 'Rightists call him an out-and-out communist, while he disappoints Leftists by rejecting communism and most aspects of doctrinaire socialism. . . . He presents no ideal solutions, but his thought is wide enough to contain the best in tradition and the best in progressive thinking.' (*Bangkok Bank Monthly Review*, December 1975). Sulak is critical of the rationalist political Buddhism which flourished especially in the 1950s and 1960s: 'Unfortunately, in countries where members of the sangha worked closely with the masses to gain independence from foreign rulers, they became so involved with politics that they neglected the constant cultivation of mindfulness. After independence quite a number of monks remained involved in political matters, so they lost the spiritual life.'[235]

Sulak and his associates work for a Buddhist-inspired economic and social development which is opposed to the dominant Western model of Third World development. He associates the latter with a widening gap between rich and poor, landlessness, environmental degradation, the growing power of transnational corporations, the militarization of society, and an insidious Western intellectual and cultural imperialism. He argues for locally based democracy, appropriate Asian social institutions and national self-reliance, and refers approvingly to Gandhi's network of 'village republics' and Schumacher's 'Buddhist economics'. Sulak's *Siamese Resurgence*[87] and *A Buddhist Vision for Renewing Society*[158] provide useful pointers to the Buddhist radicalism formulated at the start of this chapter.

Another influential figure in Thai engaged Buddhism is *Ajahn* Buddhadasa. In contrast both to traditional doctrinal and prescriptive teaching and to the modernism which secularly inverts it, Buddhadasa's Dharma teaching is experientially and meditatively based. His teaching draws freely upon Mahayana Buddhism as well as upon Theravada and he holds that all religions are ultimately and fundamentally the same. Buddhadasa is concerned with the crisis in traditional Thai Buddhism, which is being eroded and devitalized by Western secularism, leaving an increasingly empty shell of public and national ceremonial combined with quasi-magical ritual designed to bring personal good fortune. In the words of his principal Western interpreter, Donald Swearer, Buddhadasa has 'urged a return to an authentic *Buddhadhamma*, replacing merit-making with a serious quest for Nibbana/Nirvana, the memorization of endless categories of Abhidhamma philosophies with an understanding of the Suttas, the performance of magic rituals with the practice of meditation, and an undue emphasis on the monk with a concern for the entire Buddhist community, lay and monastic.'[236]

Buddhadasa's transcendental modernism in his presentation of Dharma undoubtedly complements and inspires the transcendental social radicalism of activists like Sulak Sivaraksa. The *Ajahn* (teacher) has, moreover, himself offered a vision of 'dhammic socialism' in a volume of essays which was received too late for their contents to be acknowledged adequately at various points in the present text.[237] It is noteworthy that independently, and from a South-East Asian and Theravada standpoint, it presents much the same social dharma as does this book. Specifically, Buddhadasa's dhammic socialism embodies all but the second of the seven principles of a Buddhist transcendental radicalism with which this chapter opened. Rather than duplicate so much of what is already in this book, it would seem more helpful to explore this one significant area of difference.

*Ajahn* Buddhadasa's vision of the Buddhist good society resembles in fundamentals that presented in Chapter 32. However, although he does not extend his perspective to include specific social structures and processes of change, he does argue a political ideal which harks back to the benevolent paternalism of the Asokan tradition. In the closing pages of one of the essays in his *Dhammic Socialism*, the *Ajahn* declares: 'I favour a Buddhist social democracy which is composed of *dhamma* and managed by a "dictator" whose character exemplifies the ten royal virtues [of] generosity, morality, liberality, uprightness, gentleness, self-restraint, non-anger, non-hurtfulness, forbearance and non-opposition....In some cases this form of Buddhist dictatorial socialism can solve the world's problems better than any other form of government. In particular, small countries like Thailand should have democracy in the form of a dictatorial dhammic socialism.' However, 'the character of the ruler is the crucial factor....' Furthermore, a 'ruling class of some kind is absolutely necessary; however, it should be defined by its function rather than by birth.... This kind of government, an enlightened ruling class...is in fact the kind of socialism which can save the world.'

This Platonic ruling class would apparently include persons 'of great material wealth (Sanskrit: *sresthi*)'. Whereas capitalists 'accumulate endless wealth and reinvest all the profits for themselves, while oppressing their workers, a *sresthi*, in the Buddhist sense, on the other hand, employs workers in a co-operative effort for the welfare of the entire community'. Buddhadasa recalls the times when 'slavery was socialistic and did not need to be abolished. Slave and master worked for the common good. The kind of slavery which exists under a capitalist system, in which a master treats slaves or servants like animals, should be abolished....But slaves under a socialist system want to remain with their masters because they feel at ease.'

All of the foregoing runs counter to the Dhamma-inspired radicalism associated with Sarvodaya, with the Vietnamese nonviolent movement for peace and social justice described by *Thich* Nhat Hanh, and the radical democratic perspective of Sulak Sivaraksa and his associates. These movements, like the Buddhist Peace Fellowships in the West, have affinities with the 'Green', 'libertarian' sub-culture described in Chapter 33, with which most religious radicals are now broadly aligned, in opposition to all forms of élitism of wealth and power whether capitalist or communist. We have here, I suggest, a useful reminder that although the wise and insightful can provide superb guidance and inspiration as to social fundamentals — as does *Ajahn* Buddhadasa — it does not follow that they are necessarily well informed about specific social developments, and the social science involved in *applying* those fundamentals. However, although political notions plucked from a somewhat idealized past may appear fanciful in a contemporary setting, they can be potentially harmful when taken up uncritically by people who are inclined to make a cult out of a spiritual leader's pronouncements.

It is true that in pre-industrial cultures the most probable and ready means of securing some degree of social justice was through a benevolent despot or oligarchy, inspired to use their wealth and power in the service of others. Such were the (rationally) 'enlightened despots' of eighteenth-century Europe, at a time when social, economic and technical conditions were beginning to appear that would make truly democratic social renewal possible. The ideal of engaged spirituality is at last to realize this goal on the *basis* of spiritual renewal. The *dhammaraja*'s personal benevolence was real enough when circumstances much restricted the extent, powers and functions of rulers. Holding up such an ideal in the era of the centralized, bureaucratic techno-military State has on several occasions in the past hundred years conjured up saviours who have turned out to be monsters.

Buddhadasa condemns liberal democracy because of the freedom it gives to the 'defilements' (*kilesa*) of acquisitiveness and aggression, but it at least provides, in its classic form, a certain openness, balance, and potential for personal and social development. Power tends to corrupt all who come in contact with it, but absolute power corrupts absolutely. And where absolute power is allegedly wielded for others' good, the corruption can be very delusive. Moreover, power is wielded and wealth is utilized under certain social con-

ditions and within specific economic systems. Even philanthropic Quaker capitalists (for example) have been
constrained by market forces in order to stay in business.
The public exercise of personal virtue cannot be enough.

The *dhammaraja* and the élite (*ksatriya*) were Buddhist
political forms appropriate to a specific historical era, and no
more than that. Truly rooted in Dhamma, and much older
and more enduring, is the Buddhist tradition of egalitarian
respect for the individual person. Each must light his or her
own way, and now has all the means of doing so politically
if they can but open to the full humanity within themselves.
And to honour totally the warm-blooded reality of others
and their potential is the first step in gentling that defensive/
aggressive 'Self' which is so readily moved to deny or
exploit them. Dhammic society, which starts with us here
and now, is a school for learning about the infinite interdependence of people, of beings, of all things, as a condition
for any spiritual growth. Opportunity to use others, even
from the highest self-motives and for their own good, cannot
help such learning. It may be countered that although there
*is* perennial Dharma at the root of all this, my political
implications are coloured by Western individualistic humanism and do not have the universal relevance claimed for
them. This may be so; time and experience alone will tell. I
appreciate that *Ajahn* Buddhadasa is writing out of a very
different tradition and a different contemporary social situation. Nevertheless, his transcendental modernism, as I
would call it, is shared by socially engaged Buddhists in
both East and West, and for them it seems logically to lead to
the vision of an egalitarian commonwealth, democratic and
decentralized, wherein the modest wealth and power of
each obliges them to learn to be sisters and brothers of one
another (see Chapter 32).

These contentious questions arise only in the closing
pages of one of the essays in Buddhadasa's *Dhammic Socialism*. I should be sorry if the attempt to do full justice to them
here should detract from an appreciation of the impressive

sweep of the *Ajahn*'s thinking, which offers such a welcome endorsement to the main themes developed in this book. ('Socialism', however, is a term I have avoided, because of its *adhammic* overtones of ideology, polarization and authoritarian collectivism. 'Libertarian socialism' is the rather old-fashioned and secular term for the Good Society I discuss in Chapter 32).

## VIETNAM

The third of the sources in recent South-East Asian history which contributes to the formulation of a Buddhist transcendental radicalism is the tragic Vietnam experience, involving Buddhists in both the Mahayana and Theravada traditions. Here the struggle for national independence combined with a struggle between capitalism and communism, in which foreign powers were deeply involved.

As in Burma and Ceylon, Buddhist monks were active from the end of the nineteenth century in the movements to gain independence from the colonial power. And during the 1960s, in the long and bloody struggle between governments in North and South Vietnam, the Unified Buddhist Church inspired an historic campaign of mass nonviolence for a 'third way', for a neutral Vietnam which would cherish its own cultural identity (1967 Programme of the Buddhist Socialist Bloc).

The Buddhist movement sought allies in people of other faiths and beliefs who were willing to work for peace and independence, and, in particular, large numbers of Catholics made common cause with the Buddhists. When, on 16 May 1967, a young Buddhist, Nhat Chi Mai, made of herself 'a torch in the dark night', it was a leading Catholic intellectual, Father Nguyen Ngoc Lan, who undertook the dangerous work of publishing her letters and poems.

The movement for peace was linked with action for social justice and social revolution. From the two radical Buddhist bases of Van Hanh University and the School of Youth for Social Service young people went into the country to work alongside the peasants on rural development projects, and a number of unions and other organizations were formed which also embraced urban workers, women, youth and students. An extensive anti-war literature flourished, of poetry, satire, song and prayer.

The importance of the national cultural identity was emphasized, and the Buddhist and humanistic cultural tradition of Vietnam did much to shape the nonviolent character of the 'Third Way' movement. Zen Master *Thich* Nhat Hanh, who played a leading part, stressed that 'the struggle of the Vietnamese people is not only for peace and independence. *The struggle of the Vietnamese people is to remain Vietnamese.* That is why the means of the struggle cannot be those that will destroy the Vietnamese character and the humanistic values that are so dear to the Vietnamese people. We cannot accept inhuman means that will change the Vietnamese nature. In accepting many of these means we have already permitted foreign powers to come and destroy our land.'[238]

In the annals of historic mass nonviolent movements the Vietnamese episode ranks with those of Gandhi to free India of British rule and of Martin Luther King to rid the United States of racial segregation. Two Saigon dictatorships were toppled – Diem's in 1963 and Khanh's in 1964 – and the Ky-Thieu government would also have been brought down in 1966 had not the United States flown Ky's forces into the centre of the movement (Hué) and exerted other pressures. The writings of perceptive participants like Nhat Hanh[239] can do much to deepen our insight into the character of nonviolence as a positive and compassionate force.

Today the work of the Unified Buddhist Church and its allies for religious freedom and other human rights continues in the face of much persecution, and organizations and individuals all over the world have rallied to the support of the 'prisoners of conscience' – monks, nuns, writers, artists and academics.

It is difficult to assess the contemporary situation elsewhere in Indochina. Kampuchea (Cambodia) has been devastated by aerial genocide and torn apart in the 'killing fields' of civil war, sustained by the military and diplomatic support of both Western and communist powers. The communist rulers of Laos (with a population of only 3½ million) appear anxious to retain what national autonomy and cultural identity that they can. In their concern to find a Laotian way to socialism they appear to look with some favour at the Burmese example, but their exposure to Soviet and Vietnamese pressure very much restricts their freedom of manoeuvre. Notwithstanding their concern to control the sangha they appreciate its value as an ally, and there is here some possibility of accommodation.[240]

# 25  *The Mahayana and the Mass Movements of Japan*

'The primary Buddhist position on social action,' declares the American scholar Robert Thurman, 'is one of total activism, an unswerving commitment to complete self-transformation and complete world transformation.'[241] This is an activism which, doctrinally, becomes fully explicit in Mahayana Buddhism. Individual liberation from the experience of separateness, of alienation, from other beings brings a sense of oneness from which arises the compassionate concern to put an end to all suffering, and especially through liberation from delusion as the root of existential suffering. Following the bodhisattva example, practitioners are urged to dedicate themselves selflessly to relieving the sufferings of others. On the face of it, Mahayana Buddhism would seem to be strongly missionary, but the self-help character of Buddhism gives the Mahayana little in common with the evangelizing spirit of the great proselytizing religions. And in Chapter 20 I noted the historical circumstances which reduced Far Eastern Mahayana to a comparatively private, personal religion, whilst in Tibet it remained embedded in monastic theocracy. Yet, as we have seen in Part Three, the Madhyamika, Yogacara and Avatamsaka contributions to the Mahayana tradition have the potential for valuable insight and analysis of fundamental social processes. And Nagarjuna's *Jewel Garland of Royal Counsels* (Chapter 22) offers a social prescription as comprehensive and authoritative as those found in the Theravada scriptures.

Buddhism in the People's Republic of China has, it seems,

been reduced to a marginal position and its future is uncertain. However, after more than three decades of Chinese occupation and severe persecution, it is still sustaining itself in Tibet. Tibetan Buddhism has, moreover, now achieved a remarkable and historic transmission to the West, where it is well established as the third of the great 'traditions' there (with Theravada and Zen). It does not appear to bear any marks of its feudal and theocratic past, and the present Dalai Lama has made it clear that he has no wish to see that past ever restored. For example, 'In the draft Constitution of 1963, which I announced in exile, the executive authority of the Dalai Lama is made subject to the sovereign power of a popularly elected national assembly. As for the lamas, in future it must be seen to that all monasteries are self-supporting. To achieve this the lamas have to work to feed themselves.' The Dalai Lama has made it clear that in 'New Tibet' 'the special privileges and the large estates enjoyed, whether by monasteries or the aristocratic families, will have to go.'[242]

In the West the energy of adherents to Tibetan Buddhism is understandably concentrated on conserving and consolidating the religion and culture in its new environment (for example, through institutions like the Foundation for the Preservation of the Mahayana Tradition). Social and political concerns have been confined to lobbying on behalf of their homeland and their oppressed compatriots. The Dalai Lama has, however, been for many years a tireless speaker, writer and traveller for world peace and social well-being and has widely popularized the idea of a socially responsible Buddhism.

The Far Eastern Mahayana countries of Japan, Korea and Taiwan are all industrial or industrializing societies with very distinctive Buddhist cultural traditions.

In Chapter 20 I noted how in Japan Buddhist institutions eventually achieved prestige and material security, though only at the cost of passive or even active subservience to the military and imperial politics of the establishment. For Japan, defeat in the Second World War brought deep despair and disillusionment and a search for new orientations and ideals. Japanese Buddhism was deeply involved in this process, which has some similarities with developments in Theravada Buddhism in the post-colonial period (Chapter 23). Thus in Japan also Buddhism was to be recognized as a humanism which 'promotes the dignity and free personality of every man' and 'the social solidarity between men, between man and society, and between nations.'[243] Similarly, for Zen scholar Reiho Masunaga, 'The Buddhism of the future will overcome the difference between man and woman, wise and foolish, high and low, as well as national barriers; it will be grounded in a philosophy which includes the natural sciences, and in a humanism which liberates and cultivates human nature; and it will be open to all the world.'[244] In Chapter 20 reference was made to the humanist and pacifist Zen maintained by Ichikawa Hakugen in writings such as his *War Responsibility of Buddhists*. In the latter he writes of a 'Buddhist socialism' rooted in self-emptiness and hence imbued with a humble and open spirit cleansed of the will to power and working towards a co-operative commonwealth. A number of Buddhist activists and intellectuals who had been influenced by Ichikawa formed the Gudo Society, named after a Soto Zen monk, Uchiyama Gudo, who was executed in 1911 for his opposition to the demands of the imperial regime.[245]

Such humanistic explorations of intellectuals and writers are overshadowed, however, by the post-war development of the 'New Religions'. These are Buddhist lay organizations which, with some fifteen per cent of the population in membership, are among the most striking manifestations of Buddhist activism in the world today.[246]

Although noteworthy variations exist between these different New Buddhist Movements they do share certain strongly marked characteristics. All of them undertake extensive educational, missionary, welfare and publishing activities. All engage their members in a profound concern for world peace and in strong moral and social commitment (though this is directed to reforming and morally toning up society and not to radical transformation of the existing industrial consumerism). All offer strong, simple doctrines of ready appeal to the working and lower middle classes which are disproportionately represented in their membership. They tend to require total commitment from adherents and intense personal involvement in communal activities, secured by strong and charismatic leaders at all levels.

Most of these mass movements are inspired by the Lotus Sutra (see below), and also by the peculiarly Japanese Nichiren Buddhist tradition. This messianic sect was founded in 1253 by a poor fisherman's son, Nichiren, who taught that self-transcendence could be brought about by the devotional chanting of a mantra. From the beginning the sect was marked by an intolerant missionary zeal, and is differentiated from other Buddhist schools 'by its nationalistic, pugnacious and intolerant attitude'.[247] This led the eminent scholar Edward Conze (who himself had a certain reputation for abrasiveness) to conclude that 'on this occasion Buddhism had evolved its very antithesis out of itself,' so that 'it is somewhat doubtful whether it belongs to the history of Buddhism at all.'[248]

Something of the Nichiren spirit is particularly evident in the largest and most controversial of the New Buddhist Movements, the Soka Gakkai, which also has aroused strong feelings. Even a temperate scholar like Heinrich Dumoulin was moved to write, in the late 1960s, that 'were it not for its formidable size, one might be inclined to dismiss this movement, which calls itself the only true Buddhism and the only perfect religion, as merely a group of fanatics. But the secret of its success − according to both members and opponents − is precisely its belief in itself as absolute.'[249] A few years earlier the American *Time* magazine had more racily described the movement as combining 'the evangelism of Moral Rearmament with the get-the-votes discipline of the Communist Party and lots of showbiz' and had concluded that 'the regimented unquestioning qualities of

Soka Gakkai and its political arm, Komeito, are more often Japanese than Buddhist.'[250] Subsequently Soka Gakkai appears to have mellowed somewhat and is today arguably a more problematic and complex phenomenon, with its promotion of a 'middle way' for Japanese society through the medium of its 'clean government' political party, Komeito, its New Student League and numerous similar mass organizations, its daily newspaper, and its university and other impressive educational and welfare achievements. The uncompromising evangelical fervour remains, however, together with the visionary goal of establishing 'the global unity of mankind' − 'a world-wide universalism'.

In keeping with its international vision Soka Gakkai has established formally autonomous 'Nichiren Shoshu' organizations in several parts of the world. These are affiliates of Soka Gakkai International, established 'to work for and create a movement for education, culture and peace based on the Buddhism of Nichiren Daishonon'. A study of the United States organization published in 1976 found much the same spirit of mass evangelism and hierarchical structure as in the Japanese parent body.[251] The British affiliate (NSUK) is currently receiving a good deal of attention from the media, with some sharp perception beyond the often sensational treatment. Thus, John Cunningham, writing in the (London) *Guardian* of 21 November 1985, observes that 'the sect, unlike others [in Buddhism] is aggressive and proselytizing...[it is] the brand religion of the eighties; making huge inroads in the US; smaller but significant ones in the UK. And appealing to either rather broken, vulnerable people (there is instant buddyness) or else to those in upwardly mobile careers.' Socially and psychologically the movement has much in common with Christian evangelical fundamentalism, even down to linking religious faith with entrepreneurial success. Richard Causton, Director of NSUK, explains: 'People are searching for something that gives actual proof of changing your life. You can't be happy if your material circumstances are bad. Chanting teaches you to *challenge* these circumstances. You can get the courage to set up your own small business, become creative, form a determination not to accept second best.'[252]

Another, contrasting, New Buddhist Movement is the much smaller Nihonzan Myohonji, distinguished by its particularly resolute pacifism, which was sustained in the face of severe persecution throughout the Second World War. Its drum-beating, chanting monks and nuns are often seen and heard on Western as well as Eastern peace demonstrations, and its attitude is strongly ecumenical (the consecration of its Peace Pagoda in Battersea Park, London, was a notable inter-faith event).

Rissho Koseikai, with a world membership of five million, is another, much larger movement which also has a relatively open character. Its world peace campaigning has had a strong inter-faith orientation, bringing close contacts with other forms of engaged spirituality. Nikkyo Niwano, its President, has played a leading part in the International Association for Religious Freedom, the World Conference on Religion and Peace, and the Asian Conference on Religion and Peace. In Niwano's prolific writings he is particularly fond of stressing the importance of personal development and of perfecting oneself in both personal relations and in one's role in society. A feature of Rissho Koseikai are the numerous small counselling groups to provide opportunity for personal expression (including repentence) and group support.

Niwano has commented extensively on the Lotus Sutra as 'a valuable and practical guide for living in these troubled times'.[253] His reading of the social implications of the sutra makes interesting comparison with the modernist readings of the Theravada scriptures to which Chapter 23 refers. Niwano invokes a number of key social values as he works through the successive chapters of the sutra in his book *A Buddhist Approach to Peace*.[254] 'All [things] are facets of a single universal truth' and share a common fraternity. 'The spirit of the equality of all human beings, which is one of the main pillars on which world peace must be built, is, I believe, solidly endorsed by the Lotus Sutra.' Niwano claims that chapter 4 of the sutra − a prodigal son parable − 'expounds the true Bodhisattva spirit of respecting and loving even the smallest existence, and of helping each existence to develop its own Buddha nature'. The fundamental equality of all beings lies in the potential for development in each of them. Their diversity is to be understood not so much in terms of stages of development as in terms of differing and distinctive character. Hence, in an aside, Niwano warns that we should not attempt to mould developing countries into the same pattern as developed countries.

Commenting on the parable of Devadatta in his *Guide* to the Lotus Sutra, Niwano writes that 'the idea is fully put here that all people, men and women alike, have the same Buddha nature'. Notwithstanding their 'inborn distinctiveness', 'really men and women are equal and alike, and this is the ethical and social ground of male-female equality'.

However, as to Niwano's more explicit interpretations of the meaning of the Lotus Sutra which are offered in *A Buddhist Approach to Peace*, I had the impression that, like the Theravada modernists, he was *reading back* from our contemporary social milieu meanings which it would be hard to justify from the text, and especially so if its overriding soteriological purpose were borne in mind. And it is the latter which inspires Niwano's *Guide to the Threefold Lotus Sutra*. The treatment of the parable of the Magic City (chapter 7 of the Sutra) is a case in point. The *Guide* (p. 65) has the conventional reading of a mirage which is enacted as a skilful and expedient means (a classic Mahayana device) in order to encourage flagging followers of the Way, 'but a temporary thing, a device...to give them rest and restore their spirits.' But in *A Buddhist Approach to Peace* the reading is that peacemaking in our present world can only give a 'temporary respite, a resting place' (p. 60) and an opportunity for 'the reformation of our mind by religion, which alone can bring permanent peace'. Hence the Sutra is concerned with 'changing all society', in 'conformity with the Buddha

Law' (p. 61). This can only come about not by bodhisattvas who come from beyond, but by the bodhisattvas of this world, who are 'really symbols of the people who live in this world – who are awakened to the truth and practise it.' (The reference is here to chapter 15 of the Sutra.) There is no doubt about the transcendental character of Niwano's radicalism; he undoubtedly is *spiritually* engaged. But such readings as this, direct and unqualified, can only tend to encourage an exclusively secular and social understanding and overlay the primary spiritual and existential message.

Taken as a whole, the Japanese New Buddhist Movements are certainly transcendental in spirit. However, they tend to be paternalistic mass movements rather than diverse, grass-roots networks which foster individual and group self-reliance on a basis of open learning. Although their work for world peace has been impressive and influential their social orientation is to welfare provision and reforming the standards of public life, rather than to radical social transformation. They are, I believe, very much a Japanese cultural phenomenon. Translated into other societies they tend to take on a less appropriate and desirable significance – certainly politically and socially, and, arguably, also in terms of the most appropriate *yana*, or form of Buddhism. This is not an East–West question. The several principles for an engaged Buddhism which opened Chapter 23 were drawn from the experience of Buddhist activism in *three* South East Asian countries. They also accord with a widespread and increasingly influential trend in the West, as we shall see in Part Eight. And they do, arguably, have some foundation in basic Dharma.

In the case of movements such as Soka Gakkai and its affiliates real (rather than cosmetic) communication in the matter of engaged Buddhism tends to be impeded by a combination of ideological righteousness and missionary zeal. The warmth is genuine, but it comes less from openness, trust and vulnerability than from an all-pervasive – and hence smiling – sense of collective assurance.

# 26 Buddhist Modernism —
## Transcendental or Reductive?

There have been anticipations of this chapter earlier in the book. Chapter 11 introduced secularization in general terms and as affecting Christianity. The term 'reductive modernism' was coined to denote the inversion of spiritual truths by reading exclusively secular meanings into them. Similarly, Chapters 19 and 23 were both concerned with the reading back into the Buddhist scriptures of contemporary ideas from the dominant secular culture, thereby subverting their soteriological purpose. Once an engaged spirituality has emerged from a quietistic tradition and established its validity then the secular culture finds it more 'relevant' and becomes interested in it. Secularization then becomes the hazard, constantly threatening to undercut its spiritual roots. This chapter directly addresses this problem.

'Modern Buddhism' can be modern in two opposed senses. It can either be the contemporary culture's interpretation of Buddhism, and this inevitably tends to reduce Buddhism to a rational humanism (reductive modernism). Or else it can be a Buddhist interpretation of the contemporary culture, which gives us a spiritual and root-existential understanding of that culture (transcendental modernism). However, to explain the modern world in the light of Dharma, various cultural encrustations of time may need to be gently scraped off. Archaic and misleading modes of presentation, obsolescent institutions, and extrinsic secondary beliefs may have so dimmed the light that only the most sensitive and dedicated can still read by it. When the light has become feeble and the encrustations thick, then the whole apparatus may become *widely* understandable only in secular terms. And this makes of it something altogether different. It is the task of transcendental modernism to prevent this happening and, with humility and sensitivity, to help keep open access by all to the essential Dharma. Writing this book is an exercise of this kind, in a world in which Buddhism as a spirituality at present lacks direct social significance, both for many dedicated Buddhists and for the great mass of socially concerned people. It remains to add that although the distinction between transcendental and reductive modernism is clear enough at the extremes it will be less clear in the middle ground.

The character and scope of Buddhist reductive modernism are indicated in the following two passages.

> Buddhist modernism is characterized by the emphasis laid on rationalist elements in Buddhist teachings, by the belief that the teachings of Buddhism and those of modern science are not only in conformity but identical, by the tacit elimination of the traditional cosmology, and by a reinterpretation of the objective of the Buddhist religion in terms of social reform and the building of a better world.[255]

Secondly, and further to Chapter 23:

> The Buddhists of Asia have tended to invoke Buddhism as a cultural counterforce to Westernizing influences and to show that the Occident has invented nothing and that Buddhism, for example, is democratic, since it is essentially egalitarian and the decisions of the monastic institutions were reached by majority vote; that it is humanistic, since the primitive religious community was classless and its property collectively owned; that it is rationalistic, since salvation is a matter of reason

divorced from all transcendence; that in its doctrine
of the Void and its dialectic it is Kantian and
Hegelian; that it is existentialist in its denial of all
essence and its insistence on suffering; that it is, in
the theories of the School of Knowledge, the pre-
cursor of Freud and Jung. Certain of these diverse
traits are not always present in Buddhism as it
exists, but one need only reform it to adapt it to the
modern world and put it in a condition to stand up
to Christianity and even to Marxism.[256]

Buddhism is thus reduced to being a rational humanism
which includes a political theory for radical structural
change — the 'Social Fallacy' described in Chapter 10, but
with some traditional religious paintwork remaining. Western cultural colonialism was challenged by those who had
already unbeknowingly succumbed to it, but who professed
to find in the Buddhist scriptures and traditions such secular
Western ideals as scientific rationalism and state socialism.
These could then be claimed as having been all along a part
of the Eastern cultural heritage. Comically, this was at a
time when many in the West had become disillusioned with
those very things and sought escape into an Eastern spirituality which they believed would give them other-worldly
deliverance. This black joke is still to some extent being
played out by both parties.

When the spiritual kernel of Buddhism is forgotten, the
shell of rational exposition, guiding precept and supportive
social policy become, together with the institutional traditions, no more than secular instrumentalities in the service
of secular value systems. Some modernists go further, and
specify that their concern with Buddhism is as a culture and
not as a religion. For example, Professor V. K. Thakur argues
that 'to regard Buddha as the founder of a new religion is to
prejudice our understanding of his far-reaching influence.
For, in modern usage, the word religion denotes merely one
field of human activity, now regarded as of less and less

public importance, and belonging almost entirely to man's private affairs. On the other hand, Buddhism, despite all its religiosity, is a great social and cultural tradition in Asia.'[257]

Of Western secularizers of Buddhism the most eloquent and influential is surely Professor Trevor Ling, for whom the historic role of Buddhism 'to end the disease of individualism' is perceived essentially in cultural and social terms. He implies, for example, that a major concern of early Buddhism was 'the gradual establishment of a universal republic, with the Buddhist sangha at its heart'.[258] and sees the sangha, 'in the context of the fifth century BC, as the prototype social organization of the future'. For Ling, Buddhism is a socio-cultural phenomenon based on a 'psycho-social philosophy', rather than a system of personal transcendence.[259] He does maintain that 'the reordering of human consciousness and the reordering of human society were the two complementary aspects of the Buddha's teaching.... These two complementary concerns constitute the Buddhist prescription for curing the ills of the human condition.'[260] But note that social transformation is not seen here as a supportive condition for 'reordering human consciousness' or as an outcome of that more fundamental transformation but as the other major limb of the Buddhist project. Moreover, as to this 'reordering of consciousness', the Buddha's enlightenment itself is for Ling 'a process of analytical reasoning' which is 'discovered by strenuous effort of the mind' that is 'almost superhuman'.[261] There is no sense here of an arduous path of meditative humility and self-surrender, leading to a numinous turning about at the very root of self, with a revelation 'given' by the falling away of delusion. It *is*, however, possible to write about this phenomenon in terms which illuminate rather than reduce, as scholars as varied as D. T. Suzuki, Hubert Benoit, and T. P. Kasulis, have demonstrated.

The above absolute misunderstanding of Buddhism as being no more than an historic culture or a sublime humanism or a brilliantly insightful metaphysics is helped by the assumption that there are, on the one hand, only theistic religions and, on the other, only humanisms (or religions without God). Buddhism is non-theistic, so it is a humanism, free of 'the supernatural and the superhuman', as Ling puts it, though he does not explain what he means by those words. The secularizers of Buddhism take no cognizance whatever of the two *levels* of spiritual consciousness, the theistic and the gnostic (Chapter 11), of Buddhism as the world's great gnostic religion, and of the significant gnostic or mystical traditions in the great theistic religions. They are thus readily able to oppose the divine and wrathful Old Testament lawgiver to the cool and reasonable Pali Canon Buddha. There is no way that Mahayana Buddhism can be crammed into this superficial schema, so it has to be pictured as some kind of degeneration into superstition and arcane mysticism. After Asoka the history of Buddhism is downhill all the way — 'a long process of misinterpretation, perversion and distortion', according to N. V. Banerjee.[262] In Ling's words, 'it ceased to be a civilization' and 'suffered also a transformation of its original humanistic character: it became a theistic religion.'[263] This Procrustean treatment of Buddhism ignores, for example, the phenomenon of the bodhisattva, a potent paradox, at once both mystic and humanist, contemplative and activist. And what of the strong sense of the underlying unity of the different Buddhist schools and traditions which is certainly experienced among present-day practitioners of the Way?

It is ironic that the privatized, personal, quietistic and asocial Buddhism that is common in the West complements, as well as opposes, the secularized shell of public Buddhism described above. The existence of the first is in some sense a condition for the existence of the second. Thus Ling can argue that 'there are signs that in modern times the societal and political philosophy of Buddhism has been lost sight of, and that Buddhism has been reduced from a civilization to what the modern world understands by religion, that is a system of "spiritual" beliefs to be taken over by the minority...

in the last resort, a private irrelevance, having little bearing on the real issues that shape human affairs.'[264] The failure to bear witness to the implications of Buddhism as engaged spirituality thus creates a vacuum which has been filled by misleading secularized versions of Buddhism which then pass into wider currency. It is like taking the wheels off a splendid Rolls Royce motor car, putting it in a farmyard, and then extolling its virtues as a very superior chicken coop.

# 27   Engaged Buddhism: The global perspective

Dialogue — and joint action — between socially engaged Buddhists of East and West is important for a variety of reasons, and not least because their (sometimes elusively) different perspectives could make for a fruitful synthesis.

In the West Buddhism, whatever its dilettante beginnings, is now being consolidated on a strong basis of meditation and mindfulness. In the future, teaching will increasingly be in the hands of Westerners many of whom may have trained only in the West. On this foundation there are now the beginnings of a concern for some social commitment. And in the alternative socio-cultural paradigm that is emerging in the West in many different walks of life Buddhism is influential and widely respected, although its social significance is not yet fully understood.

In the East, Buddhism is a total culture, a way of life, a sense of identity, as much as a spiritual path, and as such it is required to make positive, public response to changing social pressures. To some extent there has been an intellectual response which reinterprets Buddhism as a rational humanism, but this undercuts its spiritual roots and devitalizes it for the sake of short-term credibility. This is paralleled in the mass of the population by the erosion of traditional belief by the values of industrial consumerism (whether in capitalist or communist forms). However, in South-East Asia there has appeared also an engaged Buddhist spirituality, a transcendental radicalism much like the emergent Buddhism activism in the West. There is good reason to enter into closer dialogue and make common cause. Burma is also relevant to this configuration. Although the sangha apparently exercises little direct political influence with the military government, Buddhism remains a powerful social force in Burma, and the more so in that this is one of the very few countries in the world that is resolutely endeavouring to practise a self-reliant and culturally appropriate kind of economic and social development, independent of both the capitalist and the communist ethos.

One common cause that might be made is with Buddhists in the communist countries of Vietnam, Laos, Kampuchea and China, and in Chinese-occupied Tibet. Tibet, however, is a special case in that, as the Dalai Lama has emphasized, the occupation is simply 'the worst form of colonialism. . . . The Tibetans are a distinct people, speaking a language unrelated to Chinese and possessing a religion and culture of their own. Moreover, before the Chinese invasion the Tibetans had remained free and independent for decades.'[265]

Although Asian communist regimes may appear monolithic in their first triumphant flush, amidst the difficulties of consolidation ancient and strong-rooted cultures tend to work their way back to the surface. It is in the interest of the regime to come to terms with them, since they can offer an enduring and broadly based national unity and sense of identity. The kind of Buddhism they would wish to come to terms with is the denatured secularized kind: Marxism with a Buddhist face. A spiritually engaged Buddhism, however, is something quite different, and cannot be assimilated. But I believe that there are circumstances in which a communist regime would be willing to come to terms with it. Without secularization or other compromise of Dharma essentials, could not Buddhism wear a Marxist face just as it has worn other cultural faces? (Wearing a *communist* face, however, may be a rather more difficult matter. . .which would be worth pursuing elsewhere.)

The Dalai Lama has observed that 'it is a reality of today's world that much of Buddhist civilization, stretching from the borders of Thailand to parts of Siberia, is under the sway of communist ideology. . . . Communism, however, has not been able to eradicate people's faith in Buddhism. It may seem shocking, but when one considers the experience of the past few decades and the trend of the foreseeable future, it may be wise to attempt a dialogue between Communism and Buddhism. Millions of people have suffered due to the estrangement of these two systems. When the Buddhists view the Communists with suspicion and distrust and vice versa, the two only become more estranged and the possibility of either's effectively helping the persons in this region lessen.'[266] Speaking also very much from experience, *Thich* Nhat Hanh has advised along similar lines: 'The attitude of Buddhists vis-à-vis Communism is not antagonistic, but it is cautious. Buddhists are aware of the anti-religious nature of Communism as well as its dogmatic tendencies. But they are also able to see the efforts of the Communists in the struggle for independence and for social progress. That is why they keep the door for dialogue open wide.'[267]

In the West, Buddhists have been in touch with the authorities of communist countries in the process of lobbying on behalf of Buddhist 'prisoners of conscience'. But there is also scope for developing informal contacts through correspondence, and making contact at official level, notably with the Chinese Buddhist Association (which is a 'member organization' of the Chinese People's Association for Peace and Disarmament).[268]

Japan is another important and distinctive facet of a global Buddhist activism. An industrial nation with social problems similar to those of Europe and North America, Japan also shares with them (and to some extent with Korea and Taiwan) an economically exploitative relationship with the countries of South-East Asia (excluding Singapore). At the end of Chapter 25 it was suggested that there might be some difficulties in the way of a really meaningful communication between Western Buddhist activists and the New Buddhist

Movements of Japan. Little appears to have been attempted so far, but the world-wide movement against nuclear armaments is very vigorous in Japan and would make a good starting point.

Organizations like the World Fellowship of Buddhists and the Buddhist Union of Europe provide possible media of communication for socially active Buddhists in different countries, but on the whole I believe that the advantage lies with direct, personal contacts and, where possible, in connection with specific projects.

In short, there are in the world several varieties of engaged Buddhism. Quantitatively, these are comparatively limited but they *could* be the beginnings of a global Buddhist dynamism which, allied with other engaged spirituality, could make a worthwhile contribution to world peace and social justice.

*Part Seven*
Violence and Creativity

# 28  *Fundamentals*

The remainder of this book is devoted to the tools, strategies and perspectives for a radical social transformation which would interpenetrate the personal and fundamental transformative system outlined in Part Four

Part Seven is a discussion first of the 'problem' of violence, and then, in Chapter 29, of the different kinds of coercion, gross and subtle, at work in society. Chapters 30 and 31 look at creative nonviolent action and conflict resolution which are presented as means of unblocking further development and, at the same time, as consciousness-transforming ends in themselves.

What we may perceive as 'violent' in nature is as pervasive as the law of gravity. Even the very act of procreation has a violence about it. Aldous Huxley writes of 'Life irrepressibly living itself out' as a power 'unconscious, beneath good and evil':

> He remembered that film he had seen of the fertilization of a rabbit's ovum. Spermatozoa, a span long on the screen, ferociously struggling towards their goal — the moon-like sphere of an egg. Countless, aimed from every side, their *flagella* in frantic vibration. And now the foremost had reached their objective, were burrowing into it, thrusting through the outer wall of living matter, tearing away in their violent haste whole cells that floated off and were lost. At last one of the invaders had

penetrated to the quick of the nucleus, the act of
fertilization was consummated; and suddenly the
hitherto passive sphere stirred into movement.
There was a violent spasm of contraction; its
smooth rounded surface became corrugated and in
some way resistant to the other sperms that vainly
threw themselves upon it.[269]

Ecological 'violence' can equally be seen as ecological
'harmony' and balance. One animal supports the life of
another by becoming its prey. 'Violence' harmoniously sustains the life-affirming food chain. Humankind, before
achieving unnatural omnipotence, was part of this harmonious balance of violence-and-peacefulness. Its culture centred
upon a 'law', a 'way', conformation to which would tend to
ensure continued survival, as an assertion balanced between
overweening aggression and acquisitiveness on the one
hand and a life-denying acquiescence on the other.

Taizan Maezumi, a contemporary Zen Master has observed that if we think of the Buddhist First Precept 'on a
common sense level of "Do not kill" or "Do not take any
form of life", how could we survive?' In other words, survival
or life itself depends on killing other forms of life. The
greater our awareness, the more we realize this fact on many
different levels.[270] The carrots in the vegetable patch are not
strangled by weeds because the weeds have been torn out
by the roots. Later the carrots will also be pulled out of the
ground, dismembered and scraped on the kitchen chopping
board, and then fried in oil, boiled in water, and totally
consumed. On the other side of the fence the pines scream
as the power saw cuts through the bark and into soft flesh,
filling the air with the smell of their resin. True, at the gross,
ordinarily experienced level, that is just naïve anthropo-
morphism. But at the subtle level of Indra's Net, it is seen as
compassionate affinity. 'Violence' and 'harmony' are adjec-
tives we give the better to define self and its orientation and
intent. When each disappears, what is there then?

Humankind is and is not natural, of nature, and from this

paradox stems the unique character of human violence and human peacefulness. Violence, wilful and gratuitous, is a self-affirming expression sprung from existential fear, desolation and self-hate. It is the volitional instrument of anger, resentment, greed, defensiveness and the whole gamut of alienated passions, volcanic and oceanic. Institutionally embodied, in its kammaic momentum on the stage of history, it has become an unsurpassed multiplier of suffering.

Over against violence, there is also ordinarily experienced at least some sense of the Buddha Nature, of fellow-feeling, pity, affinity, which moves us to attempt helpfulness and harmlessness, peacefulness and harmony. In the great religions are the examples of saints who have perfected such fellow-feeling, and prescriptive ethics, moral guidelines, for those who aspire to cultivate that higher level of consciousness.

The Buddhist First Precept against taking life is also commonly interpreted as a precept of nonviolence, of 'harmlessness'. And since it is about the most fundamental relationship of self to others, all the other precepts may be read as particular applications of it. It is noteworthy that distinction is made between different degrees of wilfulness, of volition, which may move us to violence. For example, killing by a conscript soldier under orders, or killing in self-defence, carry a label of diminished responsibility.

Buddhism has a comparatively good historical record in holding to the precept against killing. There appear not to have been any Buddhist wars of religion, aimed at forcible conversion, and there have been a great many examples of positive religious toleration even of aggressive missionary religions. On the other hand, Conze has argued (questionably) that 'some of the success of the [Tibetan Buddhist] Gelug-pa [sect] was due to the military support of the Mongols, who, during the seventeenth century, frequently devastated the monasteries of the rival Red sects.'[271] The long association of Japanese Zen Buddhism with military prowess and aggressive imperialism has already been noted in Chapter 20, and Trevor Ling has argued that South-East Asian Buddhist kingdoms were as militarily aggressive and self-seeking as any others.[272] Walpola Rahula argues, however, that 'according to Buddhism there is nothing that can be called a "just war" — which is only a false term coined and put into circulation to justify and excuse hatred, cruelty, violence and massacre.'[273] However, elsewhere the same writer describes a war of national independence in Sri Lanka in the second century BC conducted under the slogan 'Not for kingdom, but for Buddhism', and he concludes that 'to fight against a foreign invader for national independence became an established Buddhist tradition, since freedom was essential to the spiritual as well as material progress of the community.'[274] The understandable and to some extent inevitable association of religion with national politics has often had regrettable consequences, as in Sri Lanka's present communal troubles involving the Buddhist Sinhalese majority and the Hindu Tamil minority. At the time of writing, after over a year of strife, the monastic sangha has so far refrained from using its influence to wean the government from its preoccupations with a purely military solution or to persuade it to offer proposals which would meet the demands of even the moderate Tamils.'[275]

In Chapter 16 it was maintained that the moral precepts must be applied situationally, rather than literally, if they were not sometimes to be violated in spirit and intent, and this applies no less to the First Precept. The example of abortion was discussed in that chapter. And many possible situations come to mind, in both personal and public life, wherein a lesser killing may be the means of avoiding a greater killing, as in the case of disease-bearing insects, for instance, or an armed murderer running amok in a crowded street and other similar arithmetic of comparative homicide. Sometimes we are condemned by circumstance to find the middle way between an immoral literalism and an immoral situationalism. We have to try to steer a course between killing the precept by the moral evasion of a self-righteous literalism in its observance which violates its intention, and, on the other hand, bending too many hurtful means to too many questionable and self-serving ends. This requires a meditative insight into self-driven predilection and its picture of the situation, penetrating through the top layer of prejudice and ideology to the underlying thrust of need and fear (including the need to be in the right), and gently disarming and informing through bringing into the light of calm awareness. It is the fully aware and unevasive suffering through the racking quandary of relative choice that can reveal what must be done. In complex situations a Higher Third may open up beyond the either/or trap, recasting the conflict in terms of larger realities and exposing an ultimately beneficial course of action. American Zen Master Robert Aitken expresses this transcendental middle way of the First Precept as follows: '"No killing" refers in some sense to prohibition, but basically it is a positive exhortation to be in touch with true nature, where negative and positive, right and wrong, birth and death, right and wrong, are simply concepts which we seek to use appropriately according to circumstance.'[276] It is only through our self-conscious separation from the situation that we cannot perceive or respond to what it requires.

Whilst always seeking to be as harmless and cherishing of all life as is possible, nevertheless in order to continue affirming the life that is given us we are obliged to kill and injure. We do this directly, of 'lower', less complex life forms, and indirectly — and unnecessarily — of other men and women, through the labyrinth of social interaction (our taxes, for example, buy killing, our cheap supermarket Third World produce buys exploitative hunger). But let all such harm be done in full empathetic awareness and hence reluctantly and reverently and minimally if at all. This requires as a rule of life the habit of restricting the demands we make upon other beings, human and non-human, and implies a modest and sufficient lifestyle (quite apart from the grosser reasoning about conserving valuable planetary resources and reducing pollution). The practice of nonviolence also implies a positive assertion of the rights of others to be as much themselves as *we* would wish to be. This requires sensitive action in both private and public life as well as the avoiding of self-indulgence at others' expense. And it requires social sanctions which are deployed in a creative and nonviolent relationship with our adversary, rather than resorting to violence to free others from the injury done by social injustice.

A final word that needs to be said about situational morality, and especially in respect of the First Precept, is that most of us have a large and unconscious capacity for deluding ourselves about our ability to view with dispassionate objectivity situations which involve self-interest, particularly if they are at all complex. After some years of meditative practice, we get to know the feel of *that* kind of confidence and to be wary of it. It were best, therefore, to try to live literally and directly by the Precepts, and especially the First, and only to go beyond literal interpretation when forced into the conviction that to do so would violate them. And in such a situation, after doing all that might make for a wise decision, we can only make the best decision we are able, taking responsibility for it and remaining aware of our ignorance. Some kind of blameless omniscience only breeds monsters, not saints.

# 29 Institutional Violence and Beyond

Henceforward I shall take 'violence' to mean 'the exercise of physical force so as to inflict injury or damage to persons or property' (*The Shorter Oxford English Dictionary*). 'Coercion' will be used with the inclusive and wider meaning of 'to restrain by force, particularly by moral force, as by law or authority; to repress; to compel to compliance; to constrain' (*New Webster Dictionary*). This meaning will be extended to cover circumstances where people are compelled to endure harm or injury because they have been placed in a situation of powerlessness.

It is important to appreciate that the sensational outbreaks of violence which hit the news headlines, whether of the state or of terrorists, liberationists or common criminals, all explode from a network of social relationships many of which are more or less *coercive* but not normally *violent*. Thus, employees may be coerced into accepting wages so low as to cause hardship, because extensive unemployment has reduced their bargaining power and they are powerless to change the overall social situation. And in other circumstances employers may be coerced, nonviolently, by strike action, to concede higher wages. The major conclusion of a widely discussed Church of England report is that 'a growing number of people are excluded by poverty or powerlessness from sharing in the common life of our nation. A substantial minority − perhaps as many as one person in every four or five across the nation... − are *forced* to live on the margins of poverty or below the threshold of an acceptable standard of living.'[277] (my italics) Racial discrimination is another form of coercion, usually nonviolent, in which the power of the dominant culture is used to attempt to coerce people into a sense of inferiority, as well as forcing them into poorer housing, employment and so on. As debtors, poor countries are coerced by rich countries with threats of withholding further aid unless they accept domestic policies which further reduce their people's living standards. Again, during the last bitter winter in Britain, the reluctance of the authorities to provide welfare fuel supplements forced many old age pensioners to endure conditions of extreme cold leading to many deaths. All these are examples of the use of power to coerce short of actual violence, whether wilfully and directly or through the workings of economic and social systems which *could* be modified or changed.

To see only the violence of those who, in desperation, answer intolerable institutional coercion with overt violence is to become party to the hypocrisy of established power. Clear recognition of widespread and systematic coercion as a way of life which diminishes the lives of the great majority of the world's peoples is therefore essential for Buddhists and other advocates of nonviolence. Of this 'institutional violence' Nhat Hanh writes:

> If nonviolence is a *stand*, then it would be an attack on violence. But the most visible form of violence is revolutionary and liberational violence. So if you stand for nonviolence, you automatically stand against actual revolution and liberation. Quite distressing! 'No! We are not against revolution or liberation. We are against the other side, the side of the institutions, the side of the oppressors. The violence of the system is much more destructive, much more harmful, although it is well hidden. We call it institutional violence. By calling ourselves nonviolent we are against *all* violence, but we are

first against *institutional* violence.'...Military in-
vasions have been used for the purpose of intervention, colonization and exploitation, yes. But
colonization, exploitation and capitalism have also
been able to operate *nonviolently* even in Europe,
not to mention in Asian-African countries. The
people of the system are very clever in 'nonviolent'
strategies. The strategies that have been used by
us within the nonviolent movement, if compared
to 'nonviolent' strategies used by capitalism and
colonialism, look like young babies. Perhaps we
need to go to them (the oppressors and exploiters),
to learn more about 'nonviolent' strategies in order
to be able to fight them back.[278]

And one of the exceptional situations in which the French
Protestant theologian, Jacques Ellul, is willing to 'condone'
violence is 'when a hypocritically just and peaceful situation
must be exposed for what it is in order to end it'. He
continues:

Violence is undoubtedly the only means for ex-
ploding façades, for exposing hypocrisy and hidden oppression for what they are. It forces the
'good boss' or the humanist politician to show
himself in his true colours – as a savage exploiter
or oppressor who does not hesitate to use violence
when he meets resistance. It reveals that the superior is affable, kind, humane, and understanding
only so far as the inferior is servile, obedient,
afraid and hardworking. Otherwise the superior
turns ferocious.[279]

Ellul makes the point well, but if coercion is met with
violence and responds with counter-violence, where can
this lead but to the escalation of violence and the hardening
of confrontation? The employment even of nonviolent means
deliberately to provoke a coercive oppressor into violence is,

I believe, a sterile and negative use of nonviolence which leads in the wrong direction. Other more imaginative means must be found to bring into the light the harmful and coercive relationships to which Ellul refers, not excluding the *creative* use of nonviolent counter-coercion in the Gandhian tradition outlined in the next chapter.

Short of the violent sanctions of fear, imprisonment and torture (increasingly routine in many countries) a social group in established dominance is coercive simply through the operation of an historically evolved social system whose workings are claimed to be impersonal and more or less inevitable, and modified only by the 'humanity' of the establishment itself....The sense of coercion, breaking occasionally into open violence, is never far below the surface in most social sectors in most countries, in the workplace and school, on the streets, in politics, in the shadow of the State and the Law, and in constant reminders in the news media. And this coercion, and the periodic clenched violence, are legitimated in the violent and coercive itch in all of us, erupting, when much provoked, in hot-righteous ill will. Wilhelm Reich observed that 'there is not a single individual who does not bear the elements of fascist feeling and thinking in his structure'. Invoking the 'class struggle' has the same gutsy, righteous excitement about it as invoking 'law and order'.

However, 'coercion' can only properly be used of circumstances where a person is compelled to act or endure against his or her own sense of their best interests, and hence feels that they *are* being compelled. A person may go off rejoicing to die in a 'just' war or endure hunger as an act of God. It is not only that sophisticated methods of 'thought control' exist. Nor is it simply that, as was noted in Chapter 3, many suffer patriotic death or loyal hardship in the service of their superiors in order that their lives should be made the more meaningful. Much of what is arguable as social control exists through a process of socialization, so that compliance becomes routine, habituated, ingrained, kammaic. Neither those in formal or informal authority nor those who act in conformity to their will may be conscious of being coercive or of being coerced. The latter may claim to act of their own free will. Others may argue that, on the contrary, such people have been socially conditioned to act against their real interests. It would be claimed by Marxists that they have had a 'false consciousness' imposed upon them, like 'Uncle Tom', the loyal old plantation slave of Negro tradition. Uncle Tom is an extreme case; there are others where the question is more open as to whose consciousness is 'false' and in what sense 'false'? The dangers inherent in A telling B what his or her true interests are and how she or he is betraying them are obvious. However, inviting B to undertake some exploration of his or her own social consciousness is another matter, and surely to be welcomed. And that some people attempt dogmatic foreclosure of the question is the more reason for open investigation.

Women's 'consciousness raising' groups are the best-known example of self-help exploration of social consciousness. Such exploration of women's social consciousness can be creatively related to the more fundamental spiritual project of the exploration of human existential consciousness. This creative relationship has still to be adequately investigated, however.

Social consciousness-raising through the women's movement has enabled many women to become aware of how much their dignity is denied in subjection to innumerable forms of discrimination — whether thoughtless, selfish, patronizing or simply contemptuous. The 'sixty Buddhist scholars, monks and laypeople' for whom James Hughes drafted *A Green Buddhist Declaration* maintain that:

> A Buddhist analysis of patriarchy points to the interdependence of social power and spiritual oppression, in that the organized power of men over women is rooted both in threat of violence, the greed to maintain privilege, and a subtle form of

> ego-ignorance, male chauvinism....We see [the
> subordination of women] as part of the more
> general problem of objectification and commodit-
> ization of human beings, alienating subject and
> object.[280]

Virtually everywhere women have to bear a triple burden of
child care, domestic labour and paid work outside the
home, with usually less recompense in time and money
than their menfolk. Overall, they still have to undertake
inferior work for less pay and with poorer promotion prospects. In many respects they remain second-class citizens. In
the mass media they are publicly paraded as sexual objects,
and are subjected to apparently widespread sexual harass-
ment at work and to increasing violence and the fear of
violence in the streets and even in their own homes. And
yet, until quite recently, all but a few women were socially
conditioned to acceptance of their 'inferior' status.

Here it is not possible to do justice to the important
question of Buddhist feminism. As James Hughes maintains,
in a stimulating essay on this subject, 'Buddhism, as a way
of living with compassion and insight, is radically liberating
for women....One can find within the Buddhist tradition
women who prefigure modern feminism by two and a half
millennia, and yet writings which equal the worst anti-
women polemics of any religion.'[281]

Patriarchy provides an instructive example of the way in
which the controlled, authoritarian personality, shaped by
existential fear, is expressed in specific historical and cultural
forms. The coercion and denial of parts of the self are
translated into institutionalized behaviour and shape a culture which *reinforces* the self-coercion of the self. Thus men
are unknowingly acculturated to do violence to the feminine
in their own natures. Dorothy Rowe refers to the pain and
fear inflicted by this process:

> A small boy who is aware of the diversity of
> feeling within him and of the infinite possibilities

of the person he could become, changes into a man who represses or isolates much of his emotional life, who argues 'logically' and 'intellectually', being unable to tolerate doubt, paradox and ambiguity, who sees women as strangers, either sexually enticing or of no value at all, and other men as competitors, and who reacts to frustration with a violence which he regards as both justified and manly.[282]

In brief, beneath overt violence there is a spirit of coerciveness which is widespread in virtually all historical cultures. Its roots in the individual psyche have already been examined in the first section of this book, which also introduced the phenomena of antithetical bonding and weighted polarization through which coerciveness is expressed and accentuated. Beneath coercion which is actively experienced as such is the passive, more or less unaware subjection to a coercion which others claim to see and of which the subject may also become aware through experience and investigation.

It is the task of Buddhist meditative practice to expose for each of us the roots of coerciveness and violence within ourselves, and of Buddhist activism and social psychology to point to the dynamic mutual reinforcement of this largely unconscious ill will and the social conditions which are intimately sustained by it. We need to be both well informed of, and sensitive to, the climate of often very subtle rejection and discrimination through which we relate to the various kinds of 'put down' people in our society, including (if we are men), the other half of the human race, the mentally and physically handicapped, people of other ethnic cultures, and those who suffer from the many different kinds of poverty and powerlessness.

Here again, compassion to be fully meaningful has to be socially informed and socially effective. We are not living now in the comparatively simple societies in which the great world religions were conceived. Personal help and example are still essential and may be all we can give, but they will fall short of fully effective helping. This requires working to change the social institutions and structures which affirm coerciveness and indifference and maintain their kammaic momentum. Again, it is the Buddhist recognition of the power of conditioning — including social conditioning — that points up the importance of a radical and transformative social activism. However, the disappointing results of legislation in support of the rights of women and ethnic minorities when it is not accompanied by a widespread change of heart, reflected in new social norms and attitudes, is evidence, once again, that legal and institutional changes are only superficially transformative. This is not to say they are not important. They *are* essential concomitants to any turnabout in how people feel. But that turnabout cannot be legislated into existence.

# 30  *Creative Nonviolence*

Since violence originates in the same fundamentally coercive mentality as do the evils which radical social change seeks to rectify, in the final analysis it is arguable that violence inflames those evils yet further. It is therefore commonly justified as an expedient which can carry a radical movement to a point at which conditions become favourable for it to go into reverse, and use and promote only what is peaceful. Violence can bring quick results, is understood by all, and gratifyingly and sensationally discharges the frustration and bitterness of the oppressed. But it habitually corrupts the peaceful (ultimate) ends to which the violent may sincerely aspire, as well as profoundly affecting the whole character of their current undertaking. The objectifying and depersonalization of other people which is inevitably involved in doing them violence not only tends to brutalize the violent but also becomes ingrained and institutionalized in deeply coercive and insensitive policies and organizational forms. In the kind of people they have become, the formerly oppressed resemble more and more their former oppressors. In Jacques Ellul's words:

> My study of politics and sociology have convinced me that violence is an altogether superficial thing; that is, it can produce apparent, superficial changes, rough facsimiles of change. But it never affects the roots of injustice — social structures, the bases of an economic system, the foundations of society.

>   Violence is not the appropriate means for a revolu-
>   tion in depth.[283]

Even when a single word is made of 'nonviolence' it is still a negative term. If we turn it round, therefore, and look at what is behind it, three different kinds of thinking can be broadly distinguished. First there is the creative nonviolence pioneered by Gandhi and others, and which is the natural expression of a Buddhist activism.

Secondly there is a pragmatic, rationalist strain of non-violent thinking, of which Gene Sharp is probably the most noteworthy exponent.[284] For Sharp nonviolence is simply a more effective means of attaining a peaceful and just world than violence. Sharp acknowledges the deep personal, as well as social, roots of violence, but he is critical of heavily ideological philosophies of nonviolence not least because the moral absolutism of extreme pacifism will always, he believes, restrict its appeal to a tiny and ineffective minority. In my view, Sharp shows hardly less faith in relying on the power of reason alone to mobilize and sustain the impressive array of nonviolent strategies set out in his books. Whether spelled out or not, Sharp's kind of nonviolence is shared by the majority of peace workers and other nonviolent activists at the present time. It limits itself to rendering the author-ities powerless through applying coercive 'sanctions' (as Sharp calls them) and thereby effecting a transfer of power.

Thirdly, there is an ideological kind of nonviolence, which mirrors that ideology of violence which believes that violence against injustice purifies and empowers the violent. As with all ideology, that of nonviolence tends to have a self-confirming and righteous quality about it which distances it from disconcerting realities. It inclines to grand gestures like 'the propaganda of the deed'. In this respect, demonstrations of one's moral superiority, even if they amount to heroism are as much likely to alienate others as persuade them of the truth of one's views. Thomas Merton particularly warned of 'the danger of ambiguity in protests that seek mainly to capture the attention of the press and to gain publicity for a cause, being more concerned with the impact upon the public than with the meaning of that impact'. Merton associated such gestures with 'the mental climate in which we live':

Our minds are filled with images which call for violent and erratic reactions. . . . We are swept by alternate fears and hopes which have no relation to deep moral truth. A protest which merely compounds these fears and hopes with a new store of images can hardly help us to become men of peace.

Merton remarked that 'perhaps the most insidious temptation to be avoided is one which is characteristic of the power structure itself: this fetishism of immediate and visible results.'[285]

Moreover, pacifism as ideology tends to make absolute claims and too readily assumes the universal instrumental effectiveness of nonviolent action. Richard Gregg, in one of the classics on nonviolence,[286] quotes successes from Hungary (1867), Gandhi's campaigns in South Africa (1906–14) and India (1917–47), Denmark and Norway under the Nazi occupation (1942–5) and the struggle which Martin Luther King led against racial segregation in the USA. To these might be added the experience of the Buddhist nonviolent movement in Vietnam to which I referred in Part Six, the Polish struggles against their Soviet client government, and the mass nonviolent movement which toppled dictator Marcos in the Philippines in 1986. But Gandhi hastened the withdrawal from India of a burnt-out colonial power whose post-war Labour government was disposing of a whole empire as rapidly as possible. Martin Luther King campaigned in a democracy which had a public conscience that could be shaken. It is their very real achievement that in both cases they accelerated an historical process that certainly would otherwise have been more violent. However, I believe that nonviolent movements should be assessed not so much in terms of instrumental success but rather as historical episodes which hopefully won some tangible concessions but at the same time shifted the moral climate a little. Danilo Dolci's work to change the character of a neglected, poverty-stricken southern Italy, subject to corrupt and inefficient government and Mafia gangsterism is a good example.

There have been many instances where conditions were such that no practicable foothold existed for a nonviolent action which could conceivably have yielded instrumental results. In the Second World War, for example, Jews and Slavs were overwhelmed by a heedless Nazi genocide. The war against Nazi Germany was also an example of the kind of situation where the timely use of violence was very likely to prove instrumentally effective in terminating the escalating violence of an extremely ruthless adversary, in circumstances extremely unfavourable for nonviolent action. Reference was made in Chapter 16 to the examples of Michael Scott and Dietrich Bonhoeffer, both men of great spiritual strength and maturity, who made the decision to fight. There were others, however, who felt that nonviolent witness and service was the only course of action they could take, and the only one which, historically, could be ultimately and profoundly effective.

To take another example, the left-wing regimes in Cuba and Nicaragua were born out of a comparatively modest violence on the part of the revolutionaries, and whatever their shortcomings they are undoubtedly less violent and more socially just and free of poverty than was the case under the crude dictatorships which preceded them. Such examples give plenty of scope for argument, of course, but my concern here is only to suggest that genuine moral dilemmas are involved.

On such dilemmas the writing of Jacques Ellul is particularly instructive, in that he combines a thoroughgoing and uncompromisingly radical political stance with a scrupulous honesty about the evil of violence. For Ellul no violence can be 'good, legitimate or just', yet he believes that violence can be 'understandable, acceptable and condonable' in the following exceptional circumstances: (a) when nonviolence is impracticable or has failed; (b) when it is demonstrable that if violence were not used, greater violence would befall; (c) violence must not be 'strategic', that is, an integral and fundamental part of policy; and (d) means must be found to mitigate the effects of violence before and afterwards. For 'the first law of violence is continuity. Once you start using violence you cannot get away from it.... Violence has brought so many clear and visible results; how then to go back to a way of acting that certainly looks ineffectual and seems to promise very doubtful results?' Although critical of some liberation theologians, Ellul is in no doubt that the Christian must take the side of the poor and oppressed: 'where man is exploited, crushed, degraded by man, the Christian can neither avoid involvement by escape into the realm of spiritual values or side by default with the dominant party.'

Ellul concludes that 'in face of the tragic problem of violence, the first truth to be discerned is that, whatever side he takes, the Christian cannot have an easy conscience.... If a Christian joins a violent movement, his presence implies that their (and his) undertaking is of a relative character.... For them he is a kind of permanent bad conscience.... He ought to be the one who, even as he acts with the others, proclaims the injustice and unacceptability of what they are doing. He ought to be the mirror of truth in which his comrades perceive the horror of their action. He ought to be the conscience of the movement.'[287] Buddhist readers might find too much casuistry and conscience-wrestling here, however. Better it were to meditate the dilemma in stillness and then to do what has to be done (or not), no more and no less, with a flame of clear resolution and as little smoke as possible...

In the great majority of social conflict situations the possibility of remedy through nonviolent action will be found to exist (always assuming that conciliatory and noncoercive attempts have been exhausted). More or less favourable conditions will variously obtain in respect of (a) the nature of the protest movement; (b) its adversaries; (c) the issue in dispute; and (d) the contextual situation (the state of 'external' opinion, for example). The kind of situations I have in mind are industrial disputes, community actions of various kinds (as against unwelcome 'development' foisted by the authorities or private enterprise for instance), the campaigns against nuclear weapons and nuclear power generation and waste disposal, communal strife such as that in Sri Lanka or Northern Ireland, resistance to occupation by a foreign power, movements to topple an oppressive and unrepresentative regime, and, most particularly, episodes in the process of overall radical social transformation outlined later in this book. Even if some violent course of action is undertaken within the kind of limits which Ellul finds 'condonable', every opportunity must surely be used to give effect to the creatively nonviolent approach outlined below.

Creative nonviolence is a natural and direct expression of Buddhadharma, which shares a common perspective with the nonviolence in other traditions of engaged spirituality. The most sophisticated and well-grounded model is undoubtedly the *satyagraha* of Mahatma Gandhi, which was rooted in Hinduism, with acknowledgements also to Thoreau, Tolstoy and Ruskin. Here I have drawn particularly on Joan Bondurant's valuable presentation of Gandhian creative nonviolence.[288]

The conventional approach to remedying a grievance (from a breach of employment contract to the threat of nuclear war) is to focus all attention on remedying the grievance by confronting and defeating the adversary. Where the conflict is ideological the conflict over the specific grievance is seen as no more than a step in a long and historic struggle which strengthens and matures the protesters and weakens the adversary (as in the example of the Marxist revolutionary perspective). The creative nonviolence of engaged spirituality, however, takes place in a perspective which is not only social but human and existential. Therefore the common humanity of the adversary is recognized as a matter for compassionate concern throughout the conflict. In particular, the protesters seek to be in full awareness of the urge to violence, confrontation, and alienation which they share with their adversary.

The philosophy of creative nonviolence recognizes that both protester and adversary are caught up in the same historical web of socially supercharged bitterness and antagonism. Like other entities in Indra's Net (Chapter 12) the specific question at issue is no more than an expression of the whole flux of kammaically freighted fear, ill will, acquisitiveness, and existential blindness. The so-called 'method' of nonviolence by which the specific affliction is to be removed is therefore more important than the specific question at issue, for it seeks to help undercut the human roots from which such afflictions arise again and again. It does this by seeking to bring into the awareness of the adversary the suffering which arises from greed and domination, and also to share with him something of a higher level of consciousness through the experience of mutual respect, genuine communication and some recognition of ultimate common interest. Thus Jack Douglass, an American war resister, writes that 'truth seeks the liberation of both sides, poor and wealthy, from the common bondage of an inhuman relationship.... Nonviolent liberation seeks the redemption of humanity from power itself.'[289] But, as Gandhi made very clear, where necessary the minds of the powerful and wealthy are to be forcefully (but not violently) concentrated upon these realities. The struggle is directed to raising the consciousness of adversaries as well as protesters, and obliging them to explore alternatives and make choices. The afflictions at issue are not just occasions for a profound learning exercise; they are real and terrible things in themselves, and Gandhi was always adamant that there should be no compromise on fundamental, reasonable and minimum demands.

'Satyagraha' is made up of two elements, 'love' and 'force', which are the creative dialectic of a spiritually inspired nonviolence. Nonviolent coerciveness is present as the motive power for transforming the situation, but it is to be a *filiative* and not an *antagonistic* coerciveness, with force used minimally, without violence or hate, to set in motion the search for a 'truth' in the conflict situation that both sides can recognize, a Higher Third on which to base a solution. Bondurant writes that the 'immediate goal' for Gandhi in a nonviolent conflict 'is not the triumph of his substantial side in the struggle − but, rather, the synthesis of the two opposing claims. He does, then, all he can to persuade the opponent of the correctness of his own position but, while he carries on his own persuasive activity, he allows the opponent every opportunity and, indeed, invites him to demonstrate the correctness of his (the opponent's) position and to dissuade him of his own position.' He makes it clear that he is open to persuasion and is not seeking a one-sided triumph: 'he seeks a victory not over the opponent but over the situation.'[290] 'A test of our sincerity,' observes Thomas Merton, 'in our practice of nonviolence is this: are we willing to learn something from the adversary? If a new truth is made known to us by him or through him, will we accept it? Are we willing to admit that he is not totally inhumane, wrong, unreasonable, cruel, etc.?'[291]

The foregoing is well illustrated by the following statement from Danilo Dolci, on the occasion of the occupation of the square of an Italian town where the protesters were to fast in order to persuade the authorities to build a much needed dam to relieve local poverty:

> We are here to be of service, to join together people of various political beliefs toward one common cause. We shall fast not to ridicule the police, nor to be photographed. Ours is a position of reason that emphasizes the distinction between force and truth. By our nonviolent action we shall show that truth has its own strength. Ours is a

strategy based on love, not hate, and should result
in a chain reaction of discussion and insight.[292]

Writers on nonviolent campaigning and conflict resolution
have variously distinguished successive stages through
which it is desirable that the action should move. The
following are based on those distinguished by Gandhi,
Sharp and Curle.[293] It will be appreciated that to some extent
the stages will overlap and parallel one another, rather than
following in successively exhausted sequence.

### 1. *Research*
In conflict situations, 'truth' serves the contending parties
through the same weighted polarization as everything else.
It is important to examine the adversary's truth carefully and
respectfully, to be equally rigorous in examining one's own
for tendentiousness and to try to enlarge the view by further
research which should be as independent as possible (perhaps through using intermediaries). The enlarged and more
fully shared 'knowledge base' can then be publicized and
attempts made to secure wider agreement simply, at this
stage, as to the facts of the situation.

### 2. *Negotiation and arbitration through established channels*
Every effort should be made to resolve the dispute at this
stage, which should be exhausted before further steps are
taken.

### 3. *Education, publicity, meetings and street demonstrations*
Gandhi attached great importance to the education of protesters, adversaries and other parties so far uninvolved, not
only in the question at issue but also in the philosophy and
practicalities of creative nonviolence.

### 4. *Making the case to the adversary*
Gandhi counsels the need to be constructive, not to drive
the adversary into a corner, not to push for more than is
really needed, to save the adversary's face, and not to press
home an advantage. By refraining from pressing the adver-

sary to the limit throughout the conflict and from taking advantage of his every weakness, he may be jolted out of the sense of confrontation and given some emotional space in which to make a constructive proposal free of being forced into doing so. For example, in his early days in South Africa Gandhi deliberately refrained from pushing his advantage at a time when the authorities had to cope with a rail strike as well as with him and his followers.

5. *Preparation of the protesters for creative nonviolent action*
Gandhi emphasized that the protester should be well integrated in a self-reliant affinity group in which strong bonds of mutual trust had been built up. This preparation is the most important single precondition for the success of creative nonviolence. Protesters need to have had opportunity to work through their more obtrusive self-needs with the support of the group so that they do not use a nonviolent demonstration or other action as opportunity to vent their anger, resentment or other unfinished emotional business upon the adversary. The practices of meditation and awareness are clearly valuable for developing a calm, unwavering, well-centred strength in the face of violence and provocation.

6. *Escalation of nonviolent action*
Escalation will begin with such constitutional action as lobbying the legislature, petitions, protest meetings and the like and continue through economic boycott and strikes to non-cooperation with the authorities (such as a boycott of State schools, or a tax strike). Beyond this lies active civil disobedience and lawbreaking (either symbolic or related to the grievance). The ability of the authorities or other target organization or institution to continue operating normally will become impaired. Authority is normally confirmed by compliance because it is assumed to be reasonable and in the interests of those who comply with it; or else they comply out of habit and social conditioning, or because they feel powerless. Concerted, large-scale and resolute refusal to comply obliges the authorities to resort to coercion and even

violent coercion to intimidate and terrorize. However, if the protest movement can remain firm, even this becomes self-defeating beyond a certain point.

Before moving on to escalate the action to a higher stage (until parallel government and the usurpation of existing government may become necessary) the protesters will at each stage attempt to open positive and creative negotiations with the adversary in the spirit described earlier in this chapter. If these fail, a further ultimatum may be issued and nonviolent sanctions further extended. However, even the ultimatums should offer the widest scope for agreement, should be constructive and reasonable in character, and avoid violent and confrontational language. Gandhi urged that adversaries at all levels be treated with respect and humanity and protected from physical violence and verbal abuse. The protesters' own willingness to suffer these can make a strong appeal to both adversaries and public.

Today, in peace, environmental protection and other social and political movements in Europe, North America and elsewhere there is much interest in mass nonviolent direct action, which is from time to time and here and there put into effect. Some of it is imaginative and good-humoured, but much of it is confrontational, antagonistic, symbolically violent and far from Gandhian *ahimsa* — 'positive harmless-ness'. This is what Gandhi called *duragraha* or 'one-sided force', a negative, confrontational nonviolence unconcerned with attempts to open meaningful communication with adversaries. Even when it is instrumentally successful such negative nonviolence leaves the social situation as divided and embittered as before, except that there is a little more triumphalism on one side and a little more bitter revenge-fulness on the other, until the next round.

Typical of the present state of thinking is an article in *Sanity*, the journal of the British Campaign for Nuclear Disarmament (CND) which gives the following four justi-fications for nonviolent direct action: First, it gives 'extra access to the news media' ('propaganda of the deed' again!); secondly, it is an opportunity for 'physical interference' with nuclear arms escalation; thirdly, it can give 'personal fulfil- ment'; and fourthly, it can 'force the State to reveal its more brutal and ugly features'.[294] The spirit of the article is clearly at variance with that of a creative nonviolent perspective, though the writer appears unaware of the distinction and even refers approvingly, in passing, to Gandhi, Martin Luther King and others in that tradition.

It is true that in many situations even a negative nonviol- ence may be more difficult to sustain than open violence. And in many others, it may be very difficult to find a creative way forward out of confrontational and narcissistic forms of nonviolence, and especially when the adversary will not open the door even a fraction of an inch to real communication. What is saddening, however, is the lack of awareness of the possibility of more creative forms of non- violent action and of at least attempts to make trial of them. Unfortunately such initiatives would be likely to prove divisive and disorientating in mass movements whose unity and morale depend very much on black-and-white picture- making and combative sloganizing. The initiation of dis- cussion and action around the theme of *creative* nonviolence would seem to be one of the more immediate tasks for Buddhist and other engaged spirituality.

# 31  *Interpersonal Disagreement and Conflict Resolution*

It is a common experience in working groups and organizations that much time and energy are consumed in frustrating interpersonal conflict and in fruitless attempts to resolve 'personality problems'. Moreover, as we saw in Chapter 7 on the two faces of Janus, the work which the group or organization exists to perform is coloured and warped by the emotional needs of its members, and hence it fails to respond adequately to the needs of the objective situation. Some members may be drawn into futile 'games playing', whilst others suffer frustration and burn-out. The personalities and the work which the group has to do tend to become mixed up in its members' minds, and they commonly fail to perceive that what is making the work difficult is not the nature of the work itself but the unacknowledged emotional needs of those who are trying to do it. Amidst defending their status, hitting back at imagined slights and threats, and confirming their own sense of power by putting down others, co-workers may continue to hurl facts and arguments at each other with a kind of mad rationality. Writing out of many years' experience as a senior consultant psychiatrist in a hospital, Dorothy Rowe confesses that:

> The only time I get really frightened and angry and despair that the human race will survive is when I see in the course of my work what men — competitive men, who want their own way no matter who gets hurt — will do....I have known administrators who, rather than compromise, will obstruct in

various petty ways those they see as competing with and challenging them, and when those tactics fail, they will use violent abuse — and all those over matters of little importance, such as modest sums of National Health Service money....I have seen doctors fight one another over the number of beds each has in a hospital and give no regard at all to the patients who may need to use those beds. Small boys squabbling over marbles behave with more dignity than these men. And even more undignified are the doctors who fall into screaming tantrums when the realities of hospital life fail to conform to the doctor's wishes.[295]

This is very much a 'tool' chapter, and is about the resolution of disagreement and conflict within groups and between individuals who are working together. So in one sense it is about improving the effectiveness of social activists by introducing, with a Buddhist slant, a variety of established perspectives and methods. However, there is a by now familiar dialectic here. To become more effective, a group (or work pair) has to become a different kind of group. So its members have to become different kinds of people. To become more self aware and interpersonally aware and skilled will carry a significance which goes beyond short-term instrumental success. Again, 'we build the road and the road builds us'.

There is considerable evidence that the very existence of an *adversary* in a problem situation tends to invoke a combative and competitive state of mind which makes satisfactory resolution of the problem very much more difficult. For example, a revealing series of experiments has been conducted in which a group of people were asked to play a problem-solving game with a computer which was programmed to respond precisely to each move of the human player, meeting aggressive play with aggressiveness and conciliatory and co-operative moves with like moves. The latter kinds of behaviour were 'rewarded' with 'earnings' credited to the human player. A second group played against live opponents who, unknown to them, were confederates of the experimenter who had instructed them to reciprocate players' behaviour in exactly the same way as the computer. Those playing against the machine 'learned' to act co-operatively with it so as to maximize their pay-off, even though by so doing they permitted the machine to 'earn' an even larger sum. Players against the machine were ninety per cent co-operative and conciliatory in their moves, but those confronting another human being were ninety per cent aggressive, even though their pay-off score was reduced by this behaviour. More alarmingly, the experiment was then successfully replicated with army staff officers.[296] Two millennia earlier, the Taoist sage Chuang-Tzu had drawn attention to the same phenomenon:

> If a man is crossing a river
> And an empty boat collides with his own skiff,
> Even though he be a bad tempered man
> He will not become very angry.
> But if he sees a man in the boat,
> He will shout at him to steer clear.
> If his shout is not heard, he will shout again.
> And yet again, and begin cursing.
> And all because there is someone in the boat.
> Yet if the boat were empty,
> He would not be shouting and angry.
>
> If you can empty your own boat
> Crossing the river of the world,
> No one will oppose you,
> No one will seek to harm you.[297]

It is noteworthy that, in laboratory experiments at least, it has been found that *unconditional* conciliatory or co-operative behaviour tends to be exploited by the other party, whereas the most liked opponents are those who, like Gandhi's *satyagrahis*, do initiate a co-operative move but at the same time request a co-operative move in return. If the response is positive, then a co-operative de-escalation is set in train. Conflict resolution strategy is concerned with creating the conditions for this momentum and then sustaining it.

A very extensive, practical literature exists on how to resolve conflicts and work through disagreement of various kinds. However, a Buddhist perspective and training can undoubtedly be valuable in making best use of these methods, which are of little value without some insightful interpersonal skill. The Buddhist diagnosis of the human condition draws attention to a fretfulness never far below the surface to sustain and advance our sense of self in interpersonal situations. This will be more evident, of course, where there is conflict and disagreement, where it may range from an ebullient triumphalism to a paranoiac defensiveness. Years of meditation and awareness training make clear these strong stirrings in the self, as well as making one more sensitive to them in other people, so that they lose much of their power over us. The practical uses of this awareness were exemplified in Chapter 17 with the case of a stormy meeting, in which self-awareness was the precondition for an effective and positive intervention.

The second part of this chapter examines successive (but overlapping) stages in resolving interpersonal conflicts and reaching agreement on a course of action. The same assumptions underlie these as in the case of the successive phases of a creative nonviolent action outlined in the previous chapter, but the following are more adapted to the needs of *interpersonal* conflict resolution. Here we shall use the word 'conflict' only to denote disagreement which is emotionally charged. You may find it useful to call to mind a (preferably ongoing) interpersonal disagreement known to you, particularly one in which you are directly involved or able to act as conciliator.

In the first place it is worth asking whether one of the disputants has not actually gone out of his way to involve himself in a problem or dispute which is not really his concern at all. Whose problem is it really? There are even motives that move people to invent problems, or to dispute a congenial problem so as to ignore a more threatening but important one! The itch to keep the world tidy, or to feel useful, or to kick up a bit of excitement may needlessly create or enlarge a disputatious problem. If someone else's doings do not notably harm us or others whose concerns we share, then the most useful thing might be to keep quiet and to look within to discover just what it is that is pushing us to interfere.

Secondly, situations are common where not only is conflict denied, both to oneself and others, but even the fact of disagreement. Some 'buttoned up' individuals and even whole cultures try to deny both inner and interpersonal conflict. Showing emotion, making a fuss, may be frowned upon. In the case of the religiously inclined, suppression of emotion may be mistaken for its sublimation and a state of repression mistaken for a state of spiritual grace. Another example of problem denial is to be found in the varieties of evasion, cosmetic optimism and wilful ignorance by which many people hope to outface the threat of nuclear destruction. Their 'refusal' of their fear disarms them from determined action, and being reminded of the danger can provoke resentful hostility.

It is therefore important at this stage somehow to give the security and 'permission' which will enable disputants to express their feelings freely. 'Letting off steam' may be the first essential step to resolving the conflict. Certainly it will be more valuable still if all that energy can be contained in full awareness without either sitting on it or blowing it off. However, this requires much determined practice, and for most people the only alternative to bottling up their feelings is to be able to vent them in a supportive situation where doing so can do more good than harm.

When the air has been cleared in this way it will be easier to follow the kind of advice given by Zen Master Dogen:

'When you say something to someone he may not accept it, but do not try to make him understand it rationally. Don't argue with him; just listen to his objections, until he himself finds something wrong with them.' Each disputant can repeat in their own words the other's point of view, so that they can feel for themself what it is like to hold it.

Now that the disputants and their mediator (if they have one) have the measure of the disagreement, and are not driven by such a head of emotional steam, it might be useful if they were to inform themselves more fully on the question at issue. It does sometimes happen that one party discovers with a sense of relief that he or she 'had their facts wrong,' and hence the fears which inspired their opposition are found to be groundless. Even if they are now determined to have an argument about something, at least the shame of an ignorance revealed will oblige them to find another pretext. On the other hand, research into organizational decision making does suggest that in the midst of uncertainty we do tend to assume that if only we had even more information than we have already then we would be more likely to make the 'right' decision. In fact, we tend to be blind to evidence which spoils our existing view of the situation and runs counter to what we really want to do, and in any case there is a law of diminishing returns which reduces the value of collecting more and more information. Researchers in this field have been 'astonished' by 'how much information most people ignore [in decision making], and how much they tend to overestimate the value of information....People are willing to pay much more for information than the information could possibly help them. This suggests a paradox...people overvalue information and at the same time ignore most of the information they receive.'[298] Here again much apparently 'objective' and 'rational' behaviour is an attempt to satisfy deep emotional needs, in this case the hankering after more and more information to give reassurance in reaching a 'correct' decision which may already have been subliminally determined.

If disagreement persists, and perhaps still with some strong feelings, this is nevertheless preferable to grudging compromise. It is no good 'burying the hatchet' if uncompleted emotional business is buried with it. Painful exhumations follow sooner or later. The temptation to 'get the matter over with' at a relatively superficial level should be resisted. Nothing can ripen unless it is given time. Much better than the traditional advice to sleep on a problem is to clear the mind by meditation and follow with calm reflection. When the mind is still the roots of conflict and its compulsive mechanisms can be observed with equanimity. As a disputant, give space to the other by giving them time. Do not insult them and deceive yourself by struggling to feel at ease with them when you are not. In place of the benevolence which you suppose yourself to be radiating, he or she may only sense threat. Try to grant the other their otherness by dissolving the self-gratifying picture you have of them. Simone Weil believed that to do another person justice requires us 'to be ever ready to admit that [he] is something quite different from what we read when he is there (or when we think about him). . . . Every being cries out silently to be read differently.'[299] Feel the difference, and its tension, between self and other. Gently push and feel the counter pressure. However clumsily, try to discover the dance steps and hear the music of this shared situation. For the common humanity which antagonists share is always greater than the differences which have brought them together.

Disagreement may remain even when feelings no longer run high and there is mutual acknowledgement and respect, so that people are now working together on a problem instead of fighting over it. The disputants may have different mental 'maps' in their heads which give them different underlying perspectives on the question at issue. These may be projections of different backgrounds, cultures and ideologies, as well as of different personality types. They may be rather rigid projections, reflecting an underlying anxiety to be right. At this stage, also, the help of a neutral, trusted and respected mediator will be valuable as facilitator but no more than that, and not as arbitrator. Without creating more disturbance than can be handled, it may be possible for the mediator to help bring to light the underlying psychological and ideological agenda which one or more of the disputants is using (or is being used by). And it may be helpful to move away from the answers that are being given to examine the questions that are being assumed, and further still to try better to define the problems that are implied behind the questions. Further back again, what are the *situations* that are being seen as *problems*? Much will depend on disputants' ability to let go of the particular questions, answers and problems on which they have become fixated through heavy pre-investment of self-esteem. Do we really want the best solution, or do we want the solution which is ours? In our present state of mind, how capable are we of making the decision? (The suggestions in Chapter 16 and 28 on situational choice may be also helpful, even where there is not any moral dilemma.)

The above approaches may generate a variety of possibilities which are much richer than the original alternatives and which may yield an *integrative* solution which meets the underlying needs of both disputants — a Higher Third which transcends the partial truth in which each had been imprisoned. And more valuable than the solution itself may have been the insights experienced into a more open and integrative level of consciousness at which life might be lived.

Instructive in all this are the ways in which, in myth and history, the wise and awakened pronounced judgements and facilitated solutions in perplexing and contentious situations. Certainly in the West the wise have been seen as judges and lawgivers, whether secular (Solomon, Solon of Athens) or religious (Moses), and God Almighty was created in that image. However, if we perceive the wise as having access to some kind of divine or absolute calculator then we fall into the dualism of a superior Good accessible 'out there'. The concern there is only for rightness rather than goodness, reason rather than volition, the light rather than its source.

The wise teach rather than judge, but, since all good teachers start with the concerns of those whom they teach, perplexing problems with conflicting moral interests have provided parables and anecdotes in all the world's religions. In these we see how the perception of the wise is unfiltered by the veils of engaged emotion and self-justification whilst at the same time it senses the workings of the self in the disputants, who are more or less their own problems making their own problems. At the same time there is a compassionate concern for the autonomy, the humanity, the clouded Buddha Nature, of the contending parties. It is a concern that they should make their own decisions and take responsibility for them. Therefore the teacher tends to rephrase the problem. 'How much is water worth?' asked the Buddha of the leaders of the armies of the Sakyans and the Koliyans, poised to contest the ownership of the irrigation waters of the River Rohini. 'Very little, Reverend Sir.' 'How much are warriors worth?' 'Warriors are beyond price, Reverend Sir.' Then said the Buddha, 'It is not fitting that because of a little water you should destroy warriors who are beyond price,' and they were silent.[300] Some vivid metaphor may prompt a new perception. A sharp-cutting paradox or riddle may jolt the listeners. Or a profound silence may open up space.

A well-known Buddhist example is the parable of the blind men and the elephant, each of whom stubbornly claimed knowledge of the whole through touching the part nearest him. To conclude that the wise 'see all sides of the question' would be to miss the point altogether. 'Seeing all sides of the question' may even mean being much less truly aware of the question, of its underlying force than are the disputants themselves. The wise *live* the question, they have its smell, they see all sides of the circle. 'It is not enough to sympathize with something to such an extent that one agrees with it. If necessary, one must sympathize to such an extent that one disagrees.'[301]

This chapter concludes with some reference to the harmonious working of individuals within a group.

The small group of, say, some six to eight people, has become a characteristic feature of radical movements. Moreover, networks of such groups have in the last two decades changed the character of many different kinds of professional and other organizations, from public libraries to the Church of England, supplementing and modifying the traditional hierarchical organization pyramid. A work group differs from a committee in that it works more informally and its effectiveness depends on the relationship built up between its members instead of the mechanical operation of rules and procedures. Its decisions, for example, are likely to be reached by consensus rather than the vote of the majority. It also happens to be a superb though neglected device for traditional Buddhist awareness training, in respect both of self and others.

A group will have tasks to undertake, problems to solve, and decisions to take, as in the case of a peacework or environmental protection group. To do these things well, the group members will have to learn how to work closely together. Through the group experience the members will have opportunity to learn more about themselves, as well as about one another, and will be able to develop new social skills and perceptions. The group can provide emotional support for its members, but it can also reflect back as a mirror in which each member can see something of themselves of which she or he may have been unaware. Assertive members, for example, will be made aware of their need to listen more and talk less, and make space for the less assertive. The Janus-like mix of instrumental activity and expressive behaviour in group work has already been noted in Chapter 7.

Learning group social skills is itself hard work, though a number of practical guides have been published.[302] It is particularly important for the group to set aside adequate time at the end of each working session to examine how well it handled its business, what helped and what hindered, who played what roles, and what steps might be taken for improvement. Where trust and openness have already developed, many members will be willing to share their feelings about the group and their place in it. But whereas some people will have a strong need to do this, others may feel threatened, and the group will need to move sensitively at their pace. Finally, a balance will need to be struck between improving outward effectiveness and this work on improving the group process through personal and interpersonal learning. In a spiritual context such learning will have to do with cultivating an outwardly positive inner peace.

Fellowship is important in Buddhism. The sangha, or fellowship of Followers of the Way, is one of the three Buddhist 'Refuges'. And something of the democratic spirit of the early monastic communities continues, notwithstanding hierarchical overlays. On the other hand, the teaching tradition is very much that of a talk by the teacher followed by questions and answers, with private, one-to-one interviews between teacher and pupil more prominent in some traditions (for example, Zen). Fundamentally, Buddhist learning and teaching is about the use and understanding of experience and not about conveying revealed truths. Small group methods in education and in humanistic therapy undoubtedly have much to offer in supplementing and modifying traditional teaching methods in a contemporary Western context. Learning needs to start where the learner is, and not where the teacher thinks he or she is. And the learner needs to take an active part in learning rather than being a passive recipient. The small group is a potential learning environment of unsurpassed value wherein a teacher's spiritual maturity and insight can be used to full effect *if* there is the skill to set up fruitful learning situations. It is noteworthy that the small discussion and co-counselling group is an important feature of some of the mass Buddhist lay movements of Japan.

*Part Eight*
# The Making of the Good Society

# 32  *Buddhist Social Values*

Part Eight explores a Buddhist contribution to the psycho-social transformation of our world which now appears possible.

Throughout the book it has been maintained that war, poverty and social injustice have existential origins and are endemic in the human condition. They can only be fundamentally remedied by profound personal transformation found in Buddhist and other traditions of spiritual training. However, if such a psycho-social transformation is to take place on a significant scale, it will require the creation of social conditions which are supportive and conducive, in contrast to those which at present tend to deepen existential ignorance and push the global society into deeper crisis.

In Parts Four and Five it was shown that psycho-spiritual training and the work of social transformation can be an integral, interactive process – the dialectic, again, of 'we make the road and the road makes us'. Each seeks his or her salvation through the service of others, and learns that ultimately, in the experience of unity, the existential liberation of self is the liberation of all beings. Hence, in Robert Thurman's words, 'the coming to Buddhahood is a social event, involving a whole field of sentient beings, whose collective existence must be developed to the point where the whole land is transformed, from an impure land of violence and exploitation and suffering into a pure land, a "Buddha land" such as are described so vividly in the Mahayana Scriptures.'[303] The Dalai Lama expressed much the same ideas when he wrote that 'we need human qualities such as moral scruples, compassion and humility. In recognition of human frailty and weakness, these qualities are only accessible through forceful individual development in a conducive social milieu, so that a more human world will come into being as an ultimate goal. . . . A dynamic revolution is deemed crucial for instigating a political culture founded on moral ethics.'[304]

This first chapter will draw upon earlier material in the book to set out specific Buddhist values and perspectives as contribution to the evolution of a Good Society. Chapter 33 will examine the increasingly influential tendency in our society made up of various 'Green', 'alternative' and 'libertarian' currents which point towards the higher level of consciousness to which Chapter 9, on the 'two mentalities', has referred. This tendency offers the prospect of a social transformation out of the present global crisis, and Buddhism has sufficient affinity with it to make common cause and fruitful dialogue. Chapter 34 explores the more pervasive influence of Buddhism as a catalyst in modern industrial society with particular reference to scientific humanism, new developments in Christianity, and the phenomenon of the religious cults. The last chapter shifts to the psycho-spiritual side of the transformatory equation. It discusses the prospects for substantial psycho-spiritual change in Western society, and considers the claims of humanistic psychotherapy and psychology to supplant, modify or supplement the traditional spiritual systems.

The various principles and characteristics of a Buddhist Good Society which are set out in this chapter are derived from the fundamental Buddhadharma − the analysis of the human condition and the project for its liberative transformation. They stem also from the implications of scripture, and particularly from Indra's Net (Chapter 12) and the ideas of Asoka and Nagarjuna (Chapter 22). They also draw upon the grass-roots transcendental radicalism pioneered by the Sarvodaya movement in Sri Lanka, by certain Buddhist radicals in Thailand, and in the nonviolent movement for peace and justice in Vietnam (Chapter 24).

This is not a blueprint for a Buddhist utopia to be achieved by a Buddhist inspired nonviolent revolution and followed by the rule of the saints! The fallacy of social reconstruction promoted by an élite to effect any really fundamental change has already been noted in Chapter 10. The paternalism of Asoka or Nagarjuna's royal friend are no longer relevant or necessary. No social system can by itself create a revolution in human consciousness, though it can provide more favourable conditions for such personal endeavour. This chapter is therefore not about grand designs, but rather about working with the grain of history.

The social values set out below coincide with quite widely held democratic and egalitarian ideals, whilst at the same time being ultimately at variance with both capitalist free enterprise and communist collectivist social systems. It is not so much that the values themselves are exclusively Buddhist; the Buddhism lies rather in the manner or their cultivation and how they are to be sustained. Like the Buddhist moral precepts they are to be taken as guidelines for personal and public learning. Only in a preliminary sense are they intellectual principles. Rather are they to be understood as social expressions of the more highly evolved consciousness to which we must aspire. Just as the traditional precepts exemplify how the compassionate and selfless person behaves, so are these values intended to suggest something of how a whole society would organize and function if it were composed of such people. The psycho-social transformation suggested here is a continuously sustained metamorphosis, in which a significant number of people change the whole social climate by actualizing these social values in their own experience. This experience will range from the quality of personal relationships to the work needed to institutionalize these values and make them the norms of public behaviour. The root personal transformatory system which is used may be a Buddhist or other spiritual one (and arguably these alone have the necessary power) or it may be the kind of humanistic growth perspective discussed in

Chapter 35. Like any other process this one will have its periods of gestation and its births, its times of growth and its times of fruition, but essentially it is a continuous process. But it is important to break free from the notion of a struggle for a new society which is 'attained' at some future date, with everything happy ever after. It is no less important to break free from the other comforting notion embodied in this kind of millennial fairy story, namely that everything has to change apart from me.

The first and most fundamental social principle is that:

1. *Each and every person is real*
And every creature too. The absolutely 'given' quality of that reality has been superbly expressed by Zen Master Dogen:

> No creature ever comes short of its own complete-
> ness;
> Wherever it stands, it does not fail to cover the
> ground.

Out of the fear of our self-need we tend always to perceive others in ways which will confirm ourselves and so as to justify the ways in which we are often moved to treat them. 'If human vices like greed and envy are systematically cultivated,' wrote E. F. Schumacher, 'there is nothing less than a collapse of the intelligence. A man driven by greed or envy loses the power *of seeing things as they really are*, of seeing things in their roundness and wholeness, and his very success becomes a failure.'[305] The more truly we are able to experience other people, the less space is there for 'I' to have my own self-consoling picture of them. (The dialectic of self and other has been noted in the paragraph on 'individualism' in Chapter 9, and more generally in Chapter 12 about Indra's Net.)

Our industrial materialist culture dehumanizes our experience of others and tends to reify or make things of them

through many different forms of dominance, distancing and depersonalization. How can our humanity truly flower unless we have dissolved the socially sanctioned exploitative and coercive relationships of wealth, power, sex and race? And in order to satisfy the by now huge complexity of insatiable wants there have evolved great impersonal and depersonalizing organizations, public and private, in which most of us work and to which we are subjected as citizens.

By contrast, we need to evolve and build-in social relationships which require and habituate common human equality, face-to-face closeness, and a hardworking co-operation which builds personal respect, trust and a profound recognition one of another.

## 2. *The pluralism of equality in diversity*
In his valuable paper on *Buddhist Politics*, William Ophuls points out that the principle of equality which recognizes the autonomy, uniqueness and potential of each person should not be confused with the mass egalitarianism which substitutes for it. The latter 'tends to reduce the social diversity that fosters genuine individuality and at the same time throws people into conflict as everyone tries to climb to the top of the same pole.'[306] So we need a social climate which encourages individuals to have confidence enough to enjoy just being who they are, doing what needs to be done, and ripening their awareness of life ever more richly, instead of feeling moved to prove they are the equals of others by aggressive and competitive behaviour at others' expense, or else by sinking into the consoling security of a mass mediocrity. (The egalitarian significance of Dharma has also been discussed in Chapter 20).

A tolerant and convivial pluralism which rejoices in the richness of human diversity implies a global fraternity, in which powerful countries encourage others to retain and develop their own distinctive cultures and self-reliant societies.[307]

Such a plural society would, at all levels, have the same

untidy harmony as nature itself, with co-operation and conflict resolution as its great social arts. Where there is failure, and outbreaks of self-centredness and intolerance infringe others' autonomy, whether locally, regionally or as between nations, then resort may be necessary to creative, nonviolent sanctions of the kind discussed in Chapter 30. Gene Sharp puts the argument thus:

> A political society with no final sanctions would have difficulty in maintaining internal compliance with certain basic norms against harming people, preventing an internal group from running rough-shod over the remainder of the population...and, finally, maintaining its own chosen way of life, institutions, beliefs, system of legitimate govern-ment, and independent existence in the face of external aggression. The need for sanctions applies even to the most altruistic, benevolent and egali-tarian society, including nonviolent and anarchist ones. All societies require some type of final sanc-tions for at least minimal purposes. The need for sanctions cannot be removed from human so-cieties, either at present or in the future.[308]

### 3. *Self-transcendence and social service*

The remainder of this chapter examines the social conditions most likely to discourage self-serving acquisitiveness and aggression and to promote both self-discovery and a deeper awareness of, and concern for, other beings. To be more deeply aware of self is to become more deeply aware of others. And, if there is skilful meditative awareness, the abrasions of our relationships with others will wear down the rough edges of self, bringing insight within and empathy without. Work, if it be of the right kind, is a good example, cited by Schumacher writing of 'Buddhist economics' in his book *Small is Beautiful*. Human work is not only needful 'to provide necessary and useful goods and services' and 'to enable every one of us to use and thereby perfect our gifts like good stewards', but also 'to do so in service to, and in co-operation with, others, and so to liberate ourselves from our inborn egocentricity'.

The foregoing suggests an economy where it is impossible to acquire and retain wealth and power by using other people. This would no longer be the normal and approved thing to do and sometimes arguably the only ready and practicable way of providing large numbers of people with work and wages. It suggests, instead, an economy which throws us back upon ourselves by requiring us to co-operate on an equal basis with other people of many kinds, bereft of the insularity and impersonality of hierarchical authority and the more alienating kinds of professionalization and specialization. It suggests arranging matters so that we do not find ourselves seduced at every turn by a spirit of selfish acquisitiveness and, on the contrary, find ourselves in situations where the experience of unqualified service and of giving are the norms.

All the evidence suggests that there would be a place in such an economy for small businesses, which can fill a wide range of demands flexibly and economically, do not individually have a great impact on the character of the economy, and where, with only one or two dozen employees, the unions can readily bring sanctions to bear on exploitative employers. 'This is a very clear-cut matter,' Schumacher argues. 'Where the person who is responsible for the assets is identified, there is a real existential relationship between man and matter, material. Where countries have tried to socialize or nationalize those small businesses, the result was that you just couldn't get the work done any more. Also the urge of many straightforward and honest people to stand on their own feet and do their own thing is frustrated...so I have no doubt in my mind that at this level private enterprise is excellent.'[309] Schumacher seems to have been unaware, however, of the enormous potential of free and autonomous co-operatives. There can be little doubt that this is the ideal form of Buddhist 'Right Livelihood'. Whatever the interim and transitional value of small businesses, Ophuls is surely ultimately right in concluding that 'business is anti-fraternal'. Of 'Right Livelihood' co-operatives, *Dharmachari* Subhuti's experience of the Friends of the Western Buddhist Order co-operatives (described in Chapter 21) is worth quoting:

> Right Livelihood businesses in the FWBO are not only ethical, not only serve a creative end, but they offer the opportunity for companionship with others who are trying to develop as individuals. The teams in which people work are, potentially, working spiritual communities. In most ordinary jobs the contact between people, though perhaps superficially positive, does not offer any possibility of real depth. Often back-stabbing, bullying, and political manoeuvring dominate the workplace, and strong friendship and real openness are not possible. Within a Right Livelihood team there is a shared commitment to growth. In this context this will mean that each is prepared to face up to difficulties in communication, each will be trying to be aware of the others and their needs, and each will have some vision of what is possible between them. Teams are not necessarily smooth-running and they certainly do not call for a cosy, artificial togetherness. If they are effective, they are often fiery confrontations and people may find themselves facing up to what they consider unpleasant truths. Nonetheless, the overall effect will be to produce greater life and energy, more happiness and friendship, and an atmosphere in which people can be themselves.[310]

To avoid the fragmentation of people's lives, the workplace and its activities needs as far as possible to be integrated in the life of the community in which the workers live. And the foregoing principles for wealth-creating work apply equally to the work of providing community services — health, education, leisure, environmental enhancement and so on.[311] If communities were smaller and more local (including communities in big cities), and were given basic responsibility for managing their public services and, where practicable, owned and developed by them, then a spirit of co-operative responsibility would arise in what were previously only 'residential areas'. At present only a small minority of people are able to break out of the comparatively narrow circle of nuclear family, neighbours, friends and workmates; beyond that, they plug themselves into various impersonally provided public services, visit the polling station every few years, and watch much of the rest of life as it is presented on the television screen. Of those who do make more creative and varied lives than this, there are arguably comparatively few who are brought into active and positive engagement with social realities which enable profound kinds of learning rather than merely furthering self-confirmation. Reviewing this multi-layered alienation of men and women in the culture of industrial materialism, William Ophuls concludes that 'we cannot expect much in the way of civic or fraternal virtue from the average man. On the contrary, lacking the community involvement that would simultaneously enhance his self-respect and restrain his self-seeking, the citizen is liable to relapse into a resentful apathy antithetical to both his own and the polity's health.'[312]

All that having been said, it is also true that overmuch interpersonal activity in the service of this and that *can* become a high-vibrating substitute for a more profound self-realization. So the orientation here may need to be bent back straight to a Middle Way which leaves sufficient time and energy not only for privacy and intimacy but for solitude, stillness and contemplation. Without that everything will slide back.... To create such space, therefore, it may be necessary to 'mechanize' some parts of life and to see some of the virtues in the 'mindless' bureaucratic processing of business, the distancing of professional roles, the high-speed drudgery of computers, and many economies-of-scale however standardized and impersonal. It may be recalled from Chapter 9 on the 'two mentalities' that scientistic mechanism has its value so long as it is subordinate and secondary to higher modes of knowing and is used skilfully and sensitively. The higher level of consciousness is precisely about not making a fetish of the higher level of consciousness!

In the same way it is also important both socially and personally to find the optimum balance between too much upsetting openness and too much deadening security. This applies not only to advanced stages in the evolution of a Good Society but to present-day cultures also. Further to Chapter 6, on the institutionalization of delusion, it is arguable that social conditions supportive of psycho-spiritual transformation are at their optimum in a society which is midway between being over- and understructured.

An overstructured society offers a stable and traditional social milieu which provides the individual with a secure niche from which he (and especially she) is not encouraged to venture. In such 'membership societies' the individual receives, as of custom and right, a great deal of psychological and material support, whether from the extended family, paternalistic employers, institutional religion or the State. Examples are the USSR, Japan and strong Catholic Latin cultures. In such cultures only exceptional individuals are able to flourish outside the strong, confirming identity of the group, and hence to be fully aware of the raw existential precariousness of being just a person, with all its potential for further evolution (as well as for regression). For example, Manuel Arce, a Latin American student of Zen Buddhism, testifies that 'the practice of Zen becomes especially difficult...in the midst of a culture with a strong, highly organized and active national religion, with family structures that bind and determine family life, and with a rather belligerent sense of history.'[313]

By contrast, understructured societies, of which the USA is the most striking example, are marked by high levels of personal insecurity and a driven, high-achievement individualism. Existential exposure is so extreme as to compel a restless, hyperactive search for self-confirmation through every imaginable form of achievement, acquisitiveness and aggressiveness.

It would therefore seem desirable to cultivate a social milieu with a middle mesh — not so close as to imprison, not so open as to make people too restless. A climate of openness and freedom would induce a sufficient sense of insecurity for people to be aware of their existential selves without too much cultural cocooning. But society should also provide a built-in fraternity and warm inducement to co-operativeness, with a sense of supportive rights balanced against reasonable duties. In such a culture of the Middle Way minds would be less clouded by consumerism, superstition, competitiveness, nationalism, or any of the other props and distractions which offer some satisfaction of desire or some temporary relief from suffering.

The hypothesis offered above is, of course, only one cultural variable which has to be set against others in any specific culture at a particular time in its history. Perhaps it is only a European reaction to William Ophuls' Jeffersonian vision of a Buddhist polity! There is some evidence, however, that spiritual efflorescence is associated with stable societies going into transition, as in the case of the rise of the world's major religions, or the flowering of mysticism in fourteenth-century Europe in regions where the traditional order of things was first disturbed by the winds of social and economic change but which did not experience severe disruption until later.

### 4. *Self-reliance and a human scale of things*
Perhaps the most pervasive phenomenon of industrial materialism is the huge public or private organization which is so complex that it can only function because work has been

broken down into specialized procedures, whether in office or factory. The worker is 'programmed' to operate these procedures precisely like a human cog in an organizational machine. The introduction of computers is eliminating this drudgery, but arguably at the cost of increasing the sense of alienation, manipulation and powerlessness. The ultimate expressions of this corporate giantism are the (so-called) nation-states, each with its labyrinthine bureaucratic apparatus, and the transnational corporations which relate to them through complex and shadowy political, military and industrial power linkages.

A corporate power of all kinds becomes more 'faceless', more bafflingly complex and interlinked, more shrouded in secrecy, and increasingly involved in quasi-legal coercion and even overt violence, it becomes more and more difficult to maintain democratic control and accountability even where this is formally supposed to happen. Out of their sense of injustice and powerlessness, the 'have-nots' of the world parallel 'legitimate' institutional, economic, nuclear and ecological violence with their own kinds of violent protest, ranging from street riots to international terrorism.

As I have demonstrated earlier, traditionally, Buddhism fosters personal autonomy, responsibility and self-reliance as conducive to well-being and as necessary conditions for undertaking the work of psycho-spiritual transformation. In terms of supportive social structures and climate, these personal qualities are best encouraged by the decentralization of economic activity to networks of small production and service units, preferably co-operatively owned and managed. Political power would similarly need to be as localized as possible. However, in addition to technical cost-effectiveness considerations there are other reasons, noted below, for striking a balance between dependence and self-sufficiency (assuming the latter were even possible), in both the political and economic spheres. Communities, districts, bio-regions, and nations and other areas of ethnic identity would therefore need to be tiered in loose confederations. It is noteworthy that computers can now provide flexible information processing and exchange systems through which small and autonomous units can co-ordinate their activities to an extent that previously would have required centralized control. The computer is a potentially liberating tool providing we can free ourselves from its mechanistic 'mentality' and from the kind of fascination which tends to make it an end in itself.

As Ophuls concedes, 'merely reducing the size of communal institutions to the appropriate level will not banish evil from the world — but it would reduce the massiveness of the evil that could be done and bring us back into the realm of personal evil, which we can understand and deal with. By contrast, the impersonal, faceless, "banal" evil and violence that have led to large-scale extermination of racial and political deviants and to potential nuclear holocaust are ineluctable consequences of great size, complexity and interdependence.'[314]

And beyond that, as the old and familiar forms of social egotism become unfashionable and shameful and, hopefully, lose some of their strength, conflict will tend to be more exclusively confined to areas of ideology, dogmatic altruism and the allegedly benevolent élitism which accompanies it.

For example, as Schumacher argued, small is undoubtedly beautiful when set against the giantism of our contemporary culture, but it is not *absolutely* beautiful. There are, for instance, operations which would be prohibitively expensive and organizationally and logistically impracticable if undertaken by units which were small and/or highly autonomous. The railway and telecommunications networks are obvious examples, and there are strong arguments for the retention of large-scale electricity supply grids.

Moreover, the question of smallness is related to that of autonomy versus interdependence. Self-reliance is a middle way between heavy dependence and an autonomy which verges on self-sufficiency. The small, localized economic and political units need to be sufficiently strong and independent for their members to be convinced that it is there that the crucial decisions are made that affect their interests and not a hundred miles away. Only thus will they feel both obliged and attracted to invest themselves in the governance and management of their workplace and community instead of seeing it as a marginal activity for 'those who are interested in that kind of thing'. And they will need to be vested with sufficient power and control over local resources and be sufficiently self-sufficing as not to be easily pressured or blackmailed by other political and economic centres of power.

On the other hand, too much local political and economic autonomy would make for insularity and lack of responsibility for wider concerns, whereas mutuality would tend to moderate local extremism, enhance communication and help maintain a more open society. Small is not beautiful, for example, if it gives zealous majorities unconditional freedom to override dissenters. Ophuls' Israelite response that 'with smaller scale tyranny flight is usually possible' is neither adequate nor practicable. There seems to be a case here for federal constitutions which guarantee certain political and economic minima to the citizens of all the autonomous constituent communities. The suggested measure of economic interdependence would enable economic sanctions to be applied in support of basic human rights.

It will be recalled from Chapter 12 that Indra's Net is one of mutual dependence which is only possible if each of the constituent 'jewels' has a real and separate existence. The foregoing discussion affords further examples of the contingent dialectic introduced in Part Three in which every position exists only as a balance defined by two extremes, neither of which, in its turn, has any absolute significance either.

## 5. *Sufficiency and simplicity*
The theme of simplicity and sufficiency, frugality and resourcefulness in Buddhist lifestyle has already been introduced in Chapter 12 on Indra's Net, and in Chapter 28, on

the relationship of frugality to violence. Moreover, the social values established earlier in this chapter lead in the same direction.

In the first place, if only a sufficiency of goods is produced, and there is no encouragement to multiply wants (by advertising, for example), and if, also, energies are engaged in more worthwhile activities, then the grosser kinds of craving and acquisitiveness are likely to diminish. A clean, lean simplicity of lifestyle can prove satisfying in itself, as well as supporting the transition from *having* to *being*.

Secondly, all the time and resources that went into mass consumerism, powered by the puritan work ethic, need to be released to make time for working with, and for, others, for self-development, and for just enjoying being still.

Thirdly, frugality and simplicity follow inevitably from the substantial abandonment of high techonology and large and complex, low-cost, mass production units, in favour of more local and less specialized production employing simpler technology.

Fourthly, if work is to be satisfying and creative, and produce things which are beautiful to live with and good to use, then we shall tend to have quality possessions, both personal and communal, but our possessions will be fewer.

Fifthly, it will be clear from Chapter 4 that only through reducing the depletion of natural resources and the waste products of large-scale production can we stop short of devastating our planet. This requires a simpler mode of life for humankind, and the recovery of the enjoyment of kinship with the non-human world, instead of having to lord it over an increasingly run-down zoological garden.

The development of the kind of Good Society outlined here is, of course, a push-and-pull matter. We are pushed by the past because only through evolving a society like this can we fundamentally reverse the drive to nucler and ecological destruction. Anything less radical can only give a breathing space before the potentially fatal historical process begins to work through again. And we are drawn forward by the prospect of contributing to the most significant step in human evolution, by embarking on a life-long project of consciousness change which is intimately combined with the work that has to be done to change the kind of world we live in. May each of us find his or her own way of going about this.

# 33 *The Movement Towards a Green, Libertarian 'New Age'*

The most positive and hopeful contemporary global phenomenon is surely the diverse movement variously described as 'Alternative', 'Green', 'Libertarian' or 'New Age', depending which of its several currents is in mind. In its underlying unity it represents an historic cultural shift from the still dominant scientistic mentality towards the higher level consciousness described in Chapter 9. Its affinity with Buddhist psychosocial values will be evident from the following conspectus by James Robertson:

> Growing numbers of people all over the world now firmly believe that the transition to the post-industrial age — or however else we prefer to describe the period of history now beginning — will involve a transformation of our existing way of life in all its aspects, and that such transformation has, indeed, already begun. The way we live, work, organize our societies, think of ourselves in relation to other people and the universe around us will change just as deeply as they changed in the course of the industrial revolution....This time the change will involve a shift of emphasis away from means towards ends; away from economic growth towards human development; away from quantitative to qualitative values and goals; away from the impersonal and the organizational to the personal and the interpersonal....A culture

339

which has been masculine, aggressive and domineering in its outlook will give place to one which is more feminine, co-operative and support-ive. A culture which has exalted the uniformly European will give place to one which values the multicultural richness and diversity of human experience. An anthropocentric world view that has licensed the human species to exploit the rest of nature as if from above and outside it, will give place to an ecological world view. We shall see that survival and self realization alike require us to act as we really are — an integral part of an eco-system much larger, more complex and more powerful than ourselves.[315]

Recent testimony to the underlying strength of these new cultural currents comes in a huge and so far unpublished study made for the (British) National Economic Develop-ment Office by Taylor Nelson Monitor. Peter Large, writing in the *Guardian*, summarized its 'main hopes' for Britain by the year 2010. These included:

Economic growth will not be the priority — the quality of life will.

Networks, or small overlapping cells, will dominate the new structures of society. There will be a reaction against any collective organization.

Individual freedom and individual responsibility will be paramount, but there will be safety nets for the deprived.

Some, but not all, big business will disappear as people reject bureaucracy and 'American' influence. Those that survive will do so by decen-tralizing.

Central government will shrink to a framework. The real political decisions will be taken through neighbourhood involvement and single-issue groups.[316]

The spectrum of active concerns associated with the 'rising culture' embraces feminism, the peace movement, environmental protection, co-operatives and communes, homesteading and organic farming, civil liberties and human rights, consumer protection, animal rights, and a wide range of local community initiatives such as food, housing and other co-operatives, community schools and playcentres, alternative health clinics, law centres, community information bureaux, community newspapers, and community care projects involving the elderly and disabled.[317] Also relevant are the increasingly influential self-help groups which have sprung up representing minorities long subject to various kinds of stigma, discrimination and neglect — ethnic minorities, homosexuals, old people, single parents, the physically and mentally handicapped, and many more. All these initiatives are independent of 'the establishment' and of its 'established' opposition (such as the trade union bureaucracy and the opposition political parties), and broadly share the same human, social and organizational values so as to form a more or less recognizable 'alternative culture'. Similar movements are evident in many Third World countries for economic, cultural, political and military self-reliance and against the attempt to impose a global, neo-colonial and militarized industrial materialism.[318] Beyond these explicit activisms there is much evidence of an increasing shift towards the higher consciousness mentality described in Chapter 9 in many different fields of academic research and professional service — in biology, physics, sociology, medicine, psychiatry, psychotherapy and education, and in the personal lifestyles of an increasing number of people.[319] At the time of going to press the 'established' culture of opposed values is in resurgence in Britain, the USA and several other countries. This I believe to be an intensification and polarization of the crisis rather than a new direction.

Shared values of these different currents are those of personal autonomy, open and caring human relations, potential for personal change, and nonviolence. Several writers have drawn attention to the apparent fusion of the grassroots activism of the 1960s with the 'consciousness movement' of the 1970s in a new synthesis of personal and social transformation. Buddhist radicals readily find commitment and fellowship here, particularly with other nonviolent resisters among the Quakers, International Fellowship of Reconciliation and Catholic Peace and Justice. Out on the hard libertarian wing, where there is hostility to institutionalized religion, they can be less sure of a welcome but nevertheless appear to have a better chance of developing friendly working relations than do theistic believers. Buddhism does seem to have reservoirs of goodwill in often unlikely places. It was the spectrum of 'Green' concerns which inspired, in 1984, *A Green Buddhist Declaration*, contributed by 'sixty Buddhist scholars, monks and laypeople...of the international Buddhist community on the occasion of the 14th General Conference of the World Fellowship of Buddhists.'[320]

There is a broadly shared perspective as to how the 'alternative culture' of today might become the pervasive global culture of tomorrow. Transformation is to begin here and now, with people's everyday experience — how they would really like to live their lives, and how, little by little, from the personal out to the institutional, acting locally but thinking globally, they might begin to lay the human foundations of the new society and undermine those of the old order. This contrasts with the traditional social structural, top downwards scenarios of conventionally élitist revolutionaries and reformers, imbued by the 'Social Fallacy' identified in Chapter 10.

Furthermore, the new social institutions and structures needed to give expression to, and to support, the kind of Green psycho-social transformation outlined in the previous chapter cannot be created by using, and attempting to transform, *existing* systems of power and control on their own terms. The organization and climate of governmental institutions, political parties and the like, and the mentality of the people who typically work them, runs counter to the transformative values of the last chapter. In Chapter 9, for example, it was shown how conventional confrontational politics squeeze out much social reality, substituting a bi-partisan black-and-white caricature. A cynical German politician has observed how Greens who enter the forcing house of conventional politics soon, like tomatoes, begin to turn a more conventional Red, and to behave like other politicians.

This is not to deny the valuable achievements of some policies of government (for example, the Welfare State), or the sincerity of many politicians, or the survival and achievements of many good men and women in conventional politics. It is simply that the Good Society cannot be created by means which contradict the end. And it is simply that we all have a huge capacity anyway to delude ourselves as to the motives which impel us, without further compounding them institutionally.

The main effort for social transformation must therefore be outside the established world of power and politics, to develop alternative and parallel enterprises and institutions of a kind which support rather than frustrate and confuse the project of personal transformation. Buddhist examples already mentioned are the Sarvodaya movement in Sri Lanka and the Right Livelihood co-operatives of the Friends of the Western Buddhist Order in Britain and elsewhere.

At the same time it is also clearly needful to reduce the coercion, exploitativeness and even outright violence of the state and other power centres, whether it be in nuclear weapons build-up, arming Third World despots against their own people, or killing whales. It is also needful to protect the powerless and reduce suffering by bringing the necessary pressure to bear in a creative and positive fashion, as, for example, in defending a caring public institution against unjustifiable closure. It is also desirable for radicals to exercise a transforming influence within institutions and organizations dominated by alien values where they are able to do so without themselves falling prey to those values. For example, unless well centred in alternative values, employees securing some formal participation in the management of an enterprise may in due course simply be assimilated into the dominant management ethos, instead of being able to use their position positively to achieve substantial change in traditional managerial attitudes.

The 'libertarian' current is well exemplified in the following passage from Howard Clark's pamphlet *Making Nonviolent Revolution*:

> The first step in a nonviolent anarchist approach is to question your own relationships — to assert yourself where you're being trodden on, to reclaim your own life, and at the same time to take responsibility for your own actions, which may mean getting off other people's backs; on the other hand, not letting yourself be pushed around, not ripping off their energies — whether it's having them cook or wash for us, or whether it's relying on food ripped off by imperialism without making any effort to supply some of our own. Questioning our own relationships also entails questioning our role in this society, making ourselves aware of the policies of domination and exploitation — both of other countries and of groups in this country — in which we acquiesce.
>
> It is not in a Christian sense of striving for individual perfection that nonviolent anarchism stresses the importance of changing ourselves and our immediate relationships. Rather it is change through building up a culture of people in struggle, a culture which contests power, a culture where people affirm each other and try to manage our own lives, a culture where people can gain a sense of ourselves as shapers of our own destiny, active agents with the power to do things for ourselves.[321]

The above has been quoted not only for its content but also for its tell-tale phrasing and flavour, which is similar to much in the influential periodical *Peace News* which published the pamphlet. Nevertheless, these strong feelings are worthy of respect. How can we open more creatively to the energies of the bitter anger which is fired by the daily experience of social affliction?

The transformative scenario is extended as follows by the American Quaker, George Lakey:

> The crises in society accumulate as a result of economic dislocation, pollution and other ecological strains, the dissolution of the old value system and conflict with Third World liberation movements....Mass boycotts and strikes accelerate the troubles of governments and corporations....The old order is buffeted by a growing people's movement which refuses conscription, boycotts consumer goods, refuses to pay taxes, strikes for worker control. Further, mass civil disobedience campaigns strain the resources of police chiefs, whose rank and file are not fully reliable. Courts become clogged with cases of conscience; hastily improvised prisons are filled....Finally, the Groups for a Living Revolution help the counter-institutions to become institutions, and the radical caucuses occupy and control the organizations of local and national life. Co-ordinating councils on local, regional, national and transnational levels help smooth a transfer of power from governments and corporations to the people's institutions.[322]

The above is very much a 'Big Bang' scenario from the heady years of the 1960s and early 1970s. After its first flush, historical change tends to be less euphoric, less tidy, more ambiguous and more disconcerting. For me Lakey's ringing phrases roused the spectre of those more Orwellian revolutions which consumed their own children. To paraphrase the Spanish proverb, 'God save me from my friends — *and from myself*; from my enemies I can save myself.' Schumacher popularized the idea of a Buddhist economics. The idea of a Buddhist revolution evidently also needs popularizing.

Overall, it is in the loose, diverse, evolving and suggestive Green-libertarian tradition that Buddhists can work most fruitfully and influentially. However, Buddhists and their spiritually engaged allies will wish to develop a positive dialogue-in-action with fellow activists still inclined to ideologically charged partisanship or to the cheer-leading idealism that can be almost as dangerous to us all. They will need to ask whether we do not need to find ways of going deeper to change the kind of people we are and hence to be better able to transform our world into what really *is* a qualitatively different kind of society. This theme is taken up in Chapter 35.

# 34 *Buddhist Influences and Affinities in the Psycho-Social Transformation in the West*

It might reasonably be asked how an apparently alien and esoteric religion, of minority appeal, could make any significant contribution in the West to the kind of psycho-social transformation suggested in the previous chapters. In this chapter some specific influences and affinities will be explored.

It will be evident by now that it would be most unlikely that Buddhist influence in the West would be exerted through the growth of mass Buddhist movements proselytizing in the Christian or Islamic fashion (though there is a tendency of this kind in one or two groups marginal to the Buddhist mainstream). As noted earlier, the very idea of converting someone to Buddhism would sound strange to most Buddhists. It is up to the *enquirer* to undertake the practice, if they choose to do so. No one can do it for someone else. The following two quotations from Eastern Buddhists resident in the West make much the same point about the nature of Buddhist influence. Venerable Dr Rewata Dhamma, a Theravada monk writes:

> Amidst a plurality of ideologies, political and religious, it would be best if Buddhism did not draw attention to itself, in a missionary way, as yet another 'ism'. Its ideal has always been to encourage what is in conformity with the Eightfold Path in other faiths and systems. It has always primarily been not so much a religion in its own right as a

system of effective practice, of use to the individual whether he or she professes to follow some other religion or none at all. This is constantly repeated, and needs to be, for our sake and the good of all. Buddhism cannot be effective unless this is borne constantly in mind.[323]

Similarly, Chögyam Trungpa, a Tibetan Buddhist teacher, when asked what he saw as the future of Buddhism in the West, replied:

It is scientific and practical, and so ideal for the Western mind. If it becomes a Church it will be a failure; if it is spiritual practice it will have a strong influence in all areas — art, music, psychology.[324]

Although there is a growing interest in the practice of Buddhist meditation, it is probable that strong and sustained commitment to Buddhist training is likely to remain very much a minority concern. However, as I pointed out in the Introduction, Buddhism has affinities with current developments in many different fields of thought and practice, and its diverse and suggestive influence will doubtless increase. As we have seen, its influence upon, and affinity with, the Green-libertarian 'alternative and rising culture' is particularly striking.

Many secular humanists find in Buddhism an attractive and sublime humanism and lifestyle. It attracts those who are spiritually inclined, but who cannot accept theism and objectively revealed religious authority. For those who feel there is something beyond existentialism and the humanistic psychotherapies Buddhism offers an experientially reasoned training system which invites personal experiment. As we shall see in the next chapter, it has been a major formative influence in the new field of transpersonal psychology and associated therapies, where it has already borne such impressive fruit as Ken Wilber's work on the evolution of human consciousness. And as we have seen in Chapter 9, intellectually Buddhism both affirms the up-and-coming organismic and holistic mentality and also *amplifies* it as a potentially higher level of consciousness.

Because Buddhism has close affinities with non-dogmatic Christian spirituality and with the 'mystical' traditions in other great religions, it is potentially a bridge between secular and religious forces and traditions both in the West and the East. Between uneasy allies in social action, Buddhists have a role to play as mediators, communicators and facilitators among conflicting ideologies. Professor Ninian Smart has characterized Buddhism as a 'transcendant pluralism':

> It is a kind of pluralism because the desires of persons are respected, the creativity which comes from many different flavours of thought and feeling is prized, and the security which comes from tolerant acknowledgement of different ethnic, national and spiritual traditions conserves vital resources from the past in the outward adventure of the future.[325]

Different contemporary *dharmas* (systems of knowledge, truths) take what they need from the *Buddhadharma*, and with 'the end of ideology' coming disturbingly into the view of more and more intellectual observers they are likely to find there an increasingly profound relevance. The 'post-dogmatic' theologian Don Cupitt refers to Keiji Nishitani, a Japanese philosopher who was a pupil of Heidegger:

> Reviewing the long process by which the Western mind became progressively undeceived, a process completed in Nietzsche and Sartre, he has said that Western thought now has nowhere else to go except towards Buddhism — but it must get there from Christian premises.[326]

Amidst the collapse of both metaphysics and theological realism, 'The West,' as Professor Huston Smith puts it, 'hears of men across the sea who have for centuries taken up their abode in the Void, come to feel at home in it, and find joy within it. How can this be? The West does not understand, but the Nothingness which it hears from across the sea sounds like something it may have to come to terms with.'[327]

On the other hand, although the Buddhist tradition of peace and nonviolence is widely known and greatly respected, I also have the impression that many Western humanist and Christian activists have reservations about what they see as oriental quietism and the absence of a spirit of social service and concern for social justice. As we have seen in Chapters 21 and 24 there are a number of contemporary developments which are beginning to rectify this impression.

In most of the remainder of this chapter I shall examine the affinities of Buddhism with Christian spirituality, through which the influence of Buddhism has been felt, and from which fellowship Buddhist activism can in turn draw strength.

The particular appeal of Buddhism for many Christians lies in its potential contribution to the recovery of the Christian tradition of non-dogmatic and meditative spirituality. This post-dogmatic current in theology associated with Tillich, Bultmann, Bonhoeffer and others surfaced publicly in the 1960s with Bishop John Robinson's *Honest to God*, and in Don Cupitt the new 'agnostic Christianity' has latterly even reached British television screens. For Cupitt, 'traditional theological realism is now an intellectual and psychological mess';[328] 'the struggle against it is essentially a struggle to extricate faith from its long metaphysical captivity.'[329]

Cupitt and others make the distinction between religion and spirituality, as in Chapter 11 of this book (though at a more subtle level this becomes problematical). Religion is seen as an institutionalized system of dogmatic authority, heavy with metaphysics and formal prescriptive morality. By contrast, Christian spirituality is about the gnostic-mystical search within, aided by contemplative prayer, personal discipline and the fellowship and counsel of others, and opening to divine revelation as a higher, spiritual level of consciousness. Buddhist monism is thus warmly recognizable to the Christian who, while he must 'cling to God, of course (for God is his truest being)... need not (and if he is a mystic, ought not) cling to views and ideas about God.'[330]

The literature of Buddhist–Christian dialogue and comparative study is now very rich and extensive. It ranges from broadly conceived works like Douglas Fox's *Buddhism, Christianity and the Future Religion*[331] and Winston King's *Buddhism and Christianity: some bridges of understanding*,[332] to more detailed studies like that of J. Edgar Bruns on *The Christian Buddhism of St John*,[333] which traces the parallels between the Fourth Gospel and Madhyamika Buddhism. There has been particular interest in Zen Buddhism, as the most directly experiential form of an essentially experiential and non-metaphysical religion.[334]

To what extent all religions do really 'meet at the top' concerns us here less than the strong similarities which undoubtedly exist between the practices and techniques, and also the experience of spiritual revelation, in Buddhism, Christianity and the other great perennial spiritual traditions.[335]

Something of the very positive religious pluralism that is found in Buddhism has already been noted in the chapter on Asoka's and Nagarjuna's 'Politics of enlightenment' (Chapter 22). The following two quotations provide interesting present-day testimony. The first is from the Dalai Lama:

> In the past centuries there have been many learned teachers who have laid down various paths to show the Truth. Among these Buddhism is one, and according to it my opinion is that, except for the differences in the names and forms of the various religions, the ultimate truth is the same.[336]

Another typically Buddhist view is that of Japanese Zen

Master Yamada Kōun, whose temple has become a training place for Christian clergy and laypeople:

> My work with my Christian students...is to guide these people in Zen practice and bring them to the *satori* [enlightenment] experience. Questions as to how this experience is to be understood from the standpoint of Christianity and what significance it has from a Christian standpoint are for Christians themselves to answer. My only wish is that both Christianity and Buddhism regain their power to bring their followers to true spiritual salvation.[337]

Much of the above is well summarized in a Christian theologian's conclusions at the end of a Christian–Zen Buddhist dialogue in Kyoto:

> An unbridgeable gulf appeared to separate those who believed in the soul, the Absolute and the objectivity of truth from those who spoke of Nirvana, Nothingness and the void....Soon it became clear that what united us was not philosophy but religious experience. While in philosophical formulations we were poles apart, when it came to the discussion of values we were one. The value of deep meditation, of poverty, of humility, of the spirit of gratitude, of non-violence and the love of peace — these were things in the discussion of which we had but one heart and soul. Indeed, it was amazing that such diverse philosophies should produce such similar experiences![338]

This considerable detour from the field of social activism will nevertheless help to explain the undoubted affinity felt by many Buddhists and Christians, and never more so than when making common cause from out of the same values and concerns. In the USA Buddhist and Christian fellowship in action has been evident since the Vietnam war resistance days, between Robert Aitken, Jack Douglass, the Berrigan brothers, Gary Snyder, Jim Forrest and *Thich* Nhat Hanh, as well as many lesser known folk. And in Vietnam itself, something of the fellow feeling and mutual respect between Christians and Buddhists was noted in Chapter 24. It is also present in Thailand and Sri Lanka, and there is even a bi-monthly journal, *Dialogue*, published in Colombo, for joint exploration of forms of socially engaged spirituality. Glob-ally, Professor Ninian Smart has advocated 'a certain outlook based on the complementarity of Buddhism and Christian-ity', and he believes that the two religions share a common historic destiny:

> The secular ideologies which have proved most powerful, nationalism and Marxism in particular, have fed upon the thirst for identity and social justice. They have made great claims on the al-legiance of men, and have elicited such splendid heroisms, such sacrifices, such rivers of nobly spilt blood. But they have also encouraged violence and hatred. We have a deep need to take collectivism with a certain scepticism, to use skilful means to tame the beasts of collective pride and economic revenge. The love which Christ self-emptyingly symbolizes, the compassionate non-violence which Buddhism expresses – these values are of even greater importance now than they were before such terrible means of destruction reposed in the hands of hard and confused men.[339]

Marxism and Islam, 'the other two great universalisms of the planet', Smart finds dogmatic, authoritarian and hostile both to cultural pluralism and scientific humanism.

I believe that Buddhists in the West can, contrariwise, find inspiration and many helpful pointers from the spiritual tradition within their own culture, not only from, say, fourteenth-century mystics like the much-quoted Eckhart but also from contemporaries as wide ranging as Simone Weil, T. S. Eliot and Thomas Merton. A particularly instructive example is the experience of a Japanese Jesuit, J.K. Kadowaki, with Zen *koans* and biblical parables, and with Zen *sesshins* and the corresponding Jesuit retreats, recorded in his *Zen and the Bible*.[340] Furthermore, an evolving Buddhist activism can learn much from the rich Christian tradition of contemplation and resistance, as well as from present-day experience and example. For, 'over the years,' writes Kenneth Leech, 'a remarkable consensus has occurred within most sections of world Christianity on the thrust of the gospel towards human liberation. Many Christians today would agree...that any theology which is indifferent to the theme of liberation is not Christian theology.'[341]

The Buddhist–Christian spirituality presented above is at variance with the new missionary fundamentalism burgeoning amidst the gathering global crisis.

Although Islamic fundamentalism has many characteristics in common with extreme forms of Christian fundamentalism it is in many ways a different and highly complex phenomenon, requiring separate treatment outside the scope of this book.

Christian fundamentalism covers a wide spectrum. At one end it shades off into traditional evangelical Protestantism, and the charismatic movement in the Anglican and Catholic churches. At the other end of the spectrum are movements which display regressive 'cultic' characteristics similar to those of the various oriental cults active in the West. Amidst the forceful good cheer of the mass movement there is little space for genuine dialogue, and a dogmatic righteousness powered by the emotional release of instant salvation makes it difficult to be aware of other people in their own light. God's plan for the world is an unalterable scenario and makes for the apolitical conservatism of millennial acquiescence. At worst it makes for 'the faith of wealth and weapons', as it has been called, of preachers like Jerry Fallwell, with their crusades to root out 'reds', 'atheists', 'homosexuals' and other 'deviants'. Now that Buddhists in the West are becoming involved in interfaith activity and social action, they will find a need to define themselves in relation to the fundamentalist movements on the basis of such common values and concerns as may be experienced. Certainly they can make common cause with the new, politically radical fundamentalism of evangelists like Jim Wallis and his 'Sojourners'. It has been said that such groups 'have energized the Left to an extent that it has not been energized since the Vietnam war.'[342]

Once when being interviewed about Buddhism on local radio, I was surprised at the great pains which the interviewer took to have me distinguish between Buddhism and cults such as Hare Krishna, Bhagwan Rajneesh and Transcendental Meditation with which he felt it might be confused in listeners' minds. Even many sociologists of religion fail to distinguish adequately between systems of authentic transpersonal exploration and psychologically regressive cults. In his book *A Sociable God*, Ken Wilber devotes several pages to doing so, but concedes the difficulty of making a distinction at what is in fact a point along a continuum. Many of the cults do provide some therapeutic emotional release, and some employ established psycho-physical therapies (for example, the Rajneeshis). These may help members to become less aggressive and better able to relate positively and openly to others, but the new-found self-identity tends to be dependent on continued group membership and the influence of a charismatic leadership. Rather than presenting a training leading to the transmutation of need the cults tend to feed desire, holding out promise of nirvanic bliss or at least experiential novelty. Research suggests that the typical cult member is likely to have low ego strength and to be low on self-esteem, merging his or her fragile sense of identity in group belongingness, assisted by participation mystiques. The experiences which the cult typically offers will affirm cultists in their tendency to pre-personal infantilism and immersion in the physical, and will relieve them of pressures towards a more integrated personality. Neurotic insecurity will make for avoidance of situations of relative

and ambiguous choice. Refuge will instead be sought in the
hedonism which the 'Dharma Bums' celebrated in the 1960s
or, at the other extreme, in the repressive and absolute
morality of fundamentalism, punitive of self and others.
'Cults,' concludes Wilber, 'do not have to brainwash such
members; all they have to do is show up and smile.'[343]

The charismatic cult leaders tend to exhibit a highly
refined form of egotism long familiar in the ancient spiritual
traditions. In Buddhist mythology this is the 'realm of the
gods' where, in Chögyam Trungpa's words:

> We no longer have a care about hope or fear. And
> quite possibly might believe this to be the perma-
> nent achievement of enlightenment or union with
> God. At that moment everything we see appears
> to be beautiful, loving, even the most grotesque
> situations of life seem heavenly. Anything that is
> unpleasant or aggressive seems beautiful because
> we have achieved oneness with ego. In other
> words, ego lost track of its intelligence. This is the
> absolute, ultimate achievement of bewilderment,
> the depths of ignorance − extremely powerful. It is
> a kind of spiritual atomic bomb, self-destructive in
> terms of compassion, in terms of communication,
> in terms of stepping out of the bondage of ego.[344]

Robert Aitken quotes the following instructive example 'of a
teacher from India who is currently very popular', and
makes the point that the experience of insight by itself is
not to be confused with the true spiritual maturity which
follows from its cultivation:

> His writings sparkle with genuine insight. Yet
> something is awry. There are sordid patches of
> anti-Semitism and sexism. Moreover, he does not
> seem to caution his students about cause and
> effect in daily life. What went wrong here? I think
> he chose a short cut to teaching. My impression is
> that he underwent a genuine religious experience,

but missed taking a vital, step-by-step training which in Zen Buddhist tradition comes *after* realization. Chao-chou trained for sixty years before he began to teach — a sobering example for us all. The religious path begins again with an experience of insight, and we must train diligently *thereafter* to become mature.[345]

Simone Weil gave many illustrations of the way in which 'the highest resembles the lowest' — 'the non-resistance of saints is outwardly indistinguishable from cowardice; supreme wisdom ends in a sense of ignorance, detachment is like indifference.' The saints' self-abandonment resembles the way in which fools fritter away their time, and just as the most spiritually evolved cannot but be moved to virtue so can the most driven and deluded not but be moved to vice with the same seeming inevitability.[346] 'Make a hair's breadth difference, and Heaven and Earth are set apart!' exclaimed the Third Zen Patriarch. Distinctions, for example, between what Wilber calls 'prepersonal helplessness and dependence on a paternal authority figure' and 'transpersonal active surrender and submission via a spiritual adept' may not be easy; 'the vast majority of orthodox psychologists and sociologists do not wish, or are not able, to tell the difference.'[347] It becomes even more difficult to do so where some members of the same group are behaving one way and others are more towards the other end of the continuum, as seems not infrequently the case even with the best attentions of the teacher. Nevertheless, it *is* a continuum with which we are concerned. It is less difficult to recognize one end from the other than it is to assess the significance of borderline cases near the middle, which problem can be left to researchers.

The above dissociation from Buddhism which had to be made clear carries us forward to the next chapter which examines, in present-day Western context, the means of personal psycho-spiritual transformation on which a truly fundamental social revolution must depend.

# 35 *The Prospects in the West for a Decisive Psycho-Spiritual Shift*

For the mainstream secular tradition of the last two centuries in the West 'development' has meant social, economic and political development. But the alternative 'rising culture' (as Capra calls it) is as much about personal and inner change as about social and outer change. It variously emphasizes improving the quality of lifestyle and personal relationships, and the cultivation of a new personal maturity and responsibility through the various therapies of the 'Human Growth' movement. These are seen as essential for the metamorphosis to an ecologically based, non-acquisitive society. This 'New Age' perspective of psycho-social change clearly has much in common with what has been proposed in these pages. However, whilst acknowledging the value of humanistic therapies as important resources for personal development, it is the contention of this book that it is only the core systems of traditional psycho-spiritual training, supplemented and adapted as may be necessary, that ultimately have the strength to effect the significant consciousness shifts that the present crisis of humanity requires. (Although I am writing with the Buddhist tradition in mind, the spiritual methodologies of the world's great religions are fundamentally similar and capable of being mutually reinforcing.)

The central question is how far are substantial shifts to a higher level of consciousness a practicable proposition for significant numbers of people in the middle future? In this chapter I shall have to confine myself to the prospects for the

West. But it is there that so much global wealth and power lies, and the culture of industrial materialism which originated there has already deeply corrupted much of the world's traditional cultures, as well as blighting in the bud the hope and the humanism of the Marxian millennium.

Before attempting a tentative answer to that central question, there are others to be considered which relate to the best means of effecting such personal transformation. The acquisitive, dynamic and fragmented industrial culture has bred a restless, rationalistic, high egoic individualism. But the traditional systems of spiritual development originated in 'membership societies' characterized by a different self-image. This died out in the West with the waning of the Middle Ages but still persists in the East. Conze reminds us that at least historically there was no 'clear cut distinction between "Eastern" and "Western" mentality. Until about 1450, as branches of the same perennial philosophy, Indian and Western philosophers disagreed less among themselves than with many of the later developments of European philosophy.'[348] Do traditional systems for spiritual transformation not need therefore to be more or less changed so as to make them more accessible and relevant to the typical personality profile found in Western societies? Does there not need to be a distinctive 'Western Buddhism'? Indeed, is there not a case for attempting to supersede the traditional consciousness transformers entirely with the newly emergent transpersonal therapies?

These are very large questions for the brief treatment that is possible here. But they are about the essential underpinning to the whole psycho-social project which this book proposes. As a preliminary, the very striking differences in the experience of personhood in East and West may be noted.

These differences have been particularly well documented in the case of Japan, a country which has been industrialized like those in the West. Attention focuses upon the Japanese awareness of the individual person and his or her relationship to others and to the social group. The question has been taken up in an intercultural Zen Buddhist context by T. P. Kasulis.[349] He cites linguistic evidence to show that in Japan it is the *context* of the relationship between two people that defines their individual personhood, rather than who the individuals are in themselves. Individuals sense their identity through membership of a group or community, rather than establishing it through standing out as individuals; they accept that ascribed identity rather than emphasizing their own individuality.[350] 'Being excluded from the group is the most appalling thing that any Japanese can imagine.'[351] This is reminiscent of Western feudal society, where self-identity and social recognition depended very much on being some lord's 'man' or membership of some corporation such as a religious order or a craft guild. 'Manless men' were an intolerable anomaly. So, whereas contemporary Western individualism 'allows one to retain self-identity in radically different settings, in Japan one's identity tends to be socially defined and it is expected to change from context to context.' Hence, in Japan, 'the monastic life establishes the uniquely Zen environment of nothingness out of which a Zen disciple will derive personal meaning.'[352] (That being said, however, the Japanese Buddhist practitioner presumably still has difficulty in 'letting go' his or her group attachment as does the Westerner in unclenching from his or her ego!)

Similarly, traditional Indian society is also, in Wilber's term, a 'membership society', except that the only group which really appears to matter is the extended family.[353]

Other strong characteristics of Japanese and many other Eastern societies are the sense of hierarchy and an authoritarian paternalism combined with impersonality and social distance. Lines and degrees of authority are very precisely defined, and authority resides in the position which is formally held, and not in the personality of the holder or their demonstrated competence in discharging the duties of their office.[354] Similarly, Hofstede, in his comparative studies of 'culture's consequences', has systematically demonstrated the high level of individualism of Britons, Americans, Netherlanders and Scandinavians (modified by strong filiative tendencies in the latter two) as compared with typical Pakistanis and Japanese, and their preference for open, unstructured, 'personalized' and informal social situations.[355] In the Western 'alternative culture' this individualism is modified by 'groupiness' — filiative preferences for close, emotionally exposed, and unstructured groups and networks. There is evidence that some Buddhist teachers in North America have had difficulty in sustaining their traditionally expected role-behaviour under pressure of a very different culture,[356] and of preference by their students for a more open, mutually sharing kind of relationship.

In the last two decades the 'Human Growth' movement in the West, founded on humanistic psychology and psychophysical therapies, has become interested in Eastern meditative traditions, and various arguments have been advanced about the appropriateness of these to Western conditions. Before examining them it will be useful to say something about humanistic psychology itself, and particularly the transpersonal psychology which is currently evolving from it.

In contrast with the behaviourist and psychoanalytic traditions humanistic psychology recognizes the client as an autonomous person with a potential for growth which could be actualized in partnership with the therapist. There is much emphasis also on interpersonal experience through working in groups. Transpersonal psychology is a recent outgrowth concerned with 'the understanding and realization of non-ordinary, mystical or "transpersonal" states of consciousness, and with the psychological conditions which represent barriers to such personal realizations. Its concerns are thus very close to those of spiritual traditions, and, indeed, a number of transpersonal psychologists are working on conceptual systems intended to bridge and integrate psychology and the spiritual quest.'[357]

Ken Wilber, one of the most influential of these 'consciousness researchers', maintains that before individual consciousness can transcend itself the person must evolve through a hierarchy of levels of consciousness. Of fundamental importance is a healthy ego, in which the rational and the emotional, the conscious mind and the subconscious 'shadow', the 'top dog' and the 'bottom dog', are integrated and in harmony. The next level Wilber calls the centaur level, where the person becomes her or his body instead of experiencing it as a kind of appendage of the self. This is not easy, because 'we fear to reclaim the body because it houses in a particularly vivid and living form, strong emotions and feelings which are socially taboo. And ultimately the body is avoided because it is the abode of death.' Beyond the centaur level are the 'transpersonal' realms of consciousness 'where we begin to touch on an awareness which transcends the individual and discloses to a person something which passes far beyond himself.'[358] These realms lead ultimately to self-transcendence in a 'unity consciousness' in which the whole spectrum of consciousness is transcended in unobstructed awareness.

Much transpersonal psychologists' criticism of traditional meditation practice appears to be of two kinds.

In an article in the (London) Buddhist Society journal *The Middle Way*, Wilber, himself 'a practitioner of Zen for over a decade', takes fellow Buddhists to task for making of ego 'our favourite dirty word', which 'we glibly denounce as a fiction'. 'We tend to overlook entirely that we cannot transcend the ego until we *have* an ego in the first place; that the construction of the ego is the great and important task of the first half of life, at which point, and not before, its contemplative transcendence can be attempted; that the whole point of the ego is to create a self strong enough to die in nirvanic release.'[359] In short, you cannot realize your nothingness until you have become a somebody and have something to let fall. Otherwise you are likely to solidify neurosis by repressing what little self-esteem you still have.

If you are a pre-egoic nobody, with a very weak self-image, emotionally regressive, and heavily dependent on others for your sense of identity, meditation, it is argued, can actually deepen your nihilistic disorientation which you may then mistake for 'enlightenment'. Whereas Eastern teachings assume that a person already has a healthy ego structure, in the West high-egoic cultural pressures prove too much for a minority, who try to escape through regression towards pre-egoic states of consciousness. Wilber remarks in his *Middle Way* article that, 'after working with neurotics – who don't have enough ego strength – and psychotics – who have no ego strength at all – the average psychologist is dumbfounded to find us Buddhists recommending, indeed, encouraging, non-ego states...meditation, far from being a cure-all, can be *extremely detrimental* to borderline and narcissistic disorders (simply because the person is desperately attempting to create a strong and viable ego structure and intensive meditation tends to dissolve what little structure the borderline has).' Similarly, John Welwood, another transpersonal psychologist, maintains that, 'if a person has not developed the ability to relate to others in a wholesome way, or is unable to acknowledge and express feelings, psychotherapy may be the first treatment of choice before he can even begin to consider meditation....To attempt to skip over this area of our development in favour of some spiritual bliss beyond is asking for trouble.'[360]

The other half of the transpersonalists' critique of meditation refers to a phenomenon which is the reverse of the above. That is where a strong but still immature and acquisitive ego attempts, self-deludingly, to simulate and appropriate higher states of consciousness. This ego-charged pseudo-spirituality has long been recognized in the ancient spiritual traditions, and some reference was made to it at the end of the last chapter and elsewhere in this book. Jung coined the term 'inflation' for it. Criticizing the vogue for spiritual practices as the panacea for 'New Age Consciousness',

Steven Hendlin, a clinical psychologist, explains:

> The trouble basically is that one has not attained
> developmental maturity. And the result of this
> premature disidentification with ego growth is a
> further strengthening of attachments – the but-
> tressing of ego itself. The quest for oneness then is
> used in the service of the ego which is not about to
> be dismissed so hastily....The tendency to view
> experiences as 'transpersonal' which are actually
> personal or prepersonal is most readily seen in
> persons who have perhaps intuited, or sometimes
> glimpsed, the very real limitations of ego.[361]

Hendlin's remedy would be to remove from the sphere of
meditative spiritual training that whole stage of consciousness development in which ego is still acquisitive, presumably to the level of self-actualization in which being begins
to become more important than even the more subtle kinds
of having. Individuals should 'first clear up as much personal
psychological material as possible (ego integrity work),'
argues Hendlin, and 'then face the "givens" of one's existence (existential vulnerability) before then beginning serious
meditative practice.' Here the aspirant is being enjoined to
drop the therapist and take on board the spiritual pilot only
for what is the last stage of the spiritual voyage (for those
who ever get that far). Wilber's stepped evolutionary schema
for consciousness development gives much the same impression. Traditional spiritual training only appears in his
spectrum of therapies in the final transition through transpersonal consciousness. Thus, Assagioli's 'Psychosynthesis
represents a sound and effective approach to the transcendent self in no uncertain terms', while for the lower level of
ego integration, for example, Transactional Analysis is
prescribed.[362]

In the same vein, Hendlin believes that the 'experience of
voidness of meaning is *first* and foremost an existential issue
– not a spiritual one, and that those people would be better
served through some type of existential therapy than through

plunging into spiritual practice.' It would seem from this that even the Buddha's First Noble Truth of existential suffering is to be mopped up with therapy before the *real* spiritual practice can begin. This contrasts with Jung's view of existential neurosis as spiritual growth point.

In my view much of the above suggests misunderstanding of certainly Buddhist meditation practice and also ignores the context of spiritual training, in which sitting meditation is only a part of an interactive system. The next part of this chapter is a response in which seven areas for discussion and clarification are identified.

In the first place, the argument about the negative effects of meditation on people who have a poorly developed sense of self-identity cannot be dismissed. Moreover, as the remarks on spiritual cults at the end of the last chapter suggest, these are the people who are particularly likely to be drawn to the warm womb of a religious practice, gratefully embracing the 'humility' which is their mark of failure in an acquisitive world, yielding up their failed struggle to assert themselves to conformity to a quasi-monastic discipline, escaping into a group membership which itself makes no difficult psycho-social demands, and finding a lost super-parent in the omniscience of bhikkhu, roshi or guru. Certainly there do appear to be some Buddhist meditation teachers like Jack Kornfield, who sends 'quite a few of the people who come to my meditation retreats to therapists who I know are good and also have some spiritual understanding and perspective.'[363]

Beyond extreme cases there is, I believe, no *clear* distinction between a professional therapist and an insightful and experienced spiritual teacher, or between a conventional therapy and meditation and other spiritual training. Indeed, the potential therapeutic value of meditation for a variety of conditions is increasingly recognized both in the West and the East. In Britain, for example, in 1985, a group of clinical psychologists, therapists, doctors, teachers and social workers founded SIGMA (the Special Interest Group in Meditation), 'to share their knowledge and interest in the pioneering field of using meditation for the personal growth and benefit of those who come to them for help, as well as for the support of the therapists/care-givers themselves.'[364] In Japan, the long-established Morita Therapy is grounded in Zen Buddhism, and there are many other examples.

The traditional spiritual training is, moreover, designed in its early stages to provide a kind of 'character building', a gathering together of focused energy and awareness which is a precondition for the subsequent work to be done. Thus, *sila* is best understood not so much as 'morality' but rather as inner-matured moral integrity. It was said of the old Zen Masters that they had a way of making men of their monks. Venerable Myokyo-ni, a Western teacher of Zen Buddhism, writes that 'the way towards wholeness falls naturally into three stages. The first is in the training yard, learning to bear with oneself, to bear emotional onslaughts, becoming gentle and stronger, acquiring not Bull-strength but bearing strength. The second stage is maturity, a kind of mastership of the bearing or enduring strength which sustained application makes possible. Both are essential pre-requisites for the third or truly religious stage where the approach towards the awesome numinosity of the totally other begins.'[365] Does this not perhaps suggest a more relevant preparation of the poorly focused self for spiritual training than, say, assertiveness and other existential therapies? And does it not suggest that for the work of spiritual training a different kind of ego-integrity needs to be built up than that required by the norms of the conventional high-egoic culture? This is very evidently a training regimen which gently but firmly braces and challenges aspirants of weak and dependent personality.

In the second place there is the opposite and more common phenomenon of the headstrong ego, dissociated from feelings and from body, manipulating (and evading) the meditative experience. Dr Hendlin concedes that 'these issues will sooner or later come to the surface in meditative practice', but he nevertheless argues that 'they could be more carefully identified and partially resolved through a verbal therapy'.[366] The notion that such implied spiritual dysfunc-

tions should first be cleared up by therapy implies a misunderstanding of the whole character of spiritual training; it
is precisely this kind of material that is needed to manure
the spiritual growth. 'In the course of spiritual practice,'
reports Jack Kornfield, 'I have observed what we would call
psychological transformation, in which people become increasingly aware of different motivation patterns, different
kinds of attachment, and different images or relationships,
in most profound ways. Through practice and through a
sitting meditation discipline which is most central in Buddhism I have observed many people going through the kind
of growth that also happens in psychotherapy.'[367] 'There is a
kind of illumination in the meditation awareness process
that's very much like doing therapy for oneself, simply by
listening and paying attention. These insights and the acceptance that comes with a nonjudgemental awareness of
our patterns promotes mental balance and understanding,
so it can lessen our neurotic identification and suffering.'[368]

The following passage from Myokyo-ni completes the
picture by conveying the flavour of a specifically religious
training in contrast to humanistic therapy:

> The training discipline is not exacted in order to
> control or cut off emotions, but constitutes a frame-
> work against which the individual reacts, thus
> becoming familiar with his emotional household.
> The religious attitude of acceptance helps one to
> endure emotional stress, from which accrues the
> strength to continue functioning in awareness.
> Thus the individual 'I' and the emotions both
> undergo a slow but sure change. A religious atti-
> tude also prevents the ever-present danger of 'I'
> appropriating the newly found strength for selfish
> purposes. As in all good husbandry, the energy
> needs to be ploughed back into the practice, so
> that it my deepen and ripen, and bear much
> fruit.[369]

Thirdly, traditional meditative practice provides deep, penetrating observation through its combination of stilling the discriminating mind in deep absorption (*samadhi*) sufficient to open up to clear and non-manipulative contemplation (*vipassana*). By contrast, in Western psychology Kornfield finds a 'predominant emphasis on the qualities known in the Abhidhamma as analysis and investigation. This is true even in the best awareness traditions, like gestalt, where people pay very close attention in a mindful way to their inner process. Still there is a real neglect for the cutting power of *samadhi*, the stillness of the mind in meditation. . . . Thus a lot of psychological tools, which are similar to spiritual techniques, achieve different results because they do not penetrate the surface of the mind. They lack these other important aspects: concentration and tranquillity and equanimity, which empower the awareness to cut the neurotic speed.'[370] 'Conversely, there is often difficulty in Eastern traditions, because of too much emphasis on concentration and tranquillity. They may lead to wonderful experiences of rapture, silence of mind, and trance of the *Jhana* states. But without the balance of investigation and energetic observation of how things are, such practice will not lead to a deeper understanding of self and the freedom of enlightenment.'[371]

Fourthly, the preparatory levels of Buddhist spiritual training are designed not only to strengthen and focus the personality but also at the same time to integrate mind, feelings and body. This is Wilber's centaur stage, or, in Zen Buddhism, the 'pondering in the heart and the practice with the body which follows on from hearing with the ear.' This stage in the spiritual journey is graphically portrayed in the famous Zen bull-taming pictures where, in the middle picture of the series, the herdsman or 'trainer' gentles and rides home with the great 'bull' of emotional and physical energy.

Fifthly, from what has been said so far, it will be evident that although there is a certain schematic convenience in visualizing the path of spiritual training proceeding through a succession of stages this can be misleading. The beginning prefigures the end, as well as simply preparing the way for it. A spirit of unclenching humility, for example, is cultivated from the very start, as the beginner learns to bow to the Buddha image, to the teacher, to food, and even to the meditation cushion. Spiritual practice is holistic and poly-chronic as much as it is sequential and linear. The practice is much more than the sum of its techniques. Proposals to sub-stitute various religiously uninformed therapies for earlier stages of the training are therefore questionable, if for this reason alone.

Sixthly, in traditional oriental societies the trainee is sup-ported by a stable and religious culture. Moreover a high proportion of Buddhist trainees will be secure in their membership of a monastic order. In the West, for the great majority of trainees these favourable conditions do not obtain. Trainees have to come to terms with the exposed individualism of a secular culture which runs counter to their aspirations, and without the support of a tight com-munity. There is thus greater need for the *active* support of their fellows, and, above all, the teacher has a more import-ant and complex role to play and must have the skills of therapist, tutor and social facilitator as well as being spir-itually mature. Many such teachers already exist in the West, but these requirements are apparently still not fully recog-nized. In certain traditions, however, there has long been a close, ongoing contractual relationship between teacher and trainee. In personal interviews the teacher provides support and encouragement, helps the students understand their experiences, monitors and advises on successive phases of the training, and heads off delusiveness and danger. The context of the teacher's work is explained by Myokyo-ni as follows:

> In conformity with all Buddhism, the Zen school
> holds that the hard shell of I want it, as it suits me,
> as it ought to be, as I won't have it, etc. is a

mistaken combination, hardened or 'baked' by the
Three Fires [of ill will, acquisitiveness and de-
lusion] into a false identity. This hard shell needs
to be ground off, which is slow and patient work;
brute shattering from outside or inside spells catas-
trophe. When ready, the new attitude, relinked,
emerges of itself and can unfold. Since sloughing
off the last vestiges of the old shell, and the new
emergence, is a difficult process, not without
danger, a guide is needed to ensure genuine transformation. The homely analogy for this is a hen
hatching out her eggs. When the chick is ready to
come out, when the time is ripe, the hen pecks the
shell to help the chick to emerge.[372]

Finally, it was made clear in Part Four of this book that
sitting meditation — on which criticism quoted earlier was
apparently exclusively focused — is only one element in a
whole interactive system of Buddhist and other traditional
spiritual training. Of at least equal importance is the round-
the-clock awareness (mindfulness) practice and the cultivation of morality as a means of inner growth. Buddhist
training is designed to develop energy, aspiration, determination and inner strength of character within a supportive
framework of belief (faith, confidence), teachings both
reasoned and inspirational, a relationship with a teacher,
and the community of other dedicated Followers of the Way.
Within such a religious context the experience of sitting
meditation will certainly be different from when it is practised as a secularized therapy.

It remains true, however, that the conditions which favour
psycho-spiritual growth in one person, fail with another
and have regressive effects in a third, remain to some extent
elusive, depending very much, for example, on the skill and
empathy of the teacher or therapist. Robyn Skynner, a
psychotherapist, testifies that 'many who follow a sacred
tradition change profoundly as regard their ordinary life

adjustment...under the influence of some subtler and finer influence that begins to permeate and alter the entire organism.' On the other hand Skynner has noticed that others who follow such traditions 'become more closed, narrow and intolerant, both of others and of their own hidden aspects. Of those I see professionally, this group is the most intractable and untreatable of all, for the knowledge derived from a religious tradition has been put to the service of perceptual defences, of complacency, of narcissistic self-satisfaction, of comfort and security....' But, contrariwise, there are those in psychotherapy, and particularly in groups, whom Skynner finds 'can reach a point of simple openness, of awareness of themselves as part of mankind and of the universe, and of direct communion with others, more intensely than many following a traditional teaching, at least as far as one can judge by the statements and external behaviour of each. *It does not last, of course, and cannot be pursued systematically* [my italics—K.J.], but in the psychotherapeutic experience it is often there, sometimes in awe-inspiring fashion, and we have to make a place for this in our ideas.'[373]

Whereas the possibility of extensive psycho-social transformation through a spiritual renaissance of some kind (perhaps integrating the new therapies) is surely imaginable, it seems much less conceivable simply through meditation becoming fashionable or through the mass application of the multi-phase therapies prescribed in Wilber's *No Boundary*.[358]

In the foregoing pages I have argued for the maintenance of the integrity of traditional Buddhist and other spiritual training, and against the extensive substitution of humanistic therapies in its earlier stages or other significant changes in its essential character. That being said, we can now return to the original question about the extent to which a distinctively Western Buddhism needs to be developed — that is, Western *yanas* or 'vehicles' to carry the perennial Buddha-dharma.

It must surely remain a very open question as to what

extent perennial Buddhism can be made more accessible to Westerners' experience than through the Theravada, Tibetan and Zen traditions in which most are at present practising. However, the history of Buddhism contains notable examples of major cultural re-adaptations, such as the creation of Ch'an (Zen) Buddhism in China out of the Indian Mahayana import. And, in turn, T. P. Kasulis has argued that 'If Zen Buddhism is to become a major influence in Western life it will have to be transformed, not merely transplanted,' even though 'for a few Westerners a traditional Zen Buddhist training may be highly effective.'[375]

The way forward is surely through sensitive experimentation, variation and modification on the basis of received oriental practice, and an amplification of the dialogue that has already begun between practitioners of Dharma and of humanistic psychology. Well-matured teachers are already feeling out the possibilities on the basis of their day-to-day experience with their students. The Buddhist virtues of openness, pluralism and of eschewing dogmatic attitudes are here as important as ever. Experiential evolution is likely to be more reliable than the 'bolting in' of new formal techniques. There are cases where a quite traditional framework of formal training actually provides the stability within which a sensitive teacher can bring the Dharma to life for Westerners. As noted in the previous chapter, the Western spiritual and cultural tradition is a relevant resource. The Friends of the Western Buddhist Order, for example, draw upon the insight and inspiration of Blake, Shakespeare, Shelley and similar writers. Myokyo-ni's *teisho* (formal Zen talks) are a rich and evocative weave spun variously from the Greek myths, European classics, the Christian tradition, Jungian case material, and folk tales as well as the traditional Zen stories and other Buddhist material. Similarly, one Western Zen Buddhist sect chants the *sutras* in the Gregorian mode and has adopted other outward Christian conventions whilst remaining Buddhist to the core.

Whilst remaining positive about the potential contribution of 'the New Therapies' to traditional Buddhist practice, there are good reasons for being wary. Of the evidently more superheated American scene, Steven Hendlin writes of 'being confronted with a New Age information glut typified by the manufacturing of blends of Eastern—Western philosophies and practices to make it all more palatable to the Western appetite for something that goes down easily. Westerners for the most part seem to want their nouveau spirituality the same way they want their drive-through hamburgers: with little substance and without waiting. No wonder that pre-packaged psycho-spiritual programs sprang up to satisfy the need for simple, painless "oneness".'[376]

Beyond the fringes, most mainstream Buddhist training available in the West has not been affected by this kind of syncretism, though it may have suffered by association in the public mind. However, the commercialized charisma of the spiritual carpet-baggers to whom Hendlin refers should not prejudice us against teachers with professional therapeutic skills who are experimenting from their grounding in traditional training methods.

An outstanding example is the work of the American Buddhist peace activist, Joanna Macy, referred to in Chapter 17. This is a pioneering instance of how psycho-spiritual practice can be taken out into the wider community, engaging deeply felt emotions in specific areas of experience. In the Macy example the focus is wide, covering denial and despair arising out of the whole planetary crisis. Certainly in Britain the frustration, anger and hopelessness created by long-term unemployment and the fact and feeling of redundancy would provide another possible focus, and at least one Buddhist centre has already welcomed the local unemployed to special afternoon meditation sessions.

Overall, Macy's work seems to lean more towards group therapies in the gestalt tradition than to Buddhist practice, though it does include this and is generally informed by it.

In Britain, John Crook, with a background of training in

several Eastern traditions, in group therapy and in psychology research, has been developing a 'Western Zen'
retreat suited to the needs of 'urban Europeans'. His account
is quoted in some detail to convey the flavour of this kind of
development.

In this five day retreat 'silence and a strict adherence to
the rules of politeness, tidiness and consideration for others
are enforced'. Within a disciplined traditional form the
retreat offers a blend of conventional Zen Buddhist meditation, intensive work on a *koan* (for example, Who am I?
What is life?) about which no discussion is allowed but,
working alternately in pairs, each respondent is 'forced into
a free association and a progressive outpouring of themes
related to the *koan*' and neo-Reichian bioenergetic exercises.
These latter assist 'the expression of blocked emotions' and
'consist mainly in various forms of vigorous breathing coupled with active body movement to music. Some are derived
from the chanting meditation of Tibetan lamas.'

Crook explains that 'the reason for collating these different
types of experience is to allow for individual variation in response.' He concludes: 'Introjected identity components are
released through self-disclosure often involving a great deal
of emotional expression. The structure of the process makes
it safe for this to happen, and the authority of the facilitator
is firmly maintained to ensure an essential group security.
Individuals often experience relief from inhibitions and
tensions, renewed confidence and vitality, and sometimes a
major shift in their attitude with respect to their existence in
the world.'[377]

Also relevant here is the well-established Western-style
*vipassana* tradition represented in the UK by the Insight
Association and in the USA by the Insight Meditation
Society, Jack Kornfield, Joseph Goldstein, Sharon Sulzberg,
Christina Feldman and Christopher Titmus. This Insight
movement has a socially responsive, Green, flavour. It is a
culturally recycled attempt to have the Theravada Buddhadharma without the format of Buddhism, the peas without

the pod, the spirituality without the religion. It merits a separate study, but is undoubtedly a valuable growing point for contemporary Buddhism.

More generally there is a tendency now at more traditional Buddhist retreats and centres to supplement the practice with such physical activity as hatha yoga, tai-chi and even jogging. Could this be a bioenergetic growing point? The traditional Dharma talk and private teacher-to-student interview is also being supplemented in a few instances by trainee experience-sharing in unstructured small groups.

I believe it is important that psycho-physical techniques from therapy should be adapted into the traditional training only by those who are well matured within the practice by many years as trainee and teacher. Contrariwise, some humanistic therapists find it helpful to reinforce their techniques by introducing meditation and other 'spiritual' practices, and their experience here can be valuable. But the Way must be protected from dilution by well-meaning professionals and academics who, themselves ungrounded in an established spiritual practice, nevertheless wish to annex the 'lower stages' of the Way or even to offer an allegedly faster and more convenient secular by-pass. The editor of a recent symposium concludes that 'therapy represents a special and limited case of the more general spiritual search, as Newton's Laws of Motion are special cases of Einstein's broader theory of Relativity.... Critical caution should prevent us [therapists] from polluting the rich harvest of insights that is available with our own overenthusiasm, and half-baked preconceptions.'[378] None of this, however, is to deny that established spiritual teachers would not in their turn find it fruitful to master certain humanistic therapies such as the gestalt and the Jungian. The above reservations are prompted by the questionable credentials of much humanistic psychology, to which Wilber has drawn attention.

There is a questionable assumption in the Human Growth Movement which goes back to Rousseau and which is shared by such diverse people as humanistic Marxists and neo-Freudians and by hugely influential figures like Erich Fromm and Carl Rogers. It is the assumption that there is a kind of innate subjective goodness in all of us which is unable to flower because of *repression*. Relieved of the distortions created by repressive family upbringing, repressive social institutions, repressive patriarchy, and so on, every personality would become naturally well balanced and fulfilled. The mirror image of this assumption (and the more vulgarly popular one) is that we are innately evil, and only objective cultural, social and other objective constraints and conditioning can mitigate our excesses and enable us to develop some humanity (Hobbes, Burke, Darwin, Herbert Spencer, Freud, Lorenz).

As between these two 'weighted polarities' the Buddhist view is that there is in the ordinary human condition an existential dread which drives the individual both to inner dissociation and repression and to personal and socio-historical behaviour which represses others both psychically and physically. The liberal-humanistic and conservative positions above are two halves of a truth that does not go deep enough. In moderation, the first can give release of blocked off parts of the self and the latter can provide a supportive framework for development. Taken to extremes, however, humanistic therapies, if they do not lead to a higher and more integrated personality, can have regressive and negative effects, creating problems equal but opposite to those that had been remedied. Thus Wilber finds it 'a great personal disappointment that so many humanistic therapies, which began with the promising understanding that awareness ought eventually to move beyond the mind, have taken the regressive way to do so and simply retreated to. . .just body therapy, just feelings, just sensory awareness, just experiental sensation. They are, in and by themselves, a perfect education in sub-humanity, and they have the nerve to call it "consciousness raising".'[379] (Assagioli's 'Psychosyn-thesis' is one instructive exception.)

The omnipotent Western ego has tended to move away

from a healthy integration of reason and instinct. Now either the top dog of reason tries to keep the bottom dog of instinct locked up and out of the way, or, more 'progressively', the instinctual dog is released beyond the call of reason and rejoices in its mindless 'liberation' (whereas it *could* have been trained to be a sensitive watchdog and playmate). So, while some — mainly those in authority — are left petrified in the increasingly mad rationality of endless consumption, exploitation and armament, others — an equally privileged minority — enjoy the liberating delusions of a regressive, pre-egoic emotional release. Escape into the cult of irrationality is mistaken for a New Spirituality.

All this must deepen doubts about the adequacy of the (otherwise welcome) 'consciousness raising', 'emotional honesty' and do-it-yourself group therapies of the grassroots campaigners of the counter-culture to effect, unaided, the profound transformation of self needed to match 'New Age' social aspirations. Howard Clark, whose views were quoted in Chapter 33 as typical of nonviolent libertarianism, has written about the persistence of a deep-rooted self-affirming dogmatism inflicted on others:

> Yet already, since the term 'the personal is political' became a cliché, the same harshness, stridency and even competitiveness that drove people out of the old-style politics have been introduced into personal-politics — people laying trips on each other about consumerism, monogamy, child rearing, whatever, rather than respecting people who are also having difficulty changing their lives.[380]

When dependence on free-flowing honesty of feelings which are insufficiently integrated and grounded proves inadequate, there is resort to the reassurance of ideology. Jonathon Porritt, a leading British 'Green', expresses what is at bottom the same kind of disillusion as Howard Clark:

The fissiparous and internecine tendencies of the German Green Party hardly prove the most convincing endorsement for a new style of politics! This may well have something to do with the emphasis they put on the development of a specific Green ideology; one certainly requires a set of minimum criteria to establish the essential nature of the Green alternative, but to fashion those criteria into an inflexible and narrow diktat is to become hooked on ideology as a substitute for real politics. Such an approach is incompatible with the fundamental Green principles of diversity (hard to achieve when everyone is being told exactly what they ought to be thinking), decentralization (impractical if party élites insist on passing down homogenized greenery from on high) and participation (which is unlikely to result from the paper politics of those who demand unanimity on every crossed 't' and dotted 'i'). The alternative to industrialism is Green, not Green-ism![381]

In conclusion, what, then, are the prospects for a comparatively rapid, large-scale global consciousness shift, as the alternative to the slide into many different kinds of violence, irrational and madly rational? In this chapter and elsewhere in the book there is evidence of the inherent inadequacy of an exclusively secular, humanistic transformer to effect the psycho-social metamorphosis to the 'New Age' that is so confidently predicted in some quarters.[382] Only historically evolved spiritual 'Ways' like Buddhism go to the root of the problem but it will be clear by now that these do not offer any ready and assured highway beyond ego-appropriated spirituality and religious dogmatism. I am therefore inclined to Wilber's conclusion 'that we are nowhere near the Millennium. In fact, at this point in history, the most radical, pervasive and earth-shaking transformation would occur simply if everybody evolved to a mature, rational and responsible ego, capable of freely participating in the open exchange of mutual self-esteem. *There* is the "edge of history". There would be a *real* New Age.'[383] Jung expressed much the same imperative when he wrote that 'the survival of mankind depends on the speed and extent to which individuals learn to withdraw their projected shadows from others and reintegrate them honourably in themselves.'

Earlier we noted how Wilber's centaur level of consciousness was represented in the ancient Zen bull-taming pictures by bull and man united, riding home at the end of the day. In the thousand and more years that have passed since the making of that picture, we now have simultaneously to tame the great monster of human society and its history, which emanates from our own fear-driven wildness, and which, like it, appears to have an out-of-control life of its own. Through learning how to work with the threatening inner energy we learn how to work more effectively to tame the social forces which threaten us and which have the same origin. In reality, the work is one and the same.

The prospects for large-scale psycho-spiritual transformation and the accompanying Greening of society which were raised earlier must, in the light of the foregoing discussion, be viewed more soberly. Both religion and Green thinking readily run into the sands of ideology and polarization. And likewise the spiritual Ways are all too easily diverted to meet the needs of self-consolation, escapism and inflation. We are back with Part One, with the Buddhist understanding of 'ego-delusion', of existential false-consciousness. The possibility of personally and collectively working our way free from that condition is, I believe, the only prospect for finding our true humanity and beginning to climb out of the abyss into which our culture is sliding. What has to be done is clear enough. It is that enough of us should give ourselves freely into what has to be done, both personally and publicly, with a determined and warm-hearted confidence.

# Epilogue: Not Hope, But Possibilities...

This epilogue is written a few days after the disaster at the Soviet nuclear power station at Chernobyl sent radioactive clouds billowing across Europe. No nuclear reactor can be unfailingly safe, and only one similar major disaster would be sufficient to devastate a small and densely populated country like Britain. Yet neither the Government nor the Opposition is willing to phase out the nuclear power industry. Radioactive rain has been falling all day out of a grey sky. Out of our sense of ultimate powerlessness at times like this, at the huge seemingly unstoppable folly of it all, arises the familiar frustration, despair, rage.

At an unripened level of consciousness we may experience such feelings almost as if we were watching a stage play through the theatre proscenium arch. We feel at once both helplessly distanced and yet mortally involved (much like our 'mind' may feel about our 'body'). Characteristic responses are, variously, evasion, denial or consolation seeking, whether disguised as hope, rationality, apathy or resignation.

Here as elsewhere the experience of unavailingly trying to escape our affliction is itself the experience of suffering. It is like the person who was chased by her shadow until she eventually died of fear and exhaustion. She was in too much of a hurry to do anything so illogical as sitting down in the sunshine. Systems of maturation like Buddhism teach that it is only through unflinchingly facing our afflictions and opening unreservedly to our feelings that we can come to experience an empowerment that is other than this trembling self. This is the purpose of the 'despair and empowerment' workshops for peace workers pioneered by Joanna Macy and described at the end of Chapter 17.

The resolute confrontation of the present threats to humanity, however, draws us into a classic paradox, the *koan* of social action. Jack Douglass explains that the very 'intensity of my recognition of evil, necessary to my resistance and humanity, heightens the consciousness of my self which is the source of my powerlessness. I resist, therefore I am; powerless to *be* a liberating force,' and so 'my resistance will become an egotistic duel with external powers because I have not come to terms with the fundamental absence of power within myself.'[384] This is the experience of many elderly radicals whose increasing sense of powerlessness has paralled their deepening sense of conviction over the years. If emotional 'burn-out' does not consume them first their escape may be into a deepening unreality of both self and the world. They become case hardened.

The only transformative way to loosen the knot which our struggles continually tighten is through the work that has to be done within, opening up to recognition that we are our own problem. For the global-political despair is a focal expression of the sense of powerlessness which can be meditatively revealed at the very root of the human condition. The Follower of the Way discovers her or himself as being much the same bundle of variously knotted, ferocious, shameful and seemingly helpless suffering as the whole of world humanity now appears to be. Each of us is a jewel in Indra's Net which replicates the whole and is the whole. Collective, cosmic kamma has now unfolded to a point where it is the equal of personal, individual kamma. For example, each of us has always tended to live each day heedless of our mortality, as if we were going to live forever. Nowadays, most of us continue to behave as if the shadow of nuclear annihilation did not exist. Our personal mortality has always been unimaginable to us. Now we have to live with the very real possibility of the extinction of the human race itself.

Awareness of social powerlessness can only become liberative empowerment if deepened meditatively to a yielding to the powerlessness at the depths of our being and an opening to the nullity of self. Thus for Douglass 'the truth which comes in solitude is that the struggle for [social] liberation must begin by recognizing the terrifying emptiness of that self of mine which is prepared to pose on the outside as a redeemer of others. . . . For the prophet goes to the depth of the double poverty in the world and himself, in the terrible suffering of the innocent and in the radical emptiness of himself. The prophet who is able to endure this double struggle defines all over again the beauty and tragedy of man: the dignity of man's commitment to his limitations.'[385]

'"What is it," said Ajita to the Buddha, "that smothers the world? What makes the world so hard to see? What would you say pollutes the world, and what threatens it most?" "It is ignorance which smothers," said the Master, "and it is carelessness and greed which make the world invisible. The hunger of desire pollutes the world, and the great source of fear is the pain of suffering." "In every direction," said Ajita, "the rivers of desire are running. How can we dam them and what will hold them back? What can we use to close the flood-gates?" "Any river can be stopped with the dam of mindfulness," said the Buddha, "I call it the flood-stopper. And with wisdom you can close the flood-gates."'[386]

What we believe to be reality 'out there' is distorted and discoloured by our own fear, alienation and self-need. As we open in *acceptance* of how it is, of the powerlessness within and the terrible power without, so, paradoxically, there arises then a freedom and a clarity which enable action which is both appropriate and unquenchable. And which is beyond both hope and despair. The practice of a totally unreserved awareness is the road to absolute inner acceptance. This acceptance unblocks the space where selfless love and fearlessness are revealed. And the inner peace from which they arise is the way to effective outer peacemaking. This real world of Dharmadhatu 'is realizable when the solid outlines of individuality melt away and the feeling of finiteness no longer oppresses us,' writes D.T. Suzuki in his rendering of the vision of reality presented in the Avatamsaka Sutra. 'In the Dharmadhatu there are space and time and individual beings, but they show none of their earthly characteristics of separateness and obduracy.'[387]

Just released from one of his periodic imprisonments, Jack Douglass was asked whether he really felt there was any hope. 'Not hope, but there are possibilities' was, I believe, the reply that he gave. 'Possibilities' is the best word. There is still a little wish-fulfilment hiding in 'opportunities'. So what is that elusive smile playing about the Buddha's face? Is it his compassionate acknowledgement of the cosmic joke? If we really care, we shall not take the self so seriously that we cannot be freed into enough space to see the black humour, the cosmic irony. Given that space we can begin to sense out the dance of possibilities.

# Prayer

May all beings be happy.

May all be joyous and live in safety.

Let no one deceive another,
   nor despise another, as weak as they may be.
Let no one by anger or by hate wish evil
   for another.

As a mother, in peril of her own life,
   watches and protects her only child.
Thus with a limitless spirit must one
   cherish all living beings.

Love the world in its entirety — above,
   below and all around.
Without limitation.
With an infinite goodness and with benevolence.

While standing or walking, sitting or
   lying down, as long as one is awake,
Let one cultivate Loving-Kindness.

This is called the Supreme Way of Living. [388]

# Notes and References

INTRODUCTION

1 See, for example, Garry Thomson, 'Buddhism and science' in *The Middle Way*, 59 (1), May 1984, pp.25—30.
2 Ursula King, *Towards a New Mysticism*, London: Collins, 1980.
3 For those interested in developing a Buddhist 'philosophy and practice for spiritually based progressive politics' James J. Hughes has compiled *Liberation Buddhism: an annotated bibliography* which also lists organizations and periodicals, Colombo: Atlas Hall Press, 1985.
4 Ken H. Jones *Buddhism and the Bomb*, Preston (UK): Buddhist Peace Fellowship, 1985; *Buddhism and Social Action*, Kandy (Sri Lanka): Buddhist Pubn. Society, 1981 (Wheel Publication no. 285/286).
5 Ken Wilber, *Up from Eden: a transpersonal view of human evolution*, London: Routledge & Kegan Paul, 1983.
6 Ken Wilber *A Sociable God: toward a new understanding of religion*, Boulder & London: Shambhala, 1984.

PART ONE: LIVING A LIFE

7 D.T. Suzuki, *Essays in Zen Buddhism: III*, London: Rider, 1970, p.214.
8 The reference is to Francis Thompson's poem of that title.
9 Rainer Maria Rilke, 'Tenth Duino Elegy', as translated by Ruth Speirs in J.M. Cohen, ed., *The Rider Book of Mystical Verse*, London: Rider, 1983.

10 The concluding lines of Philip Larkin's poem 'The life with a hole in it', first published in the 1974 Christmas Supplement of the Poetry Book Society, and reprinted in the *Observer* (London), 8 December 1985, as part of Larkin's obituary.

11 Dorothy Rowe, *Living With the Bomb: can we live without enemies?* London: Routledge & Kegan Paul, 1985, p.112.

12 Adam Curle, *Mystics and Militants: a study of awareness, identity and social action*, London: Tavistock, 1976, p.41.

13 Don Cupitt, *The World to Come*, London: S.C.M. Press, 1982, p.xv.

14 Christopher Isherwood, 'Hypothesis and belief' in C. Isherwood, ed., *Vedanta for the Western World*, London: Allen & Unwin, 1948, p.43.

15 *Ajahn* Buddhadasa, *Toward the Truth*, ed. Donald K. Swearer, Philadelphia: Westminster Press, 1971, pp.36–40.

16 Cases from the *Mumonkan* – *the gateless gate*, being a collection of problems called *koan* which Zen teachers use in guiding their students towards release.

17 Reginald Horace Blythe, *Zen and the Zen Classics*, Tokyo: Hokuseido Press, 1960–4.

PART TWO: THE DYNAMICS OF DELUSION

18 *Majjhima-nikaya* 13.

19 H. Tajfel, ed., *Differentiation Between Groups*, London: Academic Press, 1978.

20 M. Sherif, 'Superordinate goals in the reduction of group conflict', *American Journal of Sociology*, 1958, vol. 63, pp.349–56.

21 Ken Wilber, op. cit., note 5, p.284.

22 E. F. Schumacher, *Small is Beautiful*, London: Abacus (Sphere Books), 1974, p.30.

23 See, for example, Jonathan Steele, *The Limits of Soviet Power*, London: Penguin, 1985; Jim Garrison and Pyare Shivpuri, *The Russian Threat: its myths and realities*, London: Gateway, 1983.

24 Independent Commission on Disarmament and Security Issues *Common Security: a blueprint for survival*, (Palme Report), Markham (Ontario): Simon & Schuster, 1982, p.108.

25 Glyn Williams, 'From the bottom up', *New Internationalist*, no. 153, Nov. 1985, p.15, p.18.

26 David Brandon *Zen in the Art of Helping*, London: Routledge & Kegan Paul, 1976.

27 Gary Snyder, 'Buddhism and the coming revolution' in *Earth House Hold*, New York: New Directions, 1957, p.91.

28 The Global 2000 Report to the President of the United States. *Entering the 21st Century: the summary report*, Oxford: Pergamon, 1984.

29 Willy Brandt, *North—South: a programme for survival. Report of the Independent Commission on Development Issues,* Cambridge (Mass): MIT Press, 1980; Willy Brandt, *Common Crisis: North—South Co-operation for World Recovery*, London: MIT Press, 1983.

30 The Palme Report, op. cit., note 24.

31 Brian Walker, 'In the line of fire', *New Internationalist* no. 121, March 1983, p.22.

32 Carl Oglesby and Richard Shaull, *Containment and Change*, New York: Macmillan, 1967, pp.70—1.

33 'Nuclear Winter', *Sanity* (London), June 1984, pp.17—27.

34 E. F. Schumacher, op. cit., note 22, Chapter 3.

35 Maurice Ash, 'After Schumacher', *Resurgence* no. 111, July/Aug 1985, pp.22—3.

36 Helen Caldicott, *Nuclear Madness*, London: Bantam, 1980, p.1.

37 Rainer Maria Rilke, *Letters of Rainer Maria Rilke 1910—1926*, trans. J.B. Greene and M.D. Hester, New York: W.W. Norton, 1969, pp.374—5.

38 K.N. Jayatilleke, 'The conditioned genesis of the individual,' *Buddhist Quarterly*, 11 (2—3), 1978—9, p.59, p.60.

39 Walpola Rahula, *What the Buddha Taught*, London: Gordon Fraser, 1959, p.32.

40  Melford E. Spiro, *Buddhism and Society: a great tradition and its Burmese vicissitudes*, London: Allen & Unwin, 1970.

41  David L. Gosling, 'Thai Buddhism in transition', *Religion*, vol. 7, 1977, pp.18–34 (p.32).

42  See, for example, Joseph Head and S.L. Cranston, *Reincarnation: an East–West Anthology*, New York: Julian Press, 1961.

43  Ian Mangham, *Interactions and Interventions in Organizations*, New York: Wiley, 1978, p.13.

44  Eric Berne, *Games People Play*, London: Penguin, 1968.

45  Carl Gustav Jung, 'The archetypes and the collective unconscious', *Collected Works*, London: Routledge & Kegan Paul, 1959, vol. 9, p.122 ff.

PART THREE: THE DIALECTICS OF DELUSION

46  Ivan Illich and others, *Disabling Professions*, London: Marion Boyars, 1977, p.89.

47  Charles Lindblom, *The Policy Making Process*, Eaglewood Cliffs (NJ): Prentice-Hall, 1968.

48  Paul Bracken, *The Command and Control of Nuclear Forces*, Yale University Press, 1983, p.239.

49  Reported in the *Guardian* (London) 2 Jan 1985, p.13. See also Oxford Research Group, *Who decides? Accountability and nuclear weapons decision-making in Britain*, Woodstock (Oxfordshire): Oxford Research Group, [1985].

50  E.F. Schumacher, *Good Work*, London: Abacus (Sphere Books), 1980, pp.52–3.

51  Edward Conze, *Buddhism*, Oxford: Cassirer, 1974.

52  Thomas Merton, *The Way of Chuang-Tzu*, London: Unwin Books, 1970, p.88.

53  Edward Conze, op. cit., (note 51), p.163.

54  *Third Zen Patriarch* Seng-Ts'an, *On Trust in the Heart* (*Hsin-hsin-ming*).

55  *Anguttara-nikaya* I, 10, trans. I.B. Horner.

56  *Samyutta-nikaya* I, 2, 10, trans. M.O'C. Walshe.

57 David Martin, *Religious Vision and Political Reality*, Canterbury: University of Kent Centre for the Study of Religion and Society, 1985, p.17.
58 Lionel Trilling, *Liberal Imagination: essays on literature and society*, Harmondsworth: Penguin Books, 1970.
59 See T.R.V. Murti, *The Central Philosophy of Buddhism*, London: Unwin, 2nd edn. 1960.
60 For example, Michael Q. Patton, *Qualitative Evaluation Methods*, London: Sage, 1980.
61 Eugene Sharp, Interview in *Peace News*, 12 June 1981, p.13.
62 As rendered by Joseph Goldstein in 'Tasting the strawberry: Theravada Buddhism—path of awareness', *Naropa* magazine II, 1985, p.22.
63 Robert A.F. Thurman, *The Holy Teaching of Vimalakirti: a Mahayana scripture*, Pittsburgh: Pennsylvania State University Press, 1976, pp.50−1.
64 D.T. Suzuki, 'Lectures on Zen Buddhism', in D.T. Suzuki, and others *Zen Buddhism and Psychoanalysis*, London: Souvenir Press, 1974, p.38.
65 *Samyutta-nikaya* XII, 15, trans. M.O'C. Walshe.
66 Carl Gustav Jung, 'Psychology and religion, West and East', *Collected Works*, London: Routledge & Kegan Paul, 1958, vol. 11.
67 Erich Fromm, *The Revolution of Hope*, New York: Harper & Row, 1970.
68 Thomas Kuhn, *The Structure of Scientific Revolutions*, University of Chicago Press, 1969.
69 Marilyn Ferguson, *The Aquarian Conspiracy: personal and social transformation in the 1980s*, London: Routledge & Kegan Paul, 1981.
70 American astronaut Ed Mitchell, interviewed on US television.
71 Ken Wilber, 'Two modes of knowing', in Roger N. Walsh and Frances Vaughan, eds., *Beyond Ego: transpersonal dimensions in psychology*, Los Angeles: J.P. Tarcher, 1980, pp.234−48 (p.234).

72 Quoted in Ken Wilber, *Quantum Questions: mystical writings of the world's great physicists*, Boulder: Shambhala, 1984.

73 Lawrence Le Shan, 'Physicists and mystics: similarities in world view', in his *The Medium, the Mystic and the Physicist: towards a general theory of the paranormal*, New York: Viking, 1974.

74 Alan Dawe, 'The two sociologies', *British Journal of Sociology*, 21(2), June 1970, pp.207−18.

75 Nigel Nicholson and Toby Wall, 'Introductory themes in organisational psychology', in Nigel Nicholson and Toby Wall, eds., *The Theory and Practice of Organisational Psychology*, London: Academic Press, 1982, pp.1−17.

76 See, for example, Tom Burns and G.M. Stalker, *The Management of Innovation*, London: Tavistock, 1961.

77 Quoted in Roger N. Walsh and Frances Vaughan, op. cit. (note 71), p.8.

78 As, for example, in Trevor Ling, *The Buddha's Philosophy of Man*, London: Dent, 1981, p.xv.

79 Fritjof Capra, *The Tao of Physics*, London: Wildwood House, 1975.

80 From Henry Thoreau's remark in *Walden*: 'Time is a river in which I go fishing.'

81 From T.S. Eliot's poem 'The Rock', in T.S. Eliot, *Collected Poems 1909−1962*, London: Faber & Faber, 1963.

82 Ken Wilber, op. cit. (note 71), p.237.

83 H.H. the XIV Dalai Lama, Tenzin Gyatso, *Universal Responsibility and the Good Heart*, Dharamsala (India): Library of Tibetan Works & Archives, 1976, p.16.

84 Gary Snyder, 'Spel against demons', in *Turtle Island*, New York: New Directions, 1974, pp.16−17.

85 From W.H. Auden's poem 'The Quest', in W.H. Auden, *Collected Poems*, London: Faber & Faber, 1976.

86 Simone Weil, *Gravity and Grace*, London: Routledge & Kegan Paul, 1963.

87 Sulak Sivaraksa, *Siamese Resurgence*, Bangkok: Asian Cultural Forum on Development, 1985, p.108.

88 R.D. Laing, in *Knots*, London: Penguin, 1971, p.85.
89 Aldous Huxley, *The Perennial Philosophy*, London: Chatto & Windus, 1974.
90 F.C. Happold, *Mysticism*, London: Penguin, revised edn. 1970, p.38.
91 See, for example, Elaine Pagels, *The Gnostic Gospels*, London: Penguin, 1982.
92 Ken Wilber, op. cit. (note 5).
93 Jacob Needleman, *The New Religions*, London: Allen Lane, 1972, pp.16–17.
94 Thomas Merton, *Zen and the Birds of Appetite*, New York: New Directions, 1968, p.41.
95 Kenneth Leech, *True God: an exploration of spiritual theology*, London: Sheldon Press, 1985, p.1, p.7.
96 For a valuable introduction, see D.T. Suzuki, op. cit. (note 7).
97 D.T. Suzuki, in an Introduction to Beatrice L. Suzuki, *Mahayana Buddhism*, London: Allen & Unwin, 1981, p.12.
98 Arthur Koestler, *Janus*, London: Hutchinson, 1978, p.57.
99 D.T. Suzuki, op. cit. (note 7), p.99.
100 John R. Rodman, *Theory and Practice in the Environmental Movement: notes towards an ecology of experience*, Claremont (California): Pitzer College, n.d.
101 Penny Strange, 'Permaculture: practical design for town and country in permanent agriculture', *The Ecologist*, 13(2/3) 1983, pp.88–94.
102 Bill Mollison, *'Permaculture Two*, California: Tagari (ITC), 1978. Permaculture enquiries in the UK to: Permaculture UK, P.O. Box 500, 8 Elm Avenue, Nottingham.
103 Gary Snyder, op. cit. (note 84), p.101.
104 Thomas Cleary, *Entry into the Inconceivable: an introduction to Hua-yen Buddhism*, Honolulu: University of Hawaii Press, 1983, p.2.
105 From William Blake's poem 'Auguries of innocence'.
106 Francis Cook, *Hua-yen Buddhism*, Pittsburgh: Pennsyl-

vania State University Press, 1977, p.109.

107  William Blake, op. cit. (note 105).

108  D.T. Suzuki, op. cit. (note 7), p.83.


PART FOUR: TRAINING AND LIFESTYLE

109  Robert Aitken, 'Peace, Buddhism and perennial know-ledge', [*United States*] *Buddhist Peace Fellowship Newsletter* (Berkeley, California), 6(3), July 1984, p.9.

110  Harvey Cox, *Turning East: the promise and peril of the new orientalism*, London: Allen & Unwin, 1979, p.133.

111  Rainer Maria Rilke, *Letters to a Young Poet*, trans. K.W. Maurer, London: Langley, 1943, p.248.

112  *Udana* v, 5, trans. F.L. Woodward.

113  H.H. the XIVth Dalai Lama, Tenzin Gyatso 'Love, altruism, vegetarianism, anger and the responsibilities of teachers. Questions answered by H.H. the Dalai Lama', *The Middle Way*, 60(2), Aug 1985, p.69.

114  *Ajahn* Chah, *A Taste of Freedom: selected Dhamma talks*, Hung Wai Forest Monastery (Thailand), 1980, p.49.

115  Aldous Huxley, *Eyeless in Gaza*, London: Chatto & Windus, 1969, chapter LIV.

116  Irmgard Schloegl (Venerable Myokyo-ni), *Wisdom of the Zen Masters*, London: Sheldon Press, 1975, p.13.

117  David Brandon, op. cit. (note 26), p.59.

118  Lao Tzu, 'Tao Te Ching' 38, trans. Alan Watts, in Alan Watts, *The Watercourse Way*, London: Penguin, 1975, p.108.

119  Simone Weil, op. cit. (note 86), p.53

120  Ibid. p.113.

121  *Digha-nikaya* I, 124.

122  Simone Weil, op. cit. (note 86) p.112.

123  Philip Kapleau, *Zen Dawn in the West*, London: Rider, 1980, p.232.

124  *Anguttara-nikaya* x, 176.

125  *Anguttara-nikaya* v, 177.

126 Hammalava Saddhatissa, *Buddhist Ethics*, London: Allen & Unwin, 1970, p.72.

127 E.F. Schumacher, op. cit. (note 50).

128 Robert Aitken, *The Mind of Clover: essays in Zen Buddhist ethics*, San Francisco: North Point Press, 1984, pp.29–30.

129 Sulak Sivaraksa, op. cit. (note 87), pp.77–8.

130 For more on the Tiep Hien Order and its precepts see *Thich* Nhat Hanh, 'Action and compassion in the world', [*United States*] *Buddhist Peace Fellowship Newsletter*, 7(3), 1985, pp.1–15.

131 D.T. Suzuki, 'Knowledge and innocence', in Thomas Merton, op. cit. (note 94), p.112.

132 Shantideva *Bodhicaryavatara* in Lucien Stryk, ed., *World of the Buddha*, New York: Anchor Doubleday, 1969, p.303.

133 D.T. Suzuki, op. cit. (note 7), p.135.

134 See Michael Pye, *Skilful Means: a concept in Mahayana Buddhism*, London: Duckworth, 1978.

135 Robert A.F. Thurman, trans., op. cit. (note 63), p.21.

136 Ibid., pp.64–5.

137 Zen Master Rinzai Gigen, *Sayings* [*Rinzi Roku*], extract translated by D.T. Suzuki in D.T. Suzuki, and others, op. cit. (note 64), p.33.

138 Iris Murdoch, *The Sovereignty of the Good*, London: Routledge & Kegan Paul, 1970, p.54, p.59 and p.67.

139 Buddhist Churches of America Social Issues Committee (Chairperson: Ryo Imamura), 'A Shin Buddhist stance on abortion', [*United States*] *Buddhist Peace Fellowship Newsletter*, 6(3), July 1984, pp.6–7.

140 Philip Kapleau, op. cit. (note 123), p.250.

141 Robert Aitken, op. cit. (note 128), pp.21–2.

142 David Astor, Obituary for Revd Michael Scott in the *Observer* (London), 18 September 1983.

143 *Thich* Nhat Hanh, *The Miracle of Being Awake: a manual for activists* An eight page paper which has appeared in various formats. Available through the Buddhist Peace Fellowships.

144 John Welwood, 'Befriending emotion', in John Welwood, ed., *Awakening the Heart: Eastern and Western approaches to psychotherapy and the healing relationship*, Boulder: Shambhala, 1983, pp.84–90.

145 *Venerable* Nyanaponika Mahathera, *The Power of Mindfulness*, Kandy: Buddhist Publication Society, 1976 (Wheel publication 121/122), p.16.

146 Chögyam Trungpa, *The Myth of Freedom*, Boulder: Shambhala, 1976, p.70.

147 Irmgard Schloegl (*Ven.* Myokyo-ni), *The Zen Way*, London: Sheldon Press, 1977, p.69, p.95.

148 Hubert Benoit, *The Supreme Doctrine*, New York: Viking, 1959, p.239.

149 *Thich* Nhat Hanh, 'Non-violence: practising awareness', *Seeds of Peace* (Bangkok), 1(1), April 2528 (i.e. 1985), p.4.

150 *Samyutta-nikaya* xlvii, 19.

151 Howard Clark, and others, *Preparing for Non-violent Direct Action*, Nottingham: *Peace News*/London: Campaign for Nuclear Disarmament, 1984, p.45.

152 Alexandra David-Neel, *Buddhism: its doctrines and its methods*, London: Unwin, 1978, p.97.

153 Joanna R. Macy, *Despair and Personal Power in the Nuclear Age*, Philadelphia: New Society Publishers, 1983.

154 The address of UK Interhelp is 4a High Tenterfell, Kendal, Cumbria LA9 4PC.

155 Sulak Sivaraksa, op. cit. (note 87), pp.37–8.

156 Walpola Rahula, 'The problem of the *sangha* in the West', in *Zen and the Taming of the Bull*, London: Gordon Fraser, 1978, pp.54–67.

157 Stephen Batchelor, 'Monks, laity and *sangha*', *Middle Way*, 58(1), May 1983, pp.27–33 (p.33, p.28).

158 Sulak Sivaraksa, *A Buddhist Vision for Renewing Society*, Bangkok: Tienwan, 1986, p.111.

159 John Howard Griffin, in Gerald Twomey, ed., *Thomas Merton: prophet in the belly of a paradox*, New York: Paulist Press, 1978, p.84.

PART FIVE: THE RATIONALE AND THE FORMS OF BUDDHIST
SOCIAL ACTIVISM

160 Sulak Sivaraksa, op. cit. (note 158), p.160.
161 Sulak Sivaraksa op. cit. (note 87), p.80.
162 John Snelling, ed., *The Middle Way*, 59(3), November
1984, p.141.
163 *Anguttara-nikaya* iv, 280 trans. E.M. Hare.
164 Charles Upton, 'Marxism and contemplation'. Unpublished paper.
165 Balakrishna Govind Gokhale, 'Early Buddhism and the
urban revolution', *Journal of the International Association
of Buddhist Studies*, 5(2), 1982, pp.7–22 (p.7, p.19).
166 Edward Conze, *Thirty years of Buddhist Studies*, Oxford:
Cassirer, 1968, p.217.
167 *Ajahn* Buddhadasa op. cit. (note 15), p. 26.
168 Edward Conze, op. cit. (note 51), p.12.
169 *Udana* v, 5 trans. F.L. Woodward.
170 Mi-La-Ras-Pa, *Tibet's Great Yogi Milarepa*, ed. W.Y.
Evans-Wentz, 2nd edn., London: Oxford University
Press, 1951, p.271.
171 Masao Abse, 'As Zen comes to the West', *Blind Donkey*
(Honolulu), 8(1), p.19.
172 Robert Aitken, op. cit. (note 128), pp.20–1.
173 Zen Master Rinzai Gigen, op. cit. (note 137), p.39
174 Max Weber, *Religion in India*, London: Allen & Unwin,
1959, p.213.
175 Daniel Berrigan, quoted in Kenneth Leech, *The Social
God*, London: Sheldon Press, 1981, p.28.
176 Kenneth Leech op. cit. (note 175), p. 28.
177 Simone Weil, op. cit. (note 86), p.84.
178 Gary Snyder, 'Mahasangha meeting Sept 1982' [type-
script], Berkeley (Cal): [*United States*] *Buddhist Peace
Fellowship*, n.d., p.9.
179 Gary Snyder, 'Buddhism and the possibilities of a
planetary culture', in Fred Eppsteiner and Dennis

Maloney eds., *The Path of Compassion: contemporary writings on engaged Buddhism*, Berkeley: [United States] Buddhist Peace Fellowship, Buffalo: White Pine Press, 1985, pp.152—4 (p.154, p.152).

180 Gary Snyder, op. cit. (note 27), p.92.

181 Gary Snyder, op. cit. (note 178), p.10.

182 Robert Aitken, *Taking the Path of Zen*, San Francisco: North Point Press, 1982.

183 See, for example, Joseph M. Kitigawa, 'Buddhism and social change: an historical perspective', in S. Balasooriya, and others, eds., *Buddhist Studies in Honour of Walpola Rahula*, London: Gordon Fraser, 1980, pp.84—101.

184 Theodore de Bary, ed., *The Buddhist Tradition in India, China and Japan*, New York: The Modern Library, 1969, p.260.

185 Robert Aitken, op. cit. (note 128), p.5.

186 Zen Master Hakuin, 'Hebiichigo II' in Philip B. Yampolsky, trans., *Zen Master Hakuin: selected writings*, New York: Columbia Press, 1971, p.220.

187 Daizen Victoria, 'Japanese corporate Zen', *Bulletin of Concerned Asian Scholars*, 12(1), 1980, pp.61—8.

188 Daizen Victoria, Ibid., p.65.

189 Somboon Suksamran, *Buddhism and Politics in Thailand: a study of socio-political change and political activism in the Thai sangha*, Singapore: Institute of South East Asian Studies, 1982.

190 Somboon Suksamran, *Political Buddhism in South-East Asia: the role of the sangha in the modernisation of Thailand*, London: C. Hurst, 1977.

191 S.J. Tambiah, *World Conqueror: a study of Buddhist polity in Thailand against an historical background*, London: Cambridge University Press, 1976.

192 Chaiwat Satha-Anand, 'The leaders, the lotus, and the shadow of the dove', *Seeds of Peace* (Bangkok) 1(1), April 1985, pp.24—30.

193 The headquarters of the Western Buddhist Order are at

Padmaloka, Lessingham House, Surlingham, Norwich, NR14 7AL, UK.

194 *Dharmachari* Subhuti, (Alex Kennedy), *Buddhism for Today: a portrait of a new Buddhist movement*, Tisbury (Wilts): Element Books, 1983, p.161, p.184.

195 *Dharmachari* Subhuti (Alex Kennedy), *Right Livelihood Co-operatives: an introduction*, Friends of the Western Buddhist Order Inter Co-op Secretariat, 1981, p.14.

196 Stephen Levine, *Who dies? An investigation of conscious living and conscious dying*, New York: Anchor-Doubleday, 1982, p.x.

197 David Brandon, op. cit. (note 26), p.55, p.47.

198 Buddhist Peace Fellowship: P.O. Box 4650, Berkeley, CA 94704.

199 Buddhist Peace Fellowship affiliates: 16 Upper Park Road, London NW3, Britain; P.O. Box 368, Lismore 2480, NSW, Australia.

PART SIX: ENGAGED BUDDHISM:
THE ASIAN EXPERIENCE

200 These principles, and the quotations which follow, are taken from: Robert A.F. Thurman, 'The politics of enlightenment', *Lindisfarne Newsletter* 8 (Lindisfarne Association, New York). The passages in that paper which refer to Asoka have been reprinted in Fred Eppsteiner, and Dennis Maloney, eds., op. cit. (note 179), retitled 'Edicts of Asoka', pp.66–72.

201 Nikunja V. Banerjee, *Buddhism and Marxism: a study in humanism*, New Delhi: Orient Longman, 1978, p.30.

202 A.L. Basham, 'Asoka and Buddhism: a re-examination', *Journal of the International Association of Buddhist Studies*, 5(1) 1982, pp.131–43 (p.139, p.140).

203 Robert A.F. Thurman, 'Guidelines for Buddhist social activism based on Nagarjuna's *Jewel Garland of Royal*

398   *The Social Face of Buddhism*

Counsels', *Eastern Buddhist*, 16(1) NS, Spring 1983, pp.19–51. Reprinted in Fred Eppsteiner, *and* Dennis Maloney, eds., op. cit. (note 179), pp.46–65. My quotations are from pp.50, 51, 60 and 61 of that reprint.
204 Somboon Suksamran, op. cit. (note 190), p.116.
205 Walpola Rahula, *Zen and the Taming of the Bull*, London: Gordon Fraser, 1978.
206 S. J. Tambiah, 'Buddhism and this-worldly activity', *Modern Asian Studies*, 7(1), 1973, pp.1–20 (p.17). Tambiah is quoting from E. Sarkisyanz, *Buddhist Background of the Burmese Revolution*, The Hague: Nijhoff, 1965.
207 David Gosling, 'New directions in Thai Buddhism', *Modern Asian Studies* 14(3), 1980, pp.411–39 (p.429).
208 David Gosling, ibid. p.430
209 James J. Hughes, ed., *A Green Buddhist Declaration*, Moratuwa (Sri Lanka): Sarvodaya Press, 1984.
210 Trevor Ling, trans., *The Buddha's Philosophy of Man: early Indian Buddhist dialogues*, London: Dent (Everyman), 1981, p.122.
211 Trevor Ling, trans., ibid., p.93.
212 For the account which follows I am particularly indebted to Joanna R. Macy, *Dharma and development: religion as resource in the Sarvodaya self-help movement*, West Hartford (Conn.): Kumarian Press, revised edn. 1985.
213 Ibid., p.95
214 Ibid., p.32
215 Ibid., p.76
216 Ibid., p.37
217 Ibid., p.39
218 Ibid., p.66
219 Ibid., p.15
220 Detlef Kantowsky, *Sarvodaya: the other development*, New Delhi: Vikas, 1980, p.67.
221 For a very fair discussion, see Denis Goulet, *Survival With Integrity: Sarvodaya at the crossroads*, Colombo: Marga Institute, 1981.

222 For more on this typical kind of Third World development scenario see Frances Lappe and others, *Aid as Obstacle*, San Francisco: Institute of Food and Development Policy, 1980.
223 Detlef Kantowsky, op. cit. (note 220), p.216.
224 James J. Hughes, *Sangha and Sarvodaya in Sri Lanka: an inquiry into Buddhist monks' involvement in social and political change in ancient and modern Sri Lanka*, 101 page semi-published typescript dated March 1986. Enquiries to the author 5400 S. Harper #701, chicago, Ill. 60615, USA.
225 Denis Goulet, op. cit. (note 221), p.78.
226 James J. Hughes, op. cit. (note 224), p.55.
227 Joanna R. Macy, op. cit. (note 212), p.102.
228 Ibid., p.104.
229 Ibid., p.91.
230 Detlef Kantowsky, op. cit. (note 220), p.154.
231 David Radcliffe, 'Sarvodaya and the Western world', paper contributed to conference: *Sarvodaya and world development*, Moratuwa (Sri Lanka): Sarvodaya, 1978. Quoted in Detlef Kantowsky, op. cit. (note 220), pp.166–7.
232 Ibid.
233 Joanna R. Macy, op. cit. (note 212), p.105 and p.113.
234 Sulak Sivaraksa, op. cit. (note 87), p.138.
235 Sulak Sivaraksa, op. cit. (note 158), p.178.
236 *Ajahn* Buddhadasa, *Dhammic Socialism*, ed. Donald K. Swearer, Bangkok: Thai Inter-Religious Commission for Development, 1986. More generally, see *Ajahn* Buddhadasa, op. cit. (note 15), p.25. *Handbook for Mankind: principles of Buddhism explained by Buddhadasa Bhikkhu* (1984) is also particularly valuable, but published and circulated informally.
237 *Ajahn* Buddhadasa, *Dhammic Socialism* as cited above, and from which the quotations which follow are taken, pp.94–9, p.57.
238 *Thich* Nhat Hanh, *Love in Action: the non-violent struggle*

*for peace in Vietnam*, Paris: The Vietnamese Buddhist Peace Delegation, n.d., p.5.

239 For example, Thich Nhat Hanh, *The Cry of Vietnam*, Greensboro (N. Carolina): Unicorn Press, 1971.

240 John Paul Davidson, 'Buddhism in Laos: an interview', *Seeds of Peace*, (Thai Inter-Religious Commission for Development, Bangkok) 1(1), April 1985, pp.5–7.

241 Robert A.F. Thurman, op. cit. (note 203), p.46.

242 His Holiness XIVth *Dalai Lama*, Tenzin Gyatso, *Collected Statements, Interviews and Articles*, Dharamsala (India): Information Office of H.H. the Dalai Lama, 1982, p.92, p.3.

243 *Bukkyo Times* no. 697, 11 March 1967. Quoted by Heinrich Dumoulin in 'Buddhism in Modern Japan' in Heinrich Dumoulin, ed., *Buddhism in the Modern World*, New York: Collier, 1976, pp.215–76 (p.230).

244 Ibid. p.224.

245 Daizen Victoria, op. cit. (note 187), pp.61–8. (The Godukai appears now to be defunct.)

246 Tsungunari Kobo, 'Contemporary lay Buddhist movements in Japan', *Journal of the International Association of Buddhist Studies*, 6(1), 1983, pp.76–89.

247 Edward Conze, *A Short History of Buddhism*, London: Allen & Unwin, 1980, p.113.

248 Edward Conze, ibid. pp.113–14.

249 Heinrich Dumoulin, op. cit. (note 243), p.251.

250 *Time* magazine, May 1964. Quoted in Jerrold Schecter, *The New Face of Buddha: Buddhism and political power in South-East Asia*, London: Gollancz, 1967.

251 Emma McCloy Layman, *Buddhism in America*, Chicago: Nelson Hall, 1976.

252 As reported in the *Observer* colour supplement (London), 23 February 1986, p.31.

253 Nikkyo Niwano, *A Guide to the Threefold Lotus Sutra*, Tokyo: Kosei, 1981, p.7.

254 Nikkyo Niwano, *A Buddhist Approach to Peace*, Tokyo: Kosei, 1977.

255 Heinz Bechert, 'Sangha, state, society: the persistence of tradition in post-traditional Buddhist societies', *Daedalus*, 102(1), 1973, pp.85–95.

256 Paul Demieville, 'Les réligions de l'Orient et de l'Extrême-Orient: tendences actuelles,' *Encyclopédie française*, quoted in Arthur F. Wright, *Buddhism in Chinese History*, Stanford: Stanford University Press, 1959, p.112.

257 Vijay Kumar Thakur, 'The socio-political relevance of Buddhism in the modern world', *Maha Bodhi* 86(4–5), April–May 1978, pp.122–5.

258 Trevor Ling, *The Buddha*, London: Temple Smith, 1973, p.39.

259 Ibid., p.106

260 Ibid., p.151

261 Ibid., p.109.

262 Nikunja V. Banerjee, op. cit. (note 201).

263 Trevor Ling, op. cit. (note 258), p.196.

264 Ibid. pp.22–3.

265 H.H. the XIVth Dalai Lama, Tenzin Gyatso, op. cit. (note 242), p.13.

266 Ibid., p.86.

267 *Thich* Nhat Hanh, op. cit. (note 238), p.3.

268 Of the scattered Buddhist literature bearing on this subject, the following pamphlet, although already somewhat dated, was found to be of particular interest: Philip.Kapleau, *A Pilgrimage to the Buddhist Temples and Caves of China: lessons for the West, questions raised and answered*, 7 Arnold Park, Rochester, New York: the Zen Center, 1983.

PART SEVEN: VIOLENCE AND CREATIVITY

269 Aldous Huxley, op. cit. (note 115), ch.xxvi.

270 Taizan Maezumi, in *The Ten Directions* (Los Angeles Zen Center), 1(1), Spring 1983, p.1.

271 Edward Conze, op. cit. (note 51), p.65.

402    *The Social Face of Buddhism*

272  Trevor Ling, *Buddhism, Imperialism and War*, London: Allen & Unwin, 1979, p.147.
273  Walpola Rahula, op. cit. (note 39), p.84.
274  Walpola Rahula, op. cit. (note 205).
275  Report in the *Guardian* (London), 22 Feb 1986, p.7.
276  Robert Aitken, 'Two *teishos*: the First Precept', *Blind Donkey* (Diamond Sangha, Honolulu) 5(4), August 1979, p.1.
277  Archbishop of Canterbury's Commission on Urban Priority Areas, *Faith in the City: a call for action by church and nation*, London: Church House Publishing, 1985, para 15.1, p.359.
278  *Thich* Nhat Hanh, 'You call it non-violence', seven page typescript available through British Buddhist Peace Fellowship (see note 198).
279  Jacques Ellul, *Violence: reflexions from a Christian perspective*, Oxford: Mowbrays, 1978.
280  James, J. Hughes, *A Green Buddhist Declaration*, Moratuwa (Sri Lanks): Sarvodaya Press, 1984, para 2.7.
281  James J. Hughes, *Buddhist Feminism*, Colombo: Atlas Hall Press, 1985, p.1.
282  Dorothy Rowe, op. cit. (note 11), p.125.
283  Jacques Ellul, op. cit. (note 279), p.118.
284  See Gene Sharp, *Social Power and Political Freedom*, Boston: Porter Sargent, 1980.
285  Thomas Merton, *On Peace*, Oxford: Mowbrays, 1976, p.17, p.113.
286  Richard B. Gregg, *The Power of Non-violence*, London: Jas. Clarke, 2nd edn. 1960.
287  Jacques Ellul, op. cit. (note 279). Quotations are, respectively, from pp.135, 94, 134–5, 138 and 142.
288  Joan V. Bondurant, *The Conquest of Violence: the Gandhian philosophy of nonviolence*, Berkeley: University of California Press, revised edn. 1971.
289  James W. Douglass, *Resistance and Contemplation: the way of liberation*, New York: Doubleday, 1972/ Cambridge University Press, 1976, p.42, p.43.

290 Joan V. Bondurant, op. cit. (note 288), p.193.

291 Thomas Merton, op. cit. (note 285), p.114.

292 Jerre Mangione, *A Passion for Sicilians: the world around Danilo Dolci*, New York: William Morrow, 1968, p.84.

293 Adam Curle, *Making Peace*, London: Tavistock Press, 1971.

294 Pete Strauss, 'The politics of non-violent direct action', *Sanity*, (Campaign for Nuclear Disarmament, London) February 1986, pp.36—7.

295 Dorothy Rowe, op. cit. (note 11), p.108.

296 Daniel Katz and R.L. Kahn, *The Social Psychology of Organisations*, New York: Wiley, 2nd edn. 1978, pp.634—78.

297 Thomas Merton op. cit. (note 52), p.114.

298 G.M. Becker and C.G. McClintock, 'Value: behavioural decision theory', *Annual Review of Psychology* vol. 18, 1967, pp.239—86 (p.253).

299 Simone Weil, op. cit. (note 86), p.121.

300 Quoted from *Maha Sthavira* Sangharakshita, *Buddhism, World Peace and Nuclear War*, Glasgow: Windhorse, 1984, p.6.

301 *Maha Sthavira* Sangharakshita, *Peace is a Fire...writings and sayings*, London: Windhorse, 1979, p.60.

302 For example, Mike Woodcock, *Team Development Manual*, Aldershot: Gower, 1979, and Norman R. F. Maier, *Problem Solving Discussions and Conferences*, New York: McGraw Hill, 1962.


PART EIGHT: THE MAKING OF THE GOOD SOCIETY

303 Robert A. F. Thurman, op. cit. (note 200).

304 H.H. the XIVth Dalai Lama, Tenzin Gyatso, op. cit. (note 242), p.83, p.84.

305 E.F. Schumacher, op. cit. (note 22).

306 William Ophuls, 'Political values for an age of scarcity: Buddhist politics', *American Theosophist* 69(5), May 1981, pp.140—7 (p.143).

307 see Johan Galtung, *The True Worlds: a transnational perspective*, New York: Free Press, 1980.

308 Gene Sharp, op. cit. (note 284), p.297.

309 E.F. Schumacher, op. cit. (note 50), pp.66–7.

310 *Dharmachari* Subhuti (Alex Kennedy), op. cit. (note 194), pp.159–60.

311 For the arguments for making *all* work voluntary and unpaid, see Charles Handy, *The Future of Work*, Oxford: Blackwell, 1984.

312 William Ophuls, op. cit. (note 306), p.145.

313 Manuel Arce, 'The practice of Zen Buddhism in the context of a Latin culture', *Zen Bow Newsletter* (Rochester Zen Center, New York), 5(1), Winter 1981, pp.10–11.

314 William Ophuls, op. cit. (note 306), p.146

315 James Robertson, Introduction to Fritjof Capra and Charlene Spretnak, *Green Politics*, London: Hutchinson, 1984.

316 *The Guardian* (London), 7 Feb 1986, p.24.

317 See, for example, John Osmond and Angela Graham, *Alternatives: new approaches to health, education, energy, the family and the Aquarian Age*, Wellingborough (UK): Thorsons, 1984.

318 See, for example, Johan Galtung, *Self-reliance: a strategy for development and global interdependence*, Oslo University, [1977].

319 See, for example, Fritjof Capra, *The Turning Point: science, society and the rising culture*, London: Wildwood House, 1982.

320 James J. Hughes, op. cit. (note 280).

321 Howard Clark, *Making Non-violent Revolution*, Nottingham: *Peace News*, 2nd edn. 1981.

322 George Lakey, *Strategy for a Living Revolution*, San Francisco: W.H. Freeman, 1973, p.199.

323 Ven. Rewata Dhamma, 'Towards a better society: a Buddhist perspective', paper submitted at a United Nations University meeting at Thammasat University, Bangkok, 20–22 March 1985, nine page typescript.

324 Chögyam Trungpa quoted in Emma McCloy Layman, op. cit. (note 251), p.102.

325 Ninian Smart, *Beyond Ideology: religion and the future of Western civilization*, London: Collins, 1981, p.14.

326 Don Cupitt, 'A future for religious thought – I: Religion without superstition', *Listener* (London) no. 109, 13 September 1984, p.5.

327 Huston Smith, Foreword to Philip Kapleau, *Three Pillars of Zen*, Boston: Beacon Press, 1967.

328 Don Cupitt, *The World to Come*, London: S.C.M. Press, 1982, p.xv.

329 Don Cupitt, 'A future for religious thought – IV: The struggle against theological realism', *Listener* (London), no. 112, 4 October 1984.

330 William Johnston, *The Still Point: reflections on Zen and Christian mysticism*, New York: Harper & Row, 1970, p.190.

331 Douglas A. Fox, *Buddhism, Christianity and the Future Religion*, Philadelphia: Westminster Press, 1972.

332 Winston King, *Buddhism and Christianity: some bridges of understanding*, Philadelphia: Westminster Press, 1962.

333 J. Edgar Bruns, *The Christian Buddhism of St John*, New York: Paulist Press, [1971].

334 For example, Thomas Merton's numerous writings on Zen have been selected in: Thomas Merton, *Thomas Merton on Zen*, London: Sheldon Press, 1976.

335 See also Chapter 11 of this book. For further evidence for the essential unity of the spiritual traditions of the world's great religions, see: Aldous Huxley, *The Perennial Philosophy*, London: Chatto & Windus, 1974; F. Schuon, *The Transcendental Unity of Religions*, New York: Harper, 1975; Huston Smith, *The Forgotten Truth*, New York: Harper, 1976.

336 H.H. the XIVth Dalai Lama, Tenzin Gyatso, *Newsletter* (Dharamsala, India), January 1967.

337 Yamada Kōun, 'On Christianity and Zen', *Blind Donkey*, (Diamond Sangha, Honolulu) 9(1), June 1985, p.10.

338 William Johnston, op. cit. (note 330), p.xiii.

339 Ninian Smart, op. cit. (note 325), p.309, p.311.

340 J.K. Kadowaki, *Zen and the Bible: a priest's experience*, London: Routledge & Kegan Paul, 1980.

341 Kenneth Leech, op. cit. (note 95).

342 A remark by Patrick Buchanan, President Reagan's 'communications director', as reported in the *Observer* (London), June 1986, p.6.

343 Ken Wilber, op. cit. (note 6).

344 Chögyam Trungpa, *The Myth of Freedom and the Way of Meditation*, Berkeley & London: Shambala, 1976, p.26.

345 Robert Aitken, op. cit. (note 128).

346 Simone Weil, op. cit. (note 86).

347 Ken Wilber, op. cit. (note 6), p.102.

348 Edward Conze, op. cit. (note 165), pp.213—14.

349 T.P. Kasulis, *Zen Action/Zen Person*, Honolulu: University of Hawaii Press, 1981.

350 Chie Nakane, *Japanese Society*, Tokyo: Tuttle, 1984, pp.3—4.

351 Robert Christopher, *The Japanese Mind*, London: Pan, 1984, p.225.

352 T.P. Kasulis, op. cit. (note 349), p.145.

353 Sudhir Kakar, *The Inner World*, Delhi: Oxford University Press, 1981.

354 Frank Gibney, *Japan: the fragile superpower*, Tokyo: Tuttle, 1975, p.148.

355 Geert Hofstede, *Culture's Consequences: international differences in work-related values*, London: Sage, 1980.

356 For example, a number of well-substantiated cases of sexual exploitation by eminent Buddhist teachers of their students caused a crisis of confidence in certain American Buddhist centres in 1983—4. (Similar instances are not unknown, however, in the East.) The evidence was published in the Winter 1983 and Spring 1984 issues of *Co-evolution Quarterly*, and comment by two (uninvolved) teachers subsequently appeared in *Blind Donkey*, (Diamond Sangha, Honolulu) 8(3), 1984,

pp.i—iii, and *Zen Bow Newsletter*, (Rochester Zen Center, New York) 6(2—3), Summer—Fall 1984, pp.1—2.

357 Fritjof Capra, op. cit. (note 319), p.405.

358 Ken Wilber, *No Boundary: Eastern and Western approaches to personal growth*, Boulder & London: Shambhala, 1981, p.107, p.124.

359 Ken Wilber, 'In praise of ego: an uncommon Buddhist sermon', *The Middle Way*, 58(3), November 1983, pp.151—3.

360 John Welwood, 'Psychology and meditation', in John Welwood, ed., op. cit. (note 144).

361 Steven J. Hendlin, 'Pernicious oneness', *Journal of Humanistic Psychology*, 23(3), Summer 1983, pp.61—81.

362 Ken Wilber, op. cit. (note 358), p.139, p.103.

363 Jack Kornfield and others, 'Psychological adjustment is not liberation: a symposium', in *Zero: contemporary Buddhist life and thought*, (Los Angeles: Zero Press) vol. 2, 1979, p.76.

364 Announcement by Dr Robin Logie, Park Hospital, Liverpool, and Dr Peter Lofting, Dept. of Psychology, University of Warwick.

365 Venerable Myokyo-ni (Irmgard Schloegl), *Zen Traces* (The Zen Centre, London), 4(4), September 1982, p.9.

366 Steven Hendlin, op. cit. (note 361).

367 Jack Kornfield, op. cit. (note 363).

368 Jack Kornfield 'Meditation: aspects of theory and practice', in Roger Walsh and Frances Vaughan, eds., op. cit. (note 71) pp.150—3 (p.152).

369 Venerable Myokyo-ni (Irmgard Schloegl), *Zen Traces* (The Zen Centre, London), 2(4) Sept 1980, p.10.

370 Jack Kornfield, op. cit. (note 363), p.74.

371 Jack Kornfield, op. cit. (note 368), p.152.

372 Venerable Myokyo-ni (Irmgard Schloegl), op. cit. (note 369).

373 A.C. Robyn Skynner, 'Psychotherapy and spiritual tradition', in John Welwood, ed., op. cit. (note 144), pp.18—32 (pp.29—30).

374 Ken Wilber, op. cit. (note 358).

375 T.P. Kasulis, op. cit. (note 349), p.145.

376 Steven Hendlin, 355 op. cit. (note 361).

377 John Hurrell Crook, *The Evolution of Human Consciousness*, London: Oxford University Press, 1980, pp.375–80.

378 Guy Claxton, 'Therapy and beyond', in Guy Claxton, ed., *Beyond Therapy: the impact of Eastern religions on psychological theory and practice*, London: Wisdom, 1986, pp.324–5.

379 Ken Wilber, op. cit. (note 5), 307n.

380 Howard Clark, op. cit. (note 321), p.12.

381 Jonathon Porritt, *Resurgence*, no. 112, September/October 1985, p.36.

382 As, for example, in Marilyn Ferguson, op. cit. (note 69).

383 Ken Wilber, op. cit. (note 5), p.328.

EPILOGUE: NO HOPE, BUT POSSIBILITIES . . .

384 James W. Douglass, op. cit. (note 289), p.142, p.141.

385 Ibid., p.140, p.144.

386 *Sutta-Nipata*, 'Ajita's questions to the Buddha', trans. H. Saddhatissa, London: Curzon Press, 1985.

387 D.T. Suzuki, op. cit. (note 7), p.78.

PRAYER

388 A rendering from the *Metta Sutta* by Christopher Titmuss.

# Index

Abortion, 176–7
Adler, Alfred, 41
*Ahimsa*, 13, 228, 307
Aitken, Robert *Zen Master*, 151, 202–3, 209, 352, 356–7; abortion, 177; 'no killing', 287; 'no stealing', 163; 'sexual misconduct', 164
*Alayavijnana*, 64
'Angulimala' (UK Buddhist prison chaplaincy), 221
Anthropocentrism, 110, 113, 139, 340
Antithetical bonding, 44–5, 82, 223; Cold War, 55, 102; weighted polarization, 91, 100
Aristotle, 114
Ariyaratne, A.Y., 242–3, 249
Asian Cultural Forum on Development (ACFOD), 254
Asoka, 228–30, 232, 236, 256, 275, 324–5; and Sarvodaya, 242, 251
Augustine of Hippo, *Saint*, 32
Avatamsaka Buddhism, 136, 144–5
Awareness *see* Mindfulness

Bandaranaike, S.W.R.D., 234
Berrigan, Daniel, 203
Bioenergetics, 374–5
Bioregionalism, 142, 334
Blake, William, 143–4, 194, 222, 372
Bodhisattvas, 169–71; Lotus Sutra, 269–70; paradoxical

nature, 275; social action, 232, 263; vow, 194
Bonhoeffer, Dietrich, 73, 178, 350
*Brahma-vihara*, 185, 244
Brandt Commission, 52
Brown, Norman O., 29
Buddha Gotama, 86; as arbitrator, 317; enlightenment, 274; ministry, 196; social teaching, 199, 209
Buddha Nature, 33, 37, 59, 156
Buddhadharma, 89, 98, 271; Asoka, 229; *Ajahn* Buddhadasa, 263; modernism, 235–7, 349; non-missionary, 217, 256, 266, 347; *pariyatta-* and *patipatti-dhamma*, 197; social action, 193–8, 324
Buddhadasa, *Ajahn*, 36, 190, 197, 255–60
Buddhist Peace Fellowship, 257; Australia, 223; UK, 223–4; USA, 206, 223–4
Buddhist Union of Europe, 280
Bultmann, Rudolf, 350
Bureaucracy, 121, 334, 340; advocated, 331–2; Sarvodaya, 246; Max Weber, 114
Burma, 67, 231, 262; Buddhist socialism, 236–7; sangha, 228, 260; self-reliance, 278; U Nu, 234

Calvinism, 92, 132
Cambodia *see* Kampuchea

409

The publisher thanks Mr. Joshua Mailman
of New York for his kind help in
financing the production of this book.